Internationalization of the RMB

T0298613

As from 2012, the International Monetary Institution (IMI) of the Renmin University of China publishes annual reports on the internationalization of RMB. In the series of annual reports, we create and publish the Renminbi Internationalization Index (RII). Besides, we focus on one topic in each year's report. In the 2014 report, we focus on the offshore RMB markets. We study several major international currencies' historical developments to summarize theoretical implications between currency internationalization process and its offshore market development. We review the recent development of RMB offshore markets, identify key opportunities and challenges, and propose some suggestions to policy makers and market practitioners. We believe that the RII will continue to rise as the renminbi plays a more and more important role in international trades and financial transactions. The establishment and development of renminbi offshore markets will facilitate the internationalization process of the RMB.

International Monetary Institute of the RUC was established on December 20, 2009. The IMI is a nonprofit academic institution and think tank focusing on research on monetary finance theory, policy, and strategy.

China Perspectives series

The *China Perspectives* series focuses on translating and publishing works by leading Chinese scholars writing about both global topics and China-related themes. It covers humanities and social sciences, education, media, and psychology as well as many interdisciplinary themes.

This is the first time that one of these books has been translated into English for international readers. The series aims to put forward a Chinese perspective, give insights into cutting-edge academic thinking in China, and inspire researchers globally.

Sixty-two titles so far, with more to come. A full list of titles in this series is available at: www.routledge.com/series/CPH. Recently published titles:

Tax Reform and Policy in China
Peiyong Gao

Internationalization of the RMB: Establishment and Development of RMB Offshore Markets
International Monetary Institute of the RUC

Poverty Reduction and Spirit of Inclusion: Practice in China
Ling Zhu

An Advanced Study on the International Marketing of Chinese Brands
Zuohao Hu, Xi Chen, Zhilin Yang

Report on Economic Reform and Development of China 2014
Gang Lin

Regulating China's Shadow Banks
Qingmin Yan, Jianhua Li

Internet Finance in China: Introduction and Practical Approaches
Ping Xie, Chuanwei Zou, Haier Liu

Game and the Society: Incentive and Commitment
Weiying Zhang

Game and the Society: Information and Reputation
Weiying Zhang

Government Foresighted Leading: Theory and Practice of the World's Regional Economic Development
Yunxian Chen, Jianwei Qiu

Chinese Outward Direct Investment I
Yiping Huang, He Fan, Yongsheng Zhang

Chinese Outward Direct Investment II
Yiping Huang, He Fan, Yongsheng Zhang

Internationalization of the RMB

Establishment and development of RMB offshore markets

International Monetary Institute of the RUC

Routledge
Taylor & Francis Group

LONDON AND NEW YORK

First published 2016 by Routledge

2 Park Square, Milton Park, Abingdon, Oxfordshire OX14 4RN

52 Vanderbilt Avenue, New York, NY 10017

Routledge is an imprint of the Taylor & Francis Group, an informa business

First issued in paperback 2020

British Library Cataloguing in Publication Data
A catalogue record for this book is available from the British Library

Library of Congress Cataloging in Publication Data
Names: Zhongguo ren min da xue. Guo ji huo bi yan jiu suo, issuing body.
Title: Internationalization of RMB : establishment and development of RMB offshore markets / International Monetary Institute of RUC.
Description: Abingdon, Oxon ; New York, NY : Routledge, 2016. | Series: China perspectives series | Includes bibliographical references and indexes.
Identifiers: LCCN 2015041835| ISBN 9781138651708 (hardback) | ISBN 9781315624228 (ebook)
Subjects: LCSH: Renminbi. | Foreign exchange--China. | Capital market--China. | Finance--China. | Banks and banking, International. | International finance.
Classification: LCC HG1285 .I57 2016 | DDC 332.4/50951--dc23
LC record available at http://lccn.loc.gov/2015041835

ISBN: 978-1-138-65170-8 (hbk)
ISBN: 978-0-367-51656-7 (pbk)

Typeset in Bembo
by HWA Text and Data Management, London

Contents

List of figures   *vi*
List of tables   *viii*

Introduction   1

1 Renminbi Internationalization Index   6

2 Current situation of the internationalization of the renminbi   31

3 Public opinions and observations   71

4 Currency internationalization and offshore market:
  historical implications   109

5 Current situation and the future of the offshore RMB market   137

6 Challenges to building the offshore RMB market   174

7 Conclusions and suggestions   193

Postscript   205

Appendix I: Taxation comparison of offshore financial centers   *208*
Appendix II: Chronicle of events of RMB internationalization   *215*
Index   *230*

Figures

1.1 The RMB Internationalization Index   12
1.2 RII quarter growing situation   13
1.3 Cross-border trade in RMB clearing functions   16
1.4 Comprehensive index for renminbi-denominated international
     financial settlement   19
1.5 RMB international credit accounted for by global market size   20
1.6 Global RMB direct investment   22
1.7 Internationalization of RMB bonds and notes integrated
     indicators   23
1.8 Major world currency internationalization indexes   29
2.1 The scope of RMB cross-border trade settlement   32
2.2 The trend of RMB settlement scale in goods trade settlement
     and service trade settlement   33
2.3 The ratio of RMB goods trade settlement and service trade
     settlement   33
2.4 The ratio of receipt and payment in cross-border RMB
     settlement businesses   33
2.5 RMB ODI settlement and Chinese FDI   34
2.6 FDI RMB settlement over 2011 to 2013   35
2.7 The stock and issuance of RMB international bonds and notes   36
2.8 Proportion of RMB international bonds and notes on global
     market   36
2.9 Q4, 2013 Currency structure and amount of international bonds
     and notes   37
2.10 Chinese Stock Market transactions   38
2.11 The currency structure of interest rate derivatives on the global
     OTC market   39
2.12 2012–2013 RMB overseas loans and the ratio of domestic
     financial institutions   46
2.13 Development of RMB deposits and loans in Hong Kong   47
2.14 The currency swap scale of the People's Bank of China   53
2.15 The development of RMB foreign exchange derivatives market   56
2.16 Central parity rate movements of RMB   63

2.17 The nominal effective exchange rate movements of RMB 63
2.18 The nominal effective exchange rate movement of five
economies' currencies 64
2.19 RMB real effective exchange rate movements 64
2.20 The real effective exchange rate movement of five economies'
currencies 65
2.21 Daily closing price of RMB NDF 2013 65
3.1 The number of reports on RMB by the mainstream media
around the world 86
3.2 The comparison of the number of reports on RMB by the
mainstream media in different regions and nations 88
3.3 The comparison of reports on RMB by mainstream media in
different regions excluding Europe 89
3.4 The number of high-frequency words associated with RMB
around the world 90
3.5 Focuses in RMB-related reports during (2010–2013) 91
4.1 Distribution of the RMB trade in the main international
offshore financial centers 135
5.1 Offshore RMB bond issuance (0.1 billion yuan) 141
5.2 Deposit balance of London RMB market 148
5.3 Total amount of trade financing in London RMB market 149
5.4 Foreign exchange transactions in London RMB market 149
5.5 Share of Sino-British investment and trade 153
5.6 Amount of trade between China and Africa 155
5.7 Chinese direct investment into Africa 156
5.8 Net operating income of commercial banks 162
5.9 Capital adequacy ratio of commercial banks 162
5.10 Decision tree of analytic hierarchy process 167
5.11 Global distribution of offshore RMB financial centers based on
analytic hierarchy process 172
6.1 Settlement and clearing system of agency banks 183

Tables

1.1	RMB Internationalization Index indicators	10
1.2	Major world currency internationalization indexes	27
2.1	2013 product size and structure of RMB bonds in Hong Kong	37
2.2	Chinese stock market financing amount	40
2.3	Currency structure on the global FX OTC derivatives market in s4 2012 and s2 2013	41
2.4	U.S. dollar against RMB (Hong Kong) futures transactions summarized	42
2.5	Turnovers on major inter-bank markets 2012–2013	44
2.6	2012–2013 stock index futures and bonds transactions	44
2.7	The scale of currency swaps between the People's Bank of China and other monetary authorities	52
2.8	Percentages of currencies in global FER 2013	54
2.9	The trade amount of RMB to main currencies in interbank foreign exchange spot transactions market 2013	55
2.10	Current situation in 2012 of China's capital account control defined by the IMF	67
3.1	The regional distribution of media researching on public sentiment of RMB internationalization	85
3.2	The number of reports on RMB by the mainstream media around the world	87
3.3	The change of the focuses to RMB in different regions and nations over the years	94
4.1	Proportion of imported raw material over total import in Japan	125
4.2	Proportion of trade volumes of Japan in different export regions	125
4.3	Definition of main variables	130
4.4	Share of distribution of seven main international currencies in 26 countries and regions	131
4.5	Descriptive summary	132
5.1	Amount of RMB settlement in cross-border trade	145
5.2	Financial activities denominated by foreign currencies in Britain and the proportion of RMB	151
5.3	Scale of analytic hierarchy process' decision matrix	167

6.1   A comparison of Dim Sum Bonds (DSB) and Synthetic Bonds   175
6.2   CNH products   176
6.3   CHIPS and offshore RMB settlement system   185
A1.1   Characteristics of partial offshore financial centers   213
A1.2   Tax policy comparison of different offshore financial centers   214

Introduction

The Federal Reserve had declared the long-brewing exit from QE before Christmas in 2013. The recovery of the developed market economics is taking shape gradually. Nevertheless, the emerging markets suffer from economic imbalance repeatedly and face uncertainty in their future development. Nearly ten emerging economies have been defined as "vulnerable countries," and the vulnerability reflects on high domestic inflation, decreasing economic growth, current account deficits, capital flight, and exchange rate collapse, triggering concerns that the turmoil of emerging markets would cause another global financial crisis. Despite the wait-and-see attitude and the unease toward the market, the economy and currency performance of China are basically stable, and the growth of RMB Internationalization Index (RII) has maintained a strong momentum.

The RII had ushered in the single-digit era in 2013 and reached 1.69 at the end of the year. The RII increased as much as 84 percent compared with 0.92 at the beginning of 2013. The index rose faster than that of 2012. Thrillingly, the "double drive" model—trade pricing and financial valuation—to support cross-border use of RMB has taken shape. Therefore, the driving force to internationalize RMB is further balanced.

The percentage of using RMB as pricing and settlement currency rose to 2.50 percent in the global trade of 2013, increasing by 60 percent for 3 years in a row, and it contributed to nearly half of this year's RII. China continues to take the lead in the world's import and export, with the total trade volume of more than 4 trillion US dollars; China strives to explore new room for growth by bilateral trade as well as regional trade cooperation and development. Moreover, China has made continuous reforms and innovations in simplifying the examination and approval procedures and lowering the costs of local currency settlement, which has greatly boosted the confidence of the market participants from both home and abroad to use and accept RMB as pricing and settlement currency in the global trade.

By the end of 2013, the portion of RMB in the global capital and financial trade had reached 2.08 percent, contributing to 40 percent of this year's RII with a distinctly accelerated growth rate. Thereinto, the third class indicator (i.e., "RMB's share of the global direct investment") contiinues to skyrocket and ranks the first in the RII indicator system with a very impressive performance of 5.28 percent. China is now the second-largest foreign direct investment (FDI) receiver and the third-largest direct investor in the world. As the related policies become clearer, the fulfillment process of cross-border RMB direct investment becomes more standardized and convenient, and the cross-border RMB financial investment tunnels are broadened and improved gradually. As a result, more and more foreign and domestic enterprises and financial institutions are willing to use and accept RMB as pricing and settlement currency in the global capital and financial trade.

Many foreign government organizations as well as enterprises and financial institutions in the international market are interested in RMB. In November 2013, the Canadian local financial sector succeeded in selling AAA rating offshore RMB bonds to the world, which were very popular among the investors, and collected 2.5 billion yuan, setting a new issuing record of nonresidential offshore RMB bonds. The subscription amount of the bonds was far beyond expectation, within which the central banks and government financial institutions covered 62 percent. Foreign government institutions started to actually hold RMB position, showing that RMB, as a reserve currency, has undergone a historic change from being rejected to being recognized in terms of official acceptance. In 2013 alone, the monetary authorities of many countries and regions, including Australia, South Africa, Belarus, Bolivia, and Taiwan, demonstrated that they had brought RMB assets into their official foreign exchange reserves.

"Growth," "openness," and "reform" in the real economy laid the material foundation of international society's confidence in RMB, and a developed and improved offshore financial market solved the technical problems so that RMB can maintain international attraction. Therefore, the *Internationalization of RMB: 2014 Annual Report* sets its research topic as "RMB offshore market construction and development."

The research group fulfilled the following tasks. First, after sorting out the historical experience and related documents, the research group held in-depth discussion on the internal logic that the offshore financial market boosts currency internationalization, with a focus on the significance and impacts of constructing and developing offshore markets in realizing RMB internationalization in the current stage. Second, through charrettes, field visits, and questionnaires, the group thoroughly studied the current development of RMB offshore markets in places like HK, London, and Frankfurt and intensively discussed the existing problems and future prospects. Third, the group employed methods like logical deduction and empirical study to tentatively discuss the global layout of RMB offshore financial markets. In addition, the challenges and solutions to building RMB offshore markets were elaborated from two angles: "how to successfully build RMB offshore markets" and "how to minimize the negative effects of offshore markets."

The offshore financial market comes into being along with economic globalization and financial liberalization. The features of the offshore financial market (e.g., loose regulation, full competition, low trade cost, and high market openness) help it develop rapidly after its appearance in the major part of today's international financial market. The offshore financial market can offer convenience and safety when economic entities from different countries use a third-party currency in trade. A sophisticated and efficient offshore market operating mechanism plays a very important part in consolidating a currency's international status. Though America suffers from a declining trade status, the dollar remains the number one international currency even after the U.S. subprime crisis triggered the global financial tsunami. The key reason is that the dollar has always been widely used in third-party transactions, so it takes the biggest slice in official foreign exchange reserve. To some degree, that is closely related with developed global dollar offshore markets all over the world's major international financial centers.

Equally, the international usage of RMB can be achieved only with the construction and development of offshore markets. Fast-growing RMB offshore markets not only realize RMB's outflow under surplus condition but also stimulate nonresidents to use and hold RMB through diversified financial products and qualified services. Hence, the offshore RMB pool is gradually expanding. Different from the U.S. dollar and other international currencies, both the appearance of RMB offshore market as well as the initiation of RMB internationalization process are ahead of the capital account convertibility. In the long run, only by capital account reform to bring about wider and deeper international usage can RMB grow into an important international financial trade currency and reserve currency. However, before the right time to open capital account, the RMB offshore market can actually function as a substitute to some degree for capital account convertibility. In other words, to construct and develop RMB offshore markets kept the risk of transnational capital flow within the finite offshore markets and boosted RMB internationalization by loosing capital control in disguised form. Obviously, the current RMB offshore market development has created a valuable time window to push forward capital account reform in a composed, orderly, and timely way. Therefore, RMB offshore markets have extra practical significance to the current RMB internationalization.

The international experience shows that the size of offshore transaction in the international financial centers determines the currency's international status. To some sophisticated international financial centers such as London and New York, the initiative to develop RMB offshore business lies in market participants' own choices. And this automatic process can be very fast or, on the contrary, extremely slow. As for the long-term goal, RMB offshore transaction size and the percentage it takes in the sophisticated international financial centers can be considered as important standards to test whether RMB has already become one of the major international currencies. Yet, because of the global financial tsunami, the international financial centers are undergoing major adjustments. In particular, those emerging international offshore financial centers are competing fiercely against one another and fighting for RMB offshore businesses, in fear of failing to keep a head start. It means that it is possible for China to initiatively cultivate RMB offshore markets in some countries and regions. After a comprehensive study of all factors (i.e., trade, investments, geopolitics, cultures, institutional construction, etc.) through the analytic hierarchy process, the global location research of RMB offshore financial center finds out that the preferred locations for China to actively build offshore markets are HK of Asia, Switzerland of Europe, Costa Rica of America, and Mauritius of Africa, among which, HK has the most distinct advantage.

HK is now the biggest RMB offshore market in the world. HK RMB offshore financial center is the main platform for RMB settlement in cross-border trade. Moreover, it attracts many enterprises, institutions, governments, and monetary authorities from both home and abroad by the increasingly diversified RMB financial products and, therefore, the biggest offshore RMB capital pool is formed in HK as well. At the same time, HK offshore market gradually shows its demonstration effect. In the Asia-Pacific region, RMB offshore trade is also brisk in Singapore, Taiwan, and Macau, and other countries, including Korea, Japan, Australia, and Malaysia, have already shown their active attitude. In Europe, London, Paris, Luxembourg, Frankfurt, and Zurich raced to express their willingness to become the next RMB offshore financial center. In Africa and America, there are also many countries actively exploring the feasibility of building RMB offshore markets.

This report insists that efforts should be made to grasp the current favorable time window; to make full use of historical opportunities like domestic economic restructuring, international offshore financial center adjustments, and international market's searching for hedging currencies; and to promote RMB internationalization by constructing RMB offshore markets. In this process, two kinds of relations need special attention.

First, in the short run, the relation between offshore markets and the real economy should be handled properly, and the international strategy that RMB offshore markets shall serve the Chinese companies and financial institutions is underlined. The offshore market's importance in global resources allocation shall be paid attention to, the objective law to develop international financial centers respected, and the top-level design carried out under the principle of mutual benefit and reciprocity. China's trace of trade, investment, and foreign development should be followed so that RMB offshore market distribution in every continent can be rationally mapped out. Different entering policies shall be adopted in the sophisticated international financial centers and the emerging offshore financial centers. RMB internationalization should be further promoted by developing offshore market, and RMB offshore market's internationalization capability of serving Chinese companies and financial institutions needs improvement.

Second, in the mid–long term, the relation between onshore and offshore RMB financial markets shall be managed to gradually realize the ideal model that the offshore price follows onshore market price. When the development of offshore financial markets hits a certain level, it might have some impact on domestic monetary policies, causing monetary deflation pressure or imported inflation. The offshore market trade complicates the interest and exchange rate determination mechanisms in the issuing countries of the international currency. So it can be deduced that as the global RMB offshore market is heading for maturation from the growth period, China's monetary policy goals have to be shifted from quantity mode to price mode, and meanwhile challenges will be posed to anti-money-laundering and other financial regulations and even to the effectiveness of the legal system.

The *Internationalization of RMB: 2014 Annual Report* is the third annual report the research group has submitted. We have gradually widened our research views and dug deeper into some specific problems as well. Our point of view on RMB internationalization strategic positioning and its realization route is becoming clearer after we contact and exchange views with counterparts from academic and business circles, financial experts, and government officials from different countries in the world. In summary, there are three main points. First and foremost, RMB internationalization must be based on real economy internationalization. If the major players involved in foreign trade and investment are not homegrown transnational companies with competitiveness and influence in the international market, the domestic currency cannot offer sufficient confidence to the international community. As a result, the basis of its internationalization is too infirm to last. Second, China should take the historical chance of international financial center restructure to push forward the global layout of RMB offshore finance in an active and orderly manner. With a limited opening of capital account, the only way to maintain the liquidity of the RMB offshore market and to improve its attraction to nonresidents is to carry out the strategic thoughts of "interaction between domestic and oversea market." Thus, we can "walk with two legs": The first is to build RMB offshore markets, which are separated from domestic market; the second is to promote internationalization of domestic banks to extend the advantage of local currency business to the outside world. We should see that at least in the starting period of development of offshore market, it is necessary to insist that offshore financial business should serve the real economy. Developing an efficient offshore settlement system through designated clearing banks can bring up RMB internationalization level rapidly and stably. Finally, via the practices of deepening reforms and opening up of China (Shanghai) free trade area, we should actively boost the bilateral trade and financial cooperation, take the major opportunity created by silk road economic belt construction, enhance the mutual political trust, and explore new space for China to develop foreign economy. Thus, new driving force as well as enormous positive power will be given to RMB internationalization.

Chen Yulu
May 2014
Beijing

1   Renminbi Internationalization Index

RMB Internationalization Index and its principles

Internationalization of RMB

The internationalization of the RMB can be defined as the process of the RMB performing the functions of an international currency, becoming a major pricing and settlement currency in trade, and becoming a financial transaction currency and an international reserve currency. In the current extremely complicated and turbulent international economic environment, for China to implement the new urbanization, maintain a steady economic growth, and maintain its core interests, RMB internationalization is undoubtedly a very important system guarantee.

Currency internationalization requires some basic conditions. For example, the real economy should maintain steady development and play an important role in international trade and economy; there should be a higher level of domestic financial liberalization and international openness; and the basis of a market system and a macro-economy that is helpful for currency internationalization should be established. Although the currency has some preliminary conditions with the internationalization, to achieve the final goal, China will also face a long and arduous process. According to the development law of currency internationalization, the RMB internationalization must undergo peripheral–regionalization–global, the three stages of development, which takes at least 20 to 30 years.

There is no doubt that internationalization of the RMB is a process of combination of natural market formation and government policy guidance. The process is full of repeated gaming among various international forces, which requires China to make down-to-earth efforts in the aspects of politics, the economy, the military, and the culture, and to raise China's comprehensive powers in order to calmly cope with the risks and challenges of the RMB internationalization.

Definition of the RMB Internationalization Index

The international community generally measures the currency internationalization level by the proportion of one currency in official foreign exchange reserves. National governments submit the currencies that are among the top-most in their official foreign exchange reserves, in accordance with the International Monetary Fund (IMF) statistical requirements, and then the index will be published by the IMF. Since the IMF only separately censuses and publishes the currencies that are more than 1 percent of the world's official reserves, according to which they list only the dollar, euro, yen, pound, Swiss franc, Canadian dollar, and Australian dollar, that is to say, we cannot use the internationally applied indicator, the currency proportion in official foreign exchange reserves, to measure of the renminbi internationalization level.

International Monetary Institute of RUC, proceeding from the basic functions of the international currency, consider that in the case of RMB capital account's orderly opening, the international monetary function of RMB should be mainly reflected in the field of the real economy and focus on the function of RMB as a currency for trade settlement, direct investment, and international bond trading; in the guidance of which, we selected the appropriate variables and indicators and compiled a comprehensive multivariable synthesis index— the Renminbi Internationalization Index (RII)—to measure and reflect the actual level of RMB internationalization. By observing the value and the structure change of the RII, not only can we straightforwardly judge the degree of RMB internationalization and its main influence factors but also can grasp the influence direction and magnitude of different factors on the RMB internationalization, and we can conduct a dynamic comparison with the global usage of major currencies. This offers an efficient operational and management way for government decision-making sectors to accurately grasp this dynamic process, helping them to propitiously seize new opportunities and challenges from home and abroad during this process of internationalization and decisively adjust or formulate macroeconomic policies.

The compilation principles of the RMB Internationalization Index

First, the compilation of RII should be based on the international monetary function, and the index should be able to not only reflect the actual international application of the renminbi but also reflect the guidance direction of the renminbi internationalization and highlight the function of the renminbi as the means of the real economy's exchange and circulations. The compilation of RII's core purpose is to reflect objectively the present situation of the countries around the world using the renminbi, in order to provide an objective, fair, and reliable basis to the government departments' formulating relevant decisions and private department using RMB financial products and formulating the corresponding financial strategy. The global financial crisis makes people realize the danger of the overdevelopment of virtual economy; once the money was divorced from the real economy and inflated endogenously, the stable operation of the financial system would be enormously damaged. As a result, the renminbi internationalization index must not pay too much attention to the virtual economy or derivative financial transactions function but should place emphasis on the circulation function of the real economy.

Second, consider the comparability and operability comprehensively. One of the purposes of the compilation of RII is to provide the countries around the world with the choice basis of international trade and reserve currency, which requires considering the transverse comparison and dynamic comparison between different currencies of the evaluation results in the design. Through comparison and analysis of the internationalization index of the renminbi and other major currencies, we know structurally the main factors that promote or hinder the renminbi internationalization, understand the gap between the internationalization of the renminbi and other major currency, and discover the main contradictions and problems, thus providing a convenient evaluation tool to the government's speculating on the renminbi internationalization implementation and the effectiveness of promotion measures so that the Chinese government can timely seize the opportunity of the internationalization of the renminbi, formulate appropriate and targeted countermeasures, and effectively promote the internationalization of the renminbi. At the same time, the index system design should also fully consider the availability of data and the operability. For some special important indicators whose data cannot directly be collected, we should estimate them based on as much information as possible. The content of the chosen index should be easy to understand, there should be no ambiguity, to ensure that the compilation of RII can accurately and easily be calculated and applied.

Third, consideration must be given to both the stability and the flexibility. The index which the compilation of the RII is based on and the weight of each index is not suitable to change frequently, to ensure that the interpretation of the assessment result has a certain continuity and dynamic comparability. However, we should not rigidify the index and the weight of each index but maintain certain flexibility because at different stages, the internationalization of the renminbi has a different strategic target, and the periodic strategic targets need to be adjusted appropriately according to the change of international political and economic situation. In order to accurately and objectively reflect the process of RMB internationalization, the compilation of RII indexes and the weight of each index should be adapted to the RMB internationalization practices and China's strategic goal, to appropriately adjust itself in different phases.

Fourth, index compilation should be transparent and simple. The index selection principle and weight determination principle of the RII compilation should be carried out under the guidance of the scientific nature and operability. At the same time, adopt a simple and intuitive calculation method to avoid the method that is over-complicated and difficult to understand. In addition, the method of index is open, so that the government and related research department's personnel can study collaboratively on the problems of the renminbi internationalization to lay a solid foundation for the scientific development of RII.

RMB Internationalization Index Indicator system

Theoretically, a currency has three primary functions: as a unit of account, as a medium of exchange, and as a store of value. In international trade, the pricing currency is usually the settlement currency, and one of the purposes of compiling the RMB internationalization index is to focus on reflecting the actual use of the RMB in international economic activities. Therefore, this report will merge the first two functions together. The first-class indicators of RII include the international pricing and payment function and the international reserve function, and the international pricing and payment function is reflected in two aspects of trade and finance. Therefore, in the RMB internationalization index indicator system, the functions of trade pricing, finance pricing, and official foreign exchange reserves are parallelized and their weight is one third each.

According to one of the principles used in compiling the RMB internationalization index (i.e., emphasizing the circulation and transaction functions of the RMB in the real economy), the functions of the RMB in international trade should be the most important component in evaluating its internationalization. Therefore, the proportion of RMB settlement in world trade has been selected as the specific indicator.

According to the balance of payments, capital and financial accounts comprise all transactions between residents and nonresidents, which include direct investment, international security, and international credit. The RMB internationalization indicator system covers indicators from these three aspects. Corresponding indicators have been designed based on the functions of the RMB in these three categories of transactions. The following are some additional notes about indicators of securities.

International securities include bonds and stocks. Because of the great risk of information asymmetry in international finance, the scale of the international bond market with fixed income is far larger than that of international stock, which has always been in a dominant position in the international securities market. What is more, the scales of the major national stock markets are often quoted in local currency, and there is a lack of statistics concerning nonresidents' stock investment. Therefore, by taking financial theories and data availability into consideration, this report will use the international bonds and bills indicator of the Bank for International Settlements (BIS) to reflect international securities transactions. According to the BIS classification, international bonds and bills include, first, all bonds denominated in foreign currencies issued by domestic institutions and non-domestic institutions; second, the bonds denominated in domestic currency and issued by foreign institutions in the domestic market; and third, the bonds denominated in domestic currency and issued by domestic institutions in the domestic market, which are also seen as international bonds and bills if they are targeted to non-domestic investors. Thus, the international bonds and bills indicator can reflect the degree of internationalization of a country's currency in international securities markets very well. In order to reflect the transactions of the RMB international bonds more comprehensively and accurately, this report further divides the indicator into two indicators. One is the stock indicator, namely, the remaining sum of outstanding bonds and bills. The other is the flow indicator, namely, the issuance amount of bonds and bills. The reason for doing this is that the stock indicator can objectively reflect the status quo of the RMB in international bonds and bills transactions, and the flow indicator can better capture dynamic changes of the RMB international bonds and bills. Certainly, accumulation of the flow results in the stock. And the relationship between these two indicators determines that the stock indicator itself uses information from the flow indicator, thus giving greater weight to the stock indicator of the RMB international bonds and bills transactions.

The international reserve function is the most typical and centralized among all international monetary functions. Generally, the proportion of a currency held in foreign exchange reserves is the most immediate and intelligible indicator for measuring its degree of internationalization, which is published

Table 1.1 RMB Internationalization Index indicators

General indicators	Main indicators	Subordinate indicators
Function of pricing and settlement	Trade	Proportion of settlement of RMB in world trade
	Finance	Proportion of RMB overseas credit in international credit
		Proportion of RMB security in announced issues of international bonds and notes
		Proportion of RMB security in amounts outstanding of international bonds and note
		Proportion of RMB direct investment in international direct investment
Function of international reserve	Government reserve	Proportion of foreign exchange reserves of RMB in world reserve

Introduction:

Proportion of settlement of RMB in world trade = Amount of cross-border trade in RMB / Amount of cross-border trade in the world

Proportion of RMB overseas credit in international credit = RMB overseas credit / International Overseas credit

Proportion of RMB security in announced issues of international bonds and notes = Amount of RMB security in announced issues of international bonds and notes / Amount of security in announced issues of international bonds and notes

Proportion of RMB security in amounts outstanding of international bonds and notes = Amount of RMB security in amounts outstanding of international bonds and notes / Amount of security in amounts outstanding of international bonds and notes

Proportion of RMB direct investment in international direct investment = RMB direct investment / International direct investment

Proportion of foreign exchange reserves of RMB in world reserve = Foreign exchange reserves of RMB / Foreign exchange reserves.

by the IMF. In their own interests, a majority of governments in the world do not normally publish the specific currency structure of their official foreign exchange reserves, which leads to great difficulties in collecting data that reflect the international reserve function of the RMB. Despite that RMB has not been reported separately, with gradual improvement of our statistic system and deepening international cooperation the availability of data for the RMB as an official reserve is expected to increase.

Data for RII mainly come from People's Bank of China, International Monetary Fund, Bank for International Settlements, The World Bank, and the United Nations Trade and Development Organization. With the level of RMB internationalization improved, indicator and statistics of the international organizations mentioned above may be upgraded, getting access to the specific statistics of RMB usage in both overseas trade and international finance. This means modifications of indicators of RII, with more indicators included and a few changes in the different weight of existing indicators.

Calculation of RMB internationalization index method and its economic implication

In the RII index system, every index itself is a proportion (no difference of order of magnitudes), so there is no need for dimensionless processing, but we can directly conduct the weighted average and compile the RII.

$$RII_t = \frac{\sum_{j=1}^{5} X_{jt} w_j}{\sum_{j=1}^{5} w_j} \times 100 .$$

Where RII_t represents the RMB internationalization index at time t, X_{jt} represents the value of X_j at time t, and w_j represents the weight of variable X_j.

The economic implication of the RII should be interpreted like this: If the renminbi was the only international currency, the numerical value of the RII index system should equal RII equals 100. Conversely, if the renminbi was not be used in any international economic trade, the numerical value of each index should be 0 and RII 0. If the value of RII increases continuously, this means that the renminbi played greater international currency function in the international economics and that the internationalization level would be higher and higher. For example, when RII equals 10, this implies that one-tenth of the international trade, capital flow, and official reserve assets trade among the countries around the world was operated with the renminbi.

Analysis of the variation of the RMB internationalization index

Status quo of renminbi internationalization index

The RMB internationalization index has shown a steady rise in 2013; specifically, the RMB was more accepted in international trades, international financial

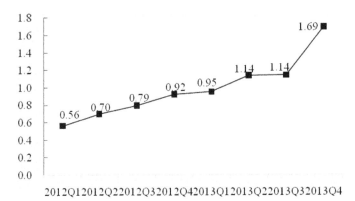

Figure 1.1 The RMB Internationalization Index

Note: Due to adjusted raw statistics, RII of four quarters in 2012 was changed from 0.55, 0.70, 0.77, and 0.87 ("RMB Internationalization Report 2013") to 0.56, 0.70, 0.79, and 0.92.

transactions, and official exchange reserves; promoting the RII represents a sustained increase. As is shown in Figure 1.1, by the fourth quarter of 2013, the RII has climbed to a new high level (1.69), with an increase of 83.80 percent. From the first quarter of 2012 to the fourth quarter of 2013, the average growth rate of RII was 15.66 percent, significantly higher than the growth rate of China's GDP and trade in the same period.

RII of Q4 2013 respectively reaches 0.95, 1.14, 1.14, and 1.69. Since related policies have been implemented in order to simplify the cross-border process in 2013, the scale and structure of RMB cross-border trade and investment settlement business have improved steadily. As is illustrated in Figure 1.2, the growth rate of RII increased from 69.15 percent (in early 2013) to 83.80 percent (2013 Q4).

Four reasons accounting for the increasing trend of RII

First, China's economy has shown a steady growth, maintaining the highest GDP growth rate all around the world. In 2013, the world economic activity began to pick up. Recovery in developed countries (like the United States and Japan) is obvious: the increasing external demand has played a significant role in stimulating the economic growth in emerging markets. However, the downside risks to the global economy and the structural vulnerability still exist. The exit of quantitative easing policy has made emerging markets confront currency depreciation, capital outflows, and other pressures. Under this complex international circumstance, the Chinese government vigorously promoted the new urbanization, adjusted economic structure, and enhanced innovation capability. As a result, China's GDP has reached 56.89 trillion yuan in 2013, with an increase of 7.7 percent. Despite the slowdown in the GDP growth rate, Chinese economic growth still took a leading place around the world. The

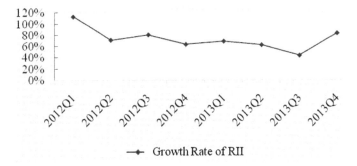

Figure 1.2 RII quarter growing situation

bright outlook of China's economy will undoubtedly provide a solid economic foundation for the RMB internationalization.

Second, the growing real economy and the expanding demand for RMB are the main forces to drive RII all the way up. China's total import and export trade topped 4 trillion dollars in 2013 for the first time, amounting to 4.16 trillion dollars, and this figure was 249.92 billion dollars more than that of the United States. China has become the world's largest trading nation, and the international trade with China is increasingly close, which highlights the advantage of using RMB-denominated settlements. The demand for international usage of RMB is expanding. Since the internationalization of the RMB started in 2011, RMB has surpassed twenty-two other currencies, ranked by leaps and bounds in the global transaction. According to the Society for Worldwide Interbank Financial Telecommunication (SWIFT) statistics, by the end of 2013, RMB had become the world's eighth-largest currency of payment, accounting for 1.12 percent of total market share, increased by 15 percent.

Third, the comprehensively deepened reforms greatly enhance the market confidence. "The Decision on Major Issues Concerning Comprehensively Deepening Reforms" was adopted at the close of the Third Plenary Session of the eighteenth CPC Central Committee; general secretary Xi Jinping worked as group leader himself during central comprehensively deepening reforms, demonstrating the ability of the Chinese government to improve governance as well as a firm belief in promoting the construction of market economy. Accelerating the market-oriented interest rate reform and the RMB capital account convertibility, improving the RMB exchange rate formation mechanism of the market, and establishing Shanghai free trade zone as a pilot to enhance open standards, this series of measures aimed at deepening the Chinese financial system is sure to release a huge bonus system, greatly boost confidence of the market for RMB, and inspire a vast potential in the RMB internationalization market.

Fourth, the rapid development of the offshore market accelerates the process of liberalization and internationalization of RMB. During 2013, the RMB offshore market has been developing rapidly with offshore RMB deposits up to 1.5 trillion yuan. Considering that China has not yet fully liberalized its capital accounts, offshore markets have become an important way to satisfy the demand of those nonresidents using RMB for trade settlement, investment, and financing. Hong Kong is the largest RMB offshore financial operations center; the scale of RMB deposits has reached 860.472 billion yuan, a 42.70 percent increase compared with 2012's. The RMB offshore business in Taiwan and Singapore is also beginning to take shape. On February 2013, a currency settlement mechanism between mainland China and Taiwan Strait was established, with forty-six banks in Taiwan starting to offer RMB deposits, loans, remittances, and wealth management business. Under the strong demand for RMB funds, RMB offshore business in Taiwan is growing faster than that in HK. Owing to the geographical advantage, Singapore has become the center for RMB business in Southeast Asian countries. About sixty-seven commercial banks in Singapore have opened RMB interbank current accounts; RMB

Box 1.1   RMB has become the world's ninth-largest currency

On April 2013, the global foreign exchange and derivatives market survey published by Bank for International Settlements every 3 years indicated that the U.S. dollar remains the dominant currency position in global foreign exchange and derivatives trading, accounting for 87 percent, followed by the euro, Japanese yen, British pound, Australian dollar, Swiss franc, Canadian dollar, and the Mexican peso, after which comes the yuan. Over the past 3 years, affected by the European sovereign debt crisis, the euro trading volume declined by 6 percentage points while its average daily trading volume is still higher than the yen by 10 percentage points. The pound trading volume also fell slightly. Under the stimulus of expected inflation target by Shinzo Abe, the exchange rate of Japanese yen fluctuated in 2013, and the trading volume increased significantly. The average daily trading volume of yen accounted for 23 percent, reaching its highest level since 1996. Additionally, the world's foreign exchange and derivatives trading is becoming more concentrated; foreign exchange transactions occurred in the United Kingdom, the United States, Singapore, and Japan and increased by 5 percent compared with 2010, accounting for 71 percent of global foreign exchange transactions.

It is noteworthy that the international status of the yuan has been significantly improved. RMB average daily trading volume increased from $34 billion in 2010 to $119.563 billion in 2013; meanwhile, the proportion of global foreign exchange transactions in RMB jumped from 0.9 percent to 2.2 percent. RMB surpassed the Swedish krona and the HK dollar for the first time, ranking in the world's top ten foreign exchange-trading currencies, becoming the ninth-largest active trading currency in the global foreign exchange market. The offshore market is a major place for RMB foreign exchange trading, and these businesses are focused on the areas of trade payment and risk hedging.

financing transactions with clearing banks have amounted to 140 billion yuan; and RMB clearing business has amounted to 2.6 trillion yuan. Furthermore, London, Luxembourg, Frankfurt, and other European financial centers are also active in offshore RMB deposits, loans, and bond business; RMB offshore financial transactions have started rushing out of Asia, expanding in Europe.

Structural analysis of RMB internationalization index changes

The proportion of RMB settlement in international trade is growing quickly

RMB-denominated cross-border trade settlement provides a solid backing for the pace of RMB internationalization. In 2013, the scale of cross-border RMB settlement has experienced a rapid growth (Figure 1.3). The RMB-denominated cross-border trade settlement business has amounted to 4.63 trillion yuan, with a significant increase of 57.5%. Specifically, in the fourth quarter of 2013, the scale of cross-border RMB trade settlement was a trillion yuan,, among which the amount of goods trade was 0.95 trillion yuan while the services and other current settlement was up to 0.52 trillion yuan. The proportion of cross-border RMB trade settlement increased from 1.03 percent in early 2012 to 2.50 percent in the fourth quarter of 2013, an increase of 143 percent.

Currently, problems of imbalances in cross-border trade by RMB clearing still exist. In 2013, the export trade settled by RMB was 1.88 trillion yuan while the import side was 2.75 trillion yuan, with receipt and payment ratio of 1:1.46. Comparing with that in 2012 (1:1.2), the problem of imbalances has worsened. A major cause of this phenomenon is the obvious trend of RMB appreciation. Considering that there is a significant difference in exchange rate between Mainland China and HK, the arbitrage operations on RMB are active, making this problem even worse.

According to SWIFT statistics, by October 2013, the market share of RMB in global traditional trade finance, that is, letters of credit and payment, has risen to 8.66 percent. It is the first time that RMB surpassed the euro, becoming the world's second-largest trade settlement currency (the U.S. dollar still holds the first place). However, compared with the U.S. dollar (which accounted for 81.08 percent of global share), the proportion of RMB in international trade settlements is not that high. Mainland China, HK, Singapore, Germany, and Australia are the top five countries and regions for RMB trade settlement business.

In 2013, the share of cross-border RMB trade settlement represented a steady growth, owing to the following three reasons.

First, the international trade environment turned to improve, which contributes to expanding the scale of RMB settlement. In 2013, Europe and other developed economies showed signs of manufacturing recovery and economic upturn; worldwide economic and trade activities as a whole have resumed growth, and the overall trading environment is better than in 2012; the "World Economic Outlook" adjusted the forecast of international trade growth to 4.5 percent. The recovery in global international trade activities is conducive

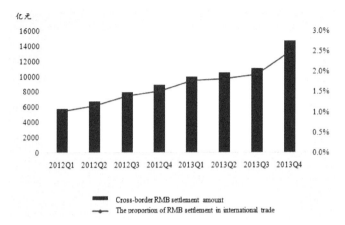

Figure 1.3 Cross-border trade in RMB clearing functions

to overall expansion in the scale of cross-border RMB trade settlements. By the end of 2013, the amount of China's total imports and exports had amounted to 4.16 trillion dollars, with an increase of 7.6 percent. It is worth mentioning that China's service trade amount has reached 539.64 billion dollars in 2013, increased by 14.7 percent. The expanding service trade and the increasing competitiveness have become important means to enhance the international trade status and bargaining power of China.

Second, the ever-increasing bilateral and regional cooperation do well in opening up new space for RMB settlements business. Under the new situation of international trade, that is, regionalization and bilateralization, China has further strengthened bilateral and regional trade cooperation, multi-seeking trade opportunities and opening up new space for trade growth. For example, in the Asia-Pacific region, China has developed closer economic and trade relations with HK, Macao, and Taiwan, taken efforts to promote with China–South Korea, and China–Australia free trade negotiations. As for Europe, China has signed free trade agreements with Iceland and Switzerland as well as cooperation agreements with Germany, Great Britain, and Ireland authorities in order to promote bilateral service trade. Apart from these, based on the historical and cultural origins, China has explored the construction of the economic zone and Maritime Silk Road with Southeast Asia, Arabia, East Africa, and Central Asian countries, which results in improving the scale and structure of trade and laying a solid foundation for enhancing the share of RMB settlement in international trade.

Third, strengthen the reform and innovation, facilitating the cross-border RMB trade settlement. Letting the market play a decisive role, reducing government intervention in economic activity is a distinctive feature of China's economic reforms in 2013. On July 10, the People's Bank of China issued "Notice on the simplification of cross-border RMB business and improving relevant policies," greatly simplifying the review process under the current cross-border RMB settlement and financing business. Taking the cross-border

Box 1.2 Further financial cooperation between Chinese market and other emerging markets in other countries

The Association of Southeast Asian Nations (ASEAN) is a strategic partner of China. During the years 2002–2012, the bilateral trade volume of China and ASEAN had increased 23.6 percent annually, and the cumulative growth of mutual investment had increased 3.4 times. Therefore, there is more and more business cycle correlation between the ASEAN and China. However, only "rice for High-speed Rail" style for complementary trade is not enough. In order to promote the upgrade of bilateral trade, President Xi Jinping presented the idea to build the "Maritime Silk Road" in the twenty-first century during his speech in the Indonesia parliament in October of 2013. And Prime Minister Li Keqiang presented to complete the "regional comprehensive economic partnership (RCEP)" negotiations. "We are completing the Asian infrastructure investment bank and strengthen infrastructure and financial cooperation by the end of 2015, so as to prepare for the future 'Diamond ten years' cooperation between Chinese-ASEAN Economic and Trade". Through a mutual set of financial institutions, the settlement of bilateral currency, and the improvement of currency swap mechanism and the clearing mechanism, the financial cooperation between ASEAN and China has been further deepened. With the aim of reaching a consensus on the market access, financial daily supervision, and some other aspects, China has signed a bilateral memorandum of supervision with seven countries in the ASEAN. As of June 2013, the Chinese funded bank had set up a total of three corporate banks, sixteen branches, and a representative office in nine countries of ASEAN, while a total of five banks of ASEAN countries had set up seven corporate banks in China. In 2013, Bank of China started cash transactions of renminbi against an Indonesia monetary shield. And Nanning offshore business innovation center of Shanghai Pudong Development Bank was established, which added new vigor to the Chinese economic exchanges and trade with ASEAN countries and offshore financial development.

Currency swaps and financial cooperation are the keys for constructing the Silk Road. On the basis of deepening the political and economic cooperation of SCO countries, the financial cooperation between China and Central Asia has entered into a new win-win stage. In August 2013, the Huoerguosi international border cooperation center, which is located in the boundary of Kazakhstan and China, carried out cross-border RMB business innovation and became the offshore renminbi financial business pilot area inland. Xinjiang is constructed to be the west bridgehead for the opening of Chinese market as well as the communication of regional financial platform for China and central Asia. At present, there are four national commercial banks that set up twelve renminbi trade settlement accounts in Xinjiang area, and the RMB against the currencies of Kazakhstan tenge also realized cash transactions.

The mechanism of BRICs (Brazil, Russia, India, China) cooperation transformed from politics cooperation to the political and economic cooperation, which implemented financial cooperation gradually and further completed the collaborative development in the new stage. On March 27, 2013, leaders in the fifth BRICs meeting had signed the "BRICs multilateral cooperation for sustainable development and co-financing agreement," "African multilateral joint infrastructure of BRIC countries financing agreement," and "Declaration of the establishment of Business Council in BRIC countries" and some other documents, which decided to establish Nuggets National Development Bank and made preparation for the establishment of the BRICs reserve pool. In September of 2013, BRIC countries had reached a basic consensus for the scale, proportion, and operation mechanism of contingency reserves and would cost $100 million, in which China would provide the largest share for BRICs' contingency reserve arrangement. The pragmatic financial cooperation with BRIC countries is of great significance for coping with the existing risk of America QE and enhancing overall financial stability and monetary status in emerging markets in other countries. Meanwhile, the cooperation can have a positive influence for China to participate in the international monetary system management and improve the influence of the RMB.

RMB settlement cost reduction and efficiency incentives into consideration, companies have a stronger incentive to use RMB settlement. Local governments have implemented institutional reforms based on their local conditions, aimed at relaxing foreign exchange controls. Both Zhejiang province (which is famous as a global commodity trade center) and Guangxi province (which is famous for its frontier trade) have begun a pilot in cross-border RMB settlement business for individuals. During the first half of 2013, cross-border RMB settlement business for individuals in Yiwu City has reached 4,598, amounting to 4.025 billion yuan, covering more than fifty countries and regions. During the second half of 2013, cross-border RMB settlement business for individuals in Dongxin City has reached 5,348, with a total scale of 6.297 billion yuan. In addition, financial institutions have carried out lots of innovation on channels and products, clearing channels for cross-border RMB financing business, reducing the cost of RMB trade financing, widening the investment channels, and providing necessary financial support to cross-border RMB settlements.

RMB international settlement and clearing functions strengthened

In 2013, RMB international financial settlement and clearing functions strengthened further, with the rising scale of renminbi financial trade, which maintained a high-speed rising trend, in international credit, direct investment, and international bond and notes trade and clearing. By the fourth quarter of 2013, the comprehensive index for renminbi-denominated international financial settlement reached 2.08 percent and grew by 86.17 percent year on year. From the first quarter of 2012 to the fourth quarter of 2013, the comprehensive index for renminbi-denominated international financial settlement year-on-year growth rate reached 127.46 percent on average, which increased very rapidly (Figure 1.4). International credit and direct invest are the two important reasons for which renminbi financial trade share increased so much.

RMB International Credit

In 2013, the scale of renminbi international credit increased rapidly, with the RMB offshore credit stock having reached 11.25 times that in the early 2010. The RMB international credit global accounted indicator increased from 0.25 percent in global share of the first quarter in 2012 to 0.42 percent in the fourth quarter in 2013 (see Figure 1.5).

It is the three powers, that is, market, financial revolution, and policy, that promoted RMB international credit to increase so quickly. First, the dependence degree of trade scale increase on trade finance has increased. With the export share of China's complete equipment having increased, trade finance demands are becoming more and more vigorous. Chinese enterprises that participated in international investment and mergers and acquisition have numbered more than 20,000, and the capital demand of overseas business is very strong. The finance demand from the real economy laid the market foundation for RMB international credit scale's steady and rapid increase. Second, Shenzhen Qianhai, China (Shanghai) Pilot Free Trade Zone, and Jiangsu Kunshan, the three pilot

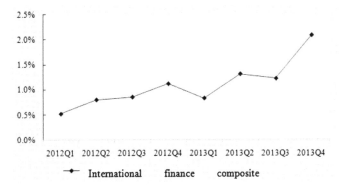

Figure 1.4 Comprehensive index for renminbi-denominated international financial settlement

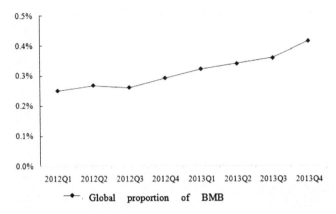

Figure 1.5 RMB international credit accounted for by global market size

areas first tried in cross-border renminbi lending business, are breaking through the limitation of the present system and thus creating favorable conditions for the international credit growth. Finally, specification and simplifying the renminbi offshore lending business processes also played a very important role to promote RMB international credit. On July 10, 2013, the People's Bank of China issued "Notice about simplifying the cross-border RMB business process and improving the relevant policies," improving the efficiency of cross-border RMB clearing further, and facilitating banking financial institutions and enterprises cross-border clearing using RMB, especially the improvement and specification of RMB overseas lending to domestic non-financial institutions, which provided a favorable policy environment system for the RMB international credit global proportion's steady increase.

In addition, from December 9 of 2013 on, commercial banks can issue and invest Negotiable Certificates of Deposit (NCD) in the interbank market, which opened the retail market of international finance business. Since then, following the foreign institutions' getting into the interbank bond market in August of 2010 and RMB Qualified Foreign Institutional Investors' (RQFII) opening in December of 2011, the renminbi bonds, stocks, and loans under capital were basically gotten through.

RMB direct investment

By the fourth quarter of 2013, total settlement of cross-border direct investment in RMB was 533.74 billion yuan, 1.9 times that of the same period in 2012. Such a large growth made the global share of RMB direct investment scale in 2013 show a trend of rapid rise in the world, with the proportion index hitting a record high of 5.28 percent in the fourth quarter (Figure 1.6).

China's steady economic growth in 2013 inspired the enthusiasm of foreign investment. Actual use of foreign direct investment reached $117.6 billion, up

Box 1.3 The three financial pilot areas become pioneers of cross-border RMB loans

The multinational company is the organizer and promoter of trade, and trade development needs financial support, which is a new characteristic of current international trade. In order to better meet the needs of cross-border renminbi trade settlement and to promote the cross-border use of renminbi under the bank's leading financial mode, promoting cross-border RMB credit business is very important.

On December 27, 2012, the People's Bank of China approved "Qianhai cross-border renminbi loans management interim measures." Qianhai cross-border RMB loan business was launched officially. Enterprises registered and practically run or invested in Qianhai can borrow RMB from RMB business operating banks in HK for the construction and development of Qianhai, with loan term independently determined by creditors and borrowers in the reasonable scope. On January 28, 2013, the first Qianhai cross-border RMB loan projects were formally signed in Shenzhen, including twenty-six loan projects where fifteen banks, such as China Development Bank, the Bank of China, Hang Seng Bank, and Standard Chartered Bank, signed with fifteen companies with a total value of RMB 2 billion yuan.

In February 2013, the State Council officially approved setting up a Kunshan pilot area to carry out the individual cross-border RMB business and allowed enterprises in Kunshan pilot area and Taiwan to try to conduct renminbi-lending business and the like within the enterprise group. In September 2013, the Bank of China Kunshan branch completed the first Taiwan-funded enterprise group internal RMB loan business, amounting to 5 million yuan.

On December 2, 2013, the People's Bank of China issued "Opinions about Financial Support to Construction of China (Shanghai) Pilot Free Trade Zone," according to which both domestic and foreign companies in the zone can borrow RMB funds from abroad. On December 5, Shanghai branch and the HK branch of Bank of Communications provided the first batch of cross-border RMB offshore loan business to Shanghai Eastday Electronic Business Co., Ltd.; The Bank of China conducted the first cross-border BMB two-way cash pool business for Wilmar (Shanghai) International Trade Co., Ltd., which received 100 million yuan and paid 150 million yuan.

From the above, Qianhai, Kunshan, and Shanghai—the three big financial reform pilot zones' cross-border RMB credit business innovation—constructed a stable and efficient mechanism for offshore RMB backflow on system and also provided the domestic enterprises with a new platform to obtain low-cost offshore RMB in favor of RMB exerting the function of the optimal allocation of resources at the two markets both at home and abroad.

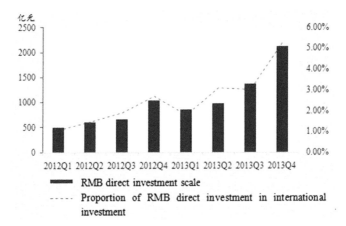

Figure 1.6 Global RMB direct investment

5.3 percent from a year earlier. Among them, the size of the RMB investment (RMB FDI) reached 448.13 billion yuan, up 76.7 percent from a year earlier, accounting for 62.4 percent of the total amount of foreign direct investment. With China's economic transformation and upgrading adjustment of industrial structure, some labor-intensive industries were transferring to Southeast Asia, South Asia, Latin America, and other developing countries and regions. In 2013, China became the third-largest overseas direct investor in the world only after the United States and Japan, which brought tremendous growth and development space for RMB overseas direct investment (ODI). The scale of overseas direct investment in RMB reached 85.61 billion yuan, 1.8 times that of last year.

Policies on RMB direct investment were further specified. On October 10, 2013, the People's Bank of China issued "notice on RMB settlement for foreign investors' investing domestic financial institutions," whereby foreign investors are allowed to invest domestic financial institutions in RMB according to provisions of relevant laws on certain domains such as green investment, capital increase, merger and acquisition, equity participation, equity transfer, profit distribution, clearing, decreasing investment, reducing holding-shares, or recovering ahead of time and so on. On December 3, 2013, the Ministry of Commerce issued no. 87: "announcements on the cross-border RMB direct investment," which further promoted RMB direct investment facilitation and completed the relevant regulations. Foreign investors no longer need a contract or constitution amendment approval when converting their original investment currency to renminbi, which simplified the application procedure of examination and approval.

In addition, the RQFLP pilot was launched, and the investment scope of foreign funds expanded further. The QE (quantative easing) funds that meet RQFLP pilot's requirement can raise RMB directly in foreign countries and remit them to PE fund management companies based in Shanghai through

RQFLP channels, to invest the domestic unlisted enterprises' equity and to share the profits of the enterprise. On August 15, 2013, the Shanghai Bank conducted the first RQFLP domestic equity investment services. The offshore renminbi funds RQFLP absorbs pertain to the foreign renminbi funds, whose investment scope shall abide by the "foreign investment industrial guidance catalogue."

RMB international bonds and notes

The bond market is one of the most important international financial markets; the currency proportion of the international bond market is an important indicator to measure the international recognition degree of a country's currency. In 2013, RMB international bonds and notes issuance reached $23.245 billion, 8.50 percent down from a year earlier; its share in the international market was 0.95 percent by the fourth quarter, with the characteristic of the large-scale fluctuation. At the same time, the balance of RMB international bonds and notes was on the rise, increasing from $40.865 billion in the first quarter of 2012 to $71.374 billion in the fourth quarter of 2013, the global proportion of 0.33 percent (Figure 1.7).

The spread home and abroad, the rapid development of the offshore market, and the inter-bank bond market's opening to the outside world are the major reasons for this continuous growth.

First, higher interest rates in China motivate domestic enterprises to issue an RMB international bond. Investment is one of the main driving forces for China to maintain a high economic growth rate, and the strong investment demand maintains the rate at a high level. From the perspective of the bond supply, the developed countries where interest rates are close to zero, are still in the quantitative easing policy, thus causing a spread of about 3 percent. In order to reduce the financing cost, many enterprises actively seek to finance by issuing foreign debt, whose demand directly promoted the scale of RMB international bond issuance. From the perspective of bond demand, the RMB international bonds' higher returns, the market's positive prospect of China's economic outlook, and the continuous rising expectations of renminbi, enhanced the attraction of RMB international bond investment, and some large international

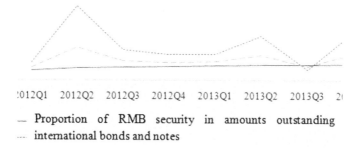

Figure 1.7 Internationalization of RMB bonds and notes integrated indicators

asset management agencies and global fund began to increase RMB bonds in its portfolio.

Second, the development of offshore markets has laid a solid market foundation for the RMB international bond issuance. Hong Kong is a major issue and trade market of RMB bonds; by the end of 2013, RMB bonds issued in HK totaled 370 billion yuan, and 85 percent of the issued securities reached the investment grade. As the RMB offshore center of the ASEAN region, Singapore launched the first batch of RMB bonds issued by HSBC and Standard Chartered Bank in May 2013 totaling 1.5 billion yuan, which were traded in the Singapore Exchange. The Industrial and Commercial Bank of China issued 2 billion yuan of the 2-year "lion city debt" in Singapore in November, which was widely welcomed and achieved a 2.6-times oversubscription. Taiwan is becoming the new renminbi bonds market. In June 2013, Deutsche Bank issued 1.1 billion yuan of RMB bonds in the Taiwan region; individual citizens can invest the bond and conduct the counter transactions in the Taiwan Stock Exchange. Agricultural Bank of China issued six Treasure Island bonds dominated in RMB in Taiwan, whose total scale reached 4 billion yuan. In addition to Asia, Europe's offshore RMB international bond issuance is also very active. Luxembourg had issued more renminbi bonds than Hong Kong and London. What's more in the first half of 2013 Luxembourg had become the second offshore RMB market after London.

Third, the inter-bank bond market's opening up improved the liquidity of the RMB international bond, which solved investors' worries. In March 2013, QFII and RQFII were allowed into the Chinese interbank bond market to participate in the trade business. By the end of 2013, more than 100 foreign institutions, including foreign central banks, international financial institutions (including the World Bank, the International Finance Corporation), sovereign wealth funds, Hong Kong and Macao clearing banks, RMB settlement in cross-border trade, foreign participating banks, foreign insurance institutions and RQFII, and the like, got into the interbank bond market. What is worth mentioning is that the World Bank, which has an important status in the international bond market, invested in China's bond market and participated in the Chinese bond market transactions, which meant the World Bank's affirmation and confidence for renminbi internationalization. This greatly enhanced the foreign institutional investors' confidence in the RMB financial markets and played a positive role to promote the demand growth of RMB bonds and notes.

RMB as a more popular foreign exchange reserve

With the development of China's economy, RMB usage share in international trade and financial transactions continues to improve; the acceptance of RMB as an international reserve currency also expands, and more and more countries (the United Kingdom and the EU included) show willingness to take RMB as their official reserve assets. Specifically, on March 17, 2013, the Central Bank of Bolivia announced an increase in the number of RMB assets to buy on the

Box 1.4 Influences of restarting the Treasury Futures Market on the RMB internationalization

In January 1976, the Chicago Mercantile Exchange launched the 90-day Treasury bond futures for the first time, then successively launched 2-year, 5-year, and 7-year and 10-year futures 1 year later, which provided investors with low-cost interest rate risk management tools. The Treasury bonds futures strengthened the attraction of the American treasury market, making the United States the world's largest Treasury market. At present, the United States, the euro zone, Britain, Japan, Canada, Mexico, Russia, and twenty-three other countries and regions have treasury bond futures markets, according to the statistics from the Bank for International Settlements (BIS) and the U.S. Futures Industry Association (FIA); and in 2012, the global interest rate futures trading accounts for about 90 percent of the world's various types of financial futures trading amount, while about half of the interest rate futures trading is Treasury bonds futures trading.

After more than five years of ruminating, on September 6, 2013 China launched three treasury bond futures, which marked the opening of the treasury bond market after being closed for 18 years. On December 18, 2013, the China Financial Futures Exchange Treasury bonds futures contracts TF1312 were delivered successfully, marking that the Treasury futures conducted the first lifecycle of a contract from listing, trading to the delivery. The products, rules, and system design of the Treasury bond futures had received the inspection of the market.

Restarting the renminbi Treasury futures is the milestone of China's financial market system construction, which had great significance in improving the competitiveness of China's financial markets. Treasury bond futures not only offered an efficient interest rate risk management tool but provided the bond market interest rate pricing with scientific basis and moreover this accumulated positive energy for the renminbi internationalization.

To expand the overseas use of RMB and stimulate foreign enterprises and institutions to hold RMB, a precondition is to preserve or increase the value. Different from the domestic financial market institutions, international finance has obvious characteristics of the securitization, which relies mainly on direct financing. While investing stocks have higher risk, a bond market of moderate risk is the object of international investors, so the size of the international bond market is greater than that of the stock market, which means that the construction of a large renminbi bond market is the necessary premise to promote the internationalization of the renminbi. In China's bond market, Treasury bonds have the largest scale and highest and best credit and liquidity; previously, because the bond underwriters lacked the hedging tools, they often chose to add the Treasury bonds to the held-to-maturity account of low-yielding operation or to sell them at the one-and-a-half market of high-risk operation, which made Treasury securities underwriters lack a reasonable pricing mechanism and suppressed the bond-trading motivation, with the demand unprosperous and the issuance efficiency low. Treasury bond futures provide a safe haven for the underwriters in the Treasury bond issuance market, which reduces largely the holding cost and transaction cost of the bond, thus reducing the issuing cost and the interest rates of Treasury bonds, which is helpful to stimulate the enthusiasm of the underwriters and investors to participate in Treasury bonds both in the primary and the secondary market, expand the scale of Treasury bond market, and meet the demand of the foreign investors to invest in bonds after the internationalization of the renminbi. In addition, according to the current system arrangement under the capital account controls, the foreign institutions conducting the renminbi business in the offshore renminbi market can access the domestic inter-bank bond market for investment and trade, and the Treasury bond futures' custody transfer mechanism means that Treasury bond futures can connect exchange market and the inter-bank market at the same time, which effectively eliminates the differences between exchange and the interbank market in pricing the same bond, thus improving the bond market's pricing ability. Therefore, the interbank market investors will be able to get more reasonable profits, offshore renminbi-holding foreign institutions can also benefit from it, thus improving the initiative of expanding renminbi business and building up more positive energy of the internationalization of the renminbi.

basis of 2012 in order to achieve diversification of international reserves and strengthen its ability to hedge against inflation. On April 24, the Central Bank of Australia made it clear that about 5 percent of its foreign exchange assets might be used to buy Chinese government bonds, including RMB as its foreign exchange reserves. On August 1, Belarus made an announcement that it would include RMB assets in the Chinese domestic market into foreign exchange reserves. On October 2, Taiwan monetary authorities took the yuan into its foreign exchange reserves for the first time. On November 12, the South African Reserve Bank announced that it would invest 1.5 billion dollars to buy Chinese bonds in order to reduce systemic risk, which accounts for about 3 percent of its reserve assets. By the end of 2013, the People's Bank of China has signed currency swap agreements with twenty-three countries and regions, amounting to 2.57 trillion yuan. These agreements would not only contribute to maintaining financial stability but facilitate bilateral trade and investment between China and other countries or economies. Through bilateral currency swap agreements, RMB has officially entered the United Kingdom, the European Union, and other major developed countries as official reserve assets in 2013, strengthening the function of RMB as foreign exchange reserves.

Comparison of major currencies' internationalization index

The diversification of international currency is a dynamic development process, and complex changes in the international trade and international financial markets tend to alter the international usage of monetary sovereignty. In order to evaluate the changes in the international monetary situation and reflect internationalization level gap between the RMB and major currency, this report would comply with RII in the same way, consisting of internationalization index in the dollar, euro, yen, and pound. In 2013, the levels of four major currencies for international use showed a rising trend. Compared to the fourth quarter in 2012, the total value of four-currency internationalization index had increased by 3.57 percent.

In 2013, American's economy recovered gradually, which helped to improve the employment situation, the consumer recovery, private investment, and export growth. Despite the financial crisis and impact of several rounds of quantitative easing to the international community's confidence in the dollar, the best hedging currency status of the dollar was still difficult to change. At the beginning of the year, the Federal Reserve System (the Fed) sent a clear signal of QE exit and promoted the appreciation of the dollar, which caused global funds to speed up the return to America and the central bank system, and the demand for dollars in the world increased. However, during the fourth quarter of 2013, the performance of the American economy was worse than expected, and the scale of the global ratio of international bonds and notes issued on the dollar fell to 39.25 percent, which decreased 11.16 percent year on year. Meanwhile, the ratio of the dollar was 61.18 percent in global foreign exchange reserves, down 0.22 percent year on year. In a word, the international status of the dollar was stable. In the fourth quarter of 2013, the dollar internationalization index had reached 52.96.

Table 1.2 Major world currency internationalization indexes

	2012Q1	2012Q2	2012Q3	2012Q4	2013Q1	2013Q2	2013Q3	2013Q4
USD	52.47	53.24	53.49	52.93	52.73	55.05	53.68	52.96
EUR	27.95	28.37	28.97	26.68	24.69	27.85	25.17	30.53
JPY	4.22	4.71	4.77	4.60	4.10	4.44	4.51	4.27
GBP	4.49	4.56	4.95	4.18	4.32	3.98	3.94	4.30
Total	89.13	90.87	92.17	88.40	85.84	91.32	87.29	92.06

The crisis of European debt remains uncertain, and the negative effect of high debt and financial state of division is still obvious. In the early part of 2013, national economic recovery in the euro area is slow and uneven, and the exchange rate fluctuations of the euro had intensified. However, during the second half of 2013, the recovery of the Eurozone economy was accelerated, and the gap between regional economies was narrowed. Substantial growth of direct investment improved the solid economic foundation for the international use of the euro. As a result, in the international bond market, the amount of global proportion of international bonds and notes issued on euro-denominated rose 44.65 percent, which increased 20.25 percent year on year. By the end of 2013, the euro proportion in the international foreign exchange reserves was 24.45 percent, up 0.92 year on year. Thus, the international status of the euro began to show an upward trend, during which the euro internationalization index reached 30.53 during the fourth quarter of 2013, and increased 3.85 percentage points compared with the same period in 2012.

Since 2013, Japanese Prime Minister Abe Shinzo continued to implement policies to stimulate the economy. The depreciation of the yen has certain positive influence on the Japanese stock market, the expansion of export, and increase business confidence. However, the international confidence in the yen dropped sharply, and hedging function is weakening due to the changes of the domestic economy and the friction of international politics and diplomatic affairs. During the fourth quarter of 2013, the global ratio of international bonds and notes balance of the yen fell to 2.21 percent, the global proportion of international credit fell by up to 9.25 percent, and the global proportion of JPY as foreign exchange reserves is 3.94 percent, down 3.74 percent year on year. Therefore, in 2013, the international status and influence of the yen declined, of which the internationalization index of the yen was 4.27 until the fourth quarter and decreased 7.25 percent year on year.

In 2013, the British economy has been growing continuously with 1.9 percent GDP growth, which indicates that the performance of economy is much better than expectation. Because of the recovery of the British economy and with sterling rate falling to a record low in the middle of 2013, pounds become one of the most essential hedge currencies in a global range. However, the problems hidden behind the British economy such as the weak exports, insufficient investment, manufacturing output, and orders not returning to pre-crisis levels cannot be ignored. What is more, the direct investment of Britain fell as did the international community's lack of confidence in the British economy. The global proportion of EUR as foreign exchange reserves is 4.01 percent, down 0.82 percent year on year. GBP performed below expectation in the international bond market, and the amount of international bonds and notes issued by GBP fell to 6.56 percent in the fourth quarter of 2013. However, the proportion of GBP in the international credit market rose slightly, up 1.41 percent year on year. On the whole, in 2013, the GBP internationalization index stayed basically stable. In the fourth quarter of 2013, the internationalization index was 4.30 (Figure 1.8).

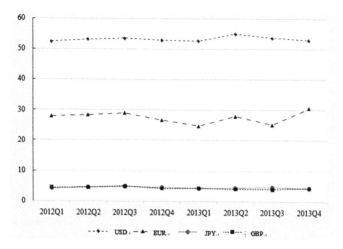

Figure 1.8 Major world currency internationalization indexes

Box 1.5 Chinese and British cooperation to build London's third financial center

The United Kingdom and China have the economies that are highly complementary; they both show the urgent needs and desires in strengthening monetary and financial cooperation. Cooperation to build a London RMB offshore center is the common bilateral mutually beneficial win-win. For London, it has a huge foreign exchange market that attracts one-third of the global foreign exchange trading volume. The market demand for RMB has had a large scale. Together with the accelerated pace of internationalization of RMB, London is clearly aware that expanding the RMB business is the indispensable method to increase financial income and to consolidate its position as an international financial center. In addition, due to the European sovereign debt crisis, the British economic recovery is still fragile. Actively strengthening China, United Kingdom economic and financial cooperation can inject new vitality into the economic recovery in the United Kingdom. For China, the EU is the largest trading partner of China; it is also the main investment area for China in recent years. The brisk demand for the RMB in real economy in the international economic activities as well needs to build nearby offshore markets to provide the RMB financial services. London is the oldest and largest global offshore financial center, which has a surprising ability of financial innovation, risk management, and market supervision. Choosing London as an RMB offshore center that covers all of Europe cannot only satisfy the market demand and improve the RMB's ability to configure domestic and foreign financial resources but also helps to expand the RMB financial transaction scale and make the RMB play a greater role in international financial transactions.

In order to create London's third financial center together, in June 22, 2013, People's Bank of China and Bank of England signed a bilateral currency swap agreement that has a scale of 200 billion yuan/200 billion pounds, providing the market with enough liquidity and eliminating the interference of liquidity risk on the offshore RMB business. In October 2013, with the British finance minister Osborne's visit to China, the British and Chinese governments achieved a number of agreements at the Fifth China United Kingdom economic and financial meeting, which promotes closer cooperation between the two countries in economy and finance. For example, the two sides agreed to make direct transaction between the RMB and pounds in Shanghai and the offshore market. China restricted British RQFII to 80 billion yuan, which constructs a stable reflux mechanism for the London offshore market and greatly enhances the attraction of London offshore RMB business. HSBC, Brazil Bank, ANZ Bank, China Construction Bank, and a number of domestic and foreign banks issued RMB bonds in the London market. In November 26, 2013, Industrial and Commercial Bank of China issued 2 billion yuan offshore renminbi bonds in London. The bond subscription rate is more than four times. High-quality financial resources injected into London lit up investment enthusiasm for yuan-denominated bonds.

In the government and the market dual driving force, London offshore RMB business has a strong and sustainable development. Compared with 2012, the trading volume of RMB forward, swap, and other interest rate products rose sharply. In June 2013, renminbi deposits amounted to 14.5 billion yuan, the credit scale up to 3.3 billion yuan, and the average daily RMB and foreign exchange transactions doubled compared to the same period in 2012. At present, London has become the world's largest outside RMB offshore market.

2 Current situation of the internationalization of the renminbi

It has been more than 4 years since 2009, when renminbi was internationalized. During the past 4 years, the scope of accepting renminbi as settlement currency has increased, and the pace of renminbi internationalization has accelerated in the field of cross-border trade settlement, direct investment, and so on. The Third Plenary Session of the Eighteenth Communist Party of China kicked off a new round of reform in China. A major market-oriented reform of interest rates, exchange rates, and capital account liberalization of the market and other changes in financial area in the system have been pushed into fast development, which is bound to add positive energy to renminbi internationalization.

RMB cross-border trade settlement

Using RMB as settlement currency for cross-border trades is a fundamental step to improve the internationalization of RMB. For enterprises, using RMB as settlement currency can effectively save the exchange cost and reduce the risk. On July 5, 2013, the People's Bank of China issued Notice on the Simplification of Cross-border Renminbi Business Processes and Improving Relevant Policies, which aims to further enhance the efficiency of cross-border renminbi settlement and bring convenience to banking financial institutions and enterprises to use the RMB for cross-border settlement. In addition, individual cross-border renminbi business started in Yiwu, Zhejiang, Dongxing, and Guangxi. In these pilot areas, individuals who are engaged in trade in goods, trade in services, and other recurring items and other services of domestic and foreign markets can open RMB settlement bank accounts in accordance with the relevant provisions for cross-border trade in RMB clearing business.

Several characters of 2013 RMB cross-border trade settlement are as follows.

Scale continues to expand, and settlement amount and settlement ratio rise rapidly

Renminbi settlement amount is steadily growing, and the proportion in the total import and export amount rises rapidly (Figure 2.1). At the end of 2013, the ratio of settlement by RMB reached 24.5 percent, which was 10 percent higher

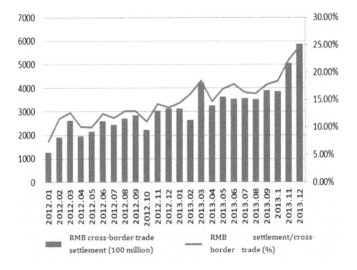

Figure 2.1 The scope of RMB cross-border trade settlement

Source: People's Bank of China, the Ministry of Commerce

than that in the beginning of 2013. In 2013, cross-border trade settled by RMB in the banking industry accumulated to 4,630 billion yuan, increasing by 1690 billion yuan which is 57.5 percent of that in 2012.

Goods trade settlement dominates, and the scope of service trade settlement expands

In the cross-border RMB settlement structure, the ratio of goods trade settlement is larger than that of service trade settlement (Figure 2.2). In 2013, the goods trade settlement amount was 3.02 trillion yuan, an increase of 0.96 trillion yuan, a growth of 47.1 percent, accounting for 65.2 percent of the total amount of RMB settlement business. The amount of service trade and other projects in the renminbi settlement amount was 1.61 trillion yuan, an increase of 0.73 trillion yuan, a growth of 83.0 percent, accounting for 34.8 percent of the total amount of RMB settlement business.

Balance in receipts and payment is stable, and export RMB settlement grows rapidly

From the perspective of renminbi settlement in the entire year of 2013, cross-border RMB trade settlement businesses were paid in 1.88 trillion yuan, an increase of 0.58 trillion yuan, a 44.6 percent increase, accounting for 40.6 percent in the amount of RMB settlement; the Real pay reached 2.75 trillion yuan, an increase of 1.18 trillion yuan, a 75.2 percent increase, accounting for 59.4 percent RMB settlement. The ratio of receipts and payment dropped from 1:1.2 in 2012

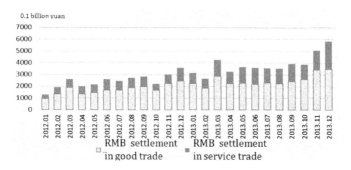

Figure 2.2   The trend of RMB settlement scale in goods trade settlement and service trade settlement

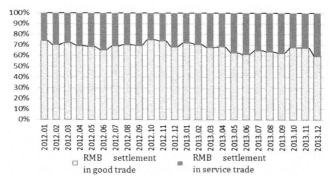

Figure 2.3   The ratio of RMB goods trade settlement and service trade settlement

Source: People's Bank of China, the Ministry of Commerce

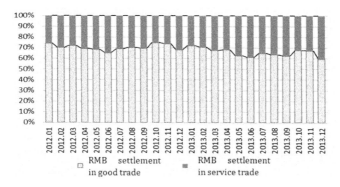

Figure 2.4   The ratio of receipt and payment in cross-border RMB settlement businesses (2010–2013)

Source: People's Bank of China

to 1:1.46. The constant exodus of RMB further increased the supplement of offshore RMB. From the change of receipts and payment ratio from 2010 to 2013, the total amount of RMB cross-border trade in receipts and payment is stable.

The current situation concerning direct investment

RMB overseas direct investment

According to the statistics of the Ministry of Commerce, in 2013, Chinese domestic investors made non-financial overseas direct investment in 5,090 foreign firms in 156 countries and regions, which amounted to $90.17 billion, up 16.8 percent over the previous year. The amount of RMB ODI was 85.61 billion RMB, accounting for 19.4 percent of the total ODI at the exchange rate at the year end, with the growth of 181.2 percent (Figure 2.5).

The fast increase in overseas investment was due to the accelerated liberation of capital account; especially the allowance for the public to do foreign direct investment has remarkably motivated the enthusiasm of Chinese civilians to invest, which has led to the rapid growth of overseas investment. On June 5, 2013, the State Council made an announcement to establish the system of individual investors' overseas investment. On December 2, 2013, the People's Bank of China promulgated the "Suggestions about Supporting (Shanghai) Pilot Free Trade Zone Financially" (abbreviated to "Suggestions"). That paper points out two measures in order to make overseas direct investment more convenient. The first measure is to allow business companies to try cross-border direct investment, which means these companies have the right to deal with cross-border payments and foreign exchange, so as to make it more convenient for them to invest. The second tends to benefit individuals, which allows qualified individuals with jobs in the zone to conduct kinds of overseas investments

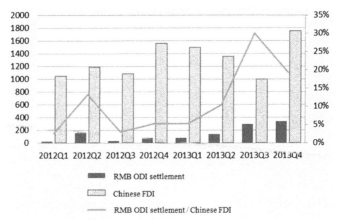

Figure 2.5   RMB ODI settlement and Chinese FDI

Source: People's Bank of China; "Chinese Monetary Policy Implementation Report"; the Ministry of Commerce.

including securities investment. Meanwhile, the individuals in the zone can convert the income abroad, and as for the individually owned business, they are allowed to provide cross-border loans to their overseas branches. Moreover, qualified foreign individuals are also allowed to open nonresident individual domestic investment accounts and to operate kinds of domestic investments including securities investment based on the regulations.

RMB foreign direct investment

The fast growth of the Chinese economy enhances the attractiveness of direct investments. In 2013, the actual use of FDI accounted for $117.586 billion, up 5.25 percent over the previous year. Foreign direct investments using RMB settlement accounted for $448.13 billion, up 76.7 percent over the previous year. RMB settlement accounted for 61.5 percent of total foreign direct investment, higher at 25.6 percent than 2012 (Figure 2.6).

In order to further standardize and facilitate RMB cross-border settlement business use when foreign investors establish, merge, and participate in financial institutions, People's Bank of China issued "Notice about foreign investors investing in domestic financial institutions by RMB settlement" on October 10, 2013. On December 3, 2013, the Ministry of Commerce published "Announcement on RBM overseas direct investment," making the RMB overseas direct investment more convenient and perfecting the related supervisions.

RMB securities investment

International bonds and bills market

In 2013, the growth of the amount of RMB bonds and notes issued declined. The annual issuance of RMB bonds and bills reached $23.242 billion, resulting

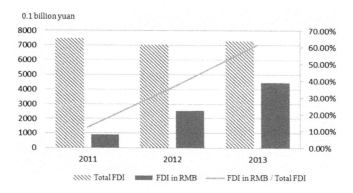

Figure 2.6 FDI RMB settlement over 2011 to 2013

Source: The Ministry of Commerce; People's Bank of China

in a year-to-year reduction of $2.063 billion, a decline of 8.12 percent (Figure 2.7).

Despite the big fluctuation on the scale of the international bonds and notes of RMB issuance, the stock amount is still in a rapid upswing. At the end of 2013, the stock of international bonds and notes of RMB reached $71.945 billion, a year-to-year increase of $14.342 billion (i.e., an increase of 24.90 percent). The balance of RMB international bonds and notes accounted for 0.33 percent of global bonds and bills, a slight increase compared with that of 2012 (0.27 percent ; Figure 2.8, Figure 2.9). Over the same period, among the global international bonds and notes balance, the dollar accounted for 35.80 percent; the euro accounted for 44.21 percent; the sterling accounted for 9.48 percent; while the Japanese yen accounted for 2.22 percent. Overall, RMB international bonds and notes accounted for a small proportion of the global balance, and there is a huge gap compared with the major international currencies.

In 2013, after bottoming out in the third quarter, RMB bonds and notes issued $8.75 billion in the fourth quarter, accounting for 0.96 percent of the

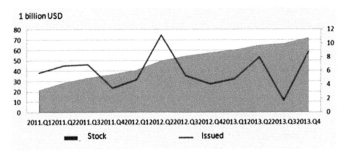

Figure 2.7 The stock and issuance of RMB international bonds and notes, 2011–2013

Source: Bank for International Settlements

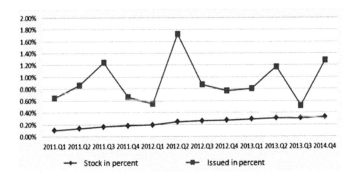

Figure 2.8 Proportion of RMB international bonds and notes on global market: in stock and issuance perspective, 2011–2013

Source: Bank for International Settlements

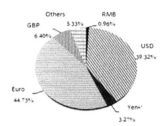

Figure 2.9 Q4, 2013 Currency structure and amount of international bonds and notes

Source: Bank for International Settlements

total bill and international bonds. Over the same period, U.S. dollars accounted for 43.96 percent of the global amount of international bonds and notes issued, and the number for the euro is 39.40 percent, for sterling is 6.39 percent, and for Japanese yen is 3.14 percent. Hong Kong is the main place for the RMB international bonds issued. RMB bonds products in HK had a substantial increase in the size of the stock in 2013, up from 241.82 billion yuan in 2012 to 290.401 billion yuan. It is worth noting that the main issuer started to expand globally from the beginner HK. Developed countries like Japan and Canada have joined the ranks of the RMB international bonds issuance. On November 5, 2013, the Department of Finance of British Columbia, Canada, announced in Beijing that the province has successfully issued 2.5 billion yuan offshore RMB bonds. This is by far the largest offshore RMB bonds issuance by foreign governments (Table 2.1).

Stock market

In 2013, the number of domestic listed companies was 2,489, five more than that at the end of 2012. Shanghai and Shenzhen stock markets were also showing a

Table 2.1 2013 product size and structure of RMB bonds in Hong Kong

Category	Stock (¥100million)	Percentage	No of bonds	Percentage
Corporate bonds	1,666.27	57.38	155.00	59.62
Financial bonds	491.27	16.92	73.00	28.08
Convertible bonds	101.47	3.49	10.00	3.85
National debt	645.00	22.21	22.00	8.46
Total	2,904.01	100.00	260.00	100.00

Source: WIND database

certain degree of differentiation. In 2013, the Shanghai Composite Index closed at 2115.98, compared to 2012, falling 153.15 points, or 6.75 percent; the Shenzhen Composite Index closed at 1057.67 points, compared with 2012, increasing by 176.50 points, or 20.03 percent. The average price-earnings ratio of the Shanghai stock market decreased from 12.30 times at the end of 2012 to 10.99 times; the average price-earnings ratio from the Shenzhen market rose from 22.01 times by the end of 2012 to 27.76 times. In 2013, market capitalization (A, B shares) totaled 23.097719 trillion yuan, an increase of 61.957 billion yuan compared with the same period of last year (i.e., an increase of 0.27 percent). The stock market circulation value totaled 19.957954 trillion yuan, an increase of 1.792128 trillion yuan, compared with the same period of last year (i.e., an increase of 9.87 percent). Trading in Shanghai and Shenzhen stock markets is very active, and the cumulative turnover was 46.87286 trillion yuan, an increase of 15.406119 trillion yuan compared with the same period of last year (i.e., an increase of 48.96 percent). Average daily turnover was 196.945 billion yuan, a year-to-year increase of 67.452 billion yuan, an increase of 52.09 percent (Figure 2.10).

Overall, China's stock market performance is poor in 2013, while there is a strong growth for stock markets in major developed countries because of the promotion from the ongoing accommodative monetary policy. In the year 2013, the Nikkei 225 index has risen 56.72 percent year-round; the U.S. Dow Jones index has risen 26.50 percent. In sharp contrast to the negative growth of the entity economy in Europe, European stock markets rose sharply. The annual increase of the French CAC40 index, the German DAX index, and the FTSE 100 Index reached 17.99 percent, 25.48 percent, and 14.43 percent, respectively. Except for China, stock market performance of other BRIC countries was more active; for example, the South African stocks have risen 19.22 percent year-round; Bombay Sensitive Index has risen 8.82 percent. The 2013 Chinese IPO

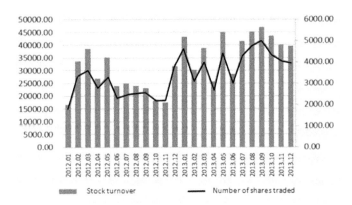

Figure 2.10 Chinese Stock Market transactions

Source: China Securities Regulatory Commission
Note: Stock turnover is in hundred million yuan; shares traded are measured in hundred million shares

market has been interrupted throughout the entire year; thus, the hematopoietic function of the stock market has been weakened. Financing is mainly in the form of private placement; in 2013, A-share private placement financing amount reached 224.659 billion yuan, an increase of 37.911 billion yuan and an increase of 20.3 percent compared with the same period of last year (Table 2.2).

Derivatives market

The market size of RMB derivatives is still small, but the product types have been continuously enriched, and the trading mechanism has been improved during the year of 2013.

Since the size of the market is small, it has not yet been included in the BIS statistics

According to the Bank for International Settlements statistics, the outstanding balance on the global OTC interest rate derivatives market is $561 trillion as of the second quarter of 2013: The dollar, euro, Japanese yen, British pound, Swiss franc, Canadian dollar, and Swedish krona account, respectively, for 30.11 percent, 40.51 percent, 9.81 percent, 8.25 percent, 0.99 percent, 1.66 percent, and 1.05 percent (Figure 2.11), whereas other currencies account for a total of less than 8 percent. Since RMB derivatives have a relatively small scale, it has not yet been included in a separate statistical currency ranking. In particular, the proportion of the market value of other currencies rose to 6.53 percent at the end of the second quarter of 2013, from 4.63 percent by the end of 2012.

From a foreign exchange derivatives perspective as of the second quarter of 2013, the outstanding notional principal amount on global OTC foreign exchange derivatives market reached $73,120,540,000,000, among which dollar-involved foreign exchange derivatives contracts amounted to $64.30884 trillion, accounting for 87.95 percent. Compared with the number of 85.51 percent (at the end of

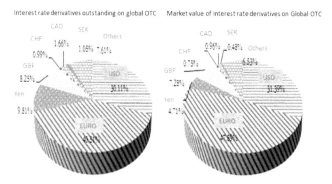

Figure 2.11 The currency structure of interest rate derivatives on the global OTC market in late S2 of 2013

Source: Bank for International Settlements.

Table 2.2 Chinese stock market financing amount

| | Initial Issue Amount | | | Refinancing Amount | | | | | |
| | A | B | H | A | | | | B | H |
				Public Additional	Directional Additional	Placement	Warrants Exercise		
2011	2825.07	0.00	67.82	132.05	1664.50	421.96	29.49	0.00	45.36
2012	1034.32	0.00	82.50	104.74	1867.48	121.00	0.00	0.00	77.14
2013Q1	0.00	0.00	0.00	10.27	776.73	66.93	0.00	0.00	36.55
2013Q2	0.00	0.00	28.93	24.15	584.27	62.09	0.00	0.00	4.99
2013Q3	0.00	0.00	0.00	14.00	340.49	297.50	0.00	0.00	11.80
2013Q4	0.00	0.30	84.24	32.00	545.10	49.23	0.00	0.00	6.17
2013	0.00	0.00	113.17	80.42	2246.59	475.75	0.00	0.00	59.51

Source: China Securities Regulatory Commission
Note: A Shares in million yuan. B Shares in hundred million U.S. dollars. H Shares in hundred million U.S. dollars

Table 2.3 Currency structure on the global FX OTC derivatives market in s4 2012 and s2 2013

Currency	FX Derivatives global OTC Notional principal outstanding ($0.1billion)		FX Derivatives global OTC Notional principal outstanding (%)	
	s4.2012	s2.2013	s4.2012	s2.2013
CAD	3098.53	3280.29	4.60%	4.49%
EUR	23796.23	24398.88	35.33%	33.37%
JPY	14113.05	15217.25	20.95%	20.81%
GBP	7824.99	8444.66	11.62%	11.55%
SEK	1453.38	1389.38	2.16%	1.90%
CHF	3832.08	4180.82	5.69%	5.72%
USD	57599.23	64308.84	85.51%	87.95%
Others	22999.31	25020.96	34.14%	34.22%

Source: Bank for International Settlements

Note: The total of proportion of the currency and foreign exchange derivatives is 200%

2012), it increased by about 2 percentage points. The amount involved in the euro foreign exchange derivatives contracts was $24.39888 trillion, accounting for 33.37 percent and decreasing approximately 2 percentage points compared with 33.53 percent by the end of 2012. The proportion of contracts amount in other currencies was less volatile. RMB foreign exchange derivatives were of low scale relatively, so it has not yet been ranked solely (Table 2.3).

RMB derivative products on the international market have been further enriched

Although from the perspective of total amount, RMB derivatives scale is relatively small, varieties of derivative products on the international market have been further enriched due to the promotion of market-oriented interest rate reform in China and the improvement of RMB exchange rate formation mechanism. In August 2013, HKEx launched its first cross-border stock index futures—China 120 Index futures—to provide investors with the trading and hedging instruments to simultaneously capture investment opportunities on both markets. On the futures transactions of the U.S. dollar against the RMB, which were launched by HKEx in September 2012, the size of the monthly turnover has significantly increased over 2012. At the end of 2013, HKEx RMB futures open interest reached 18,701 hands, and the average daily contract volume was 568 hands, increased by 278 hands, an increase of 95.86 percent compared with 2012 (Table 2.4).

Table 2.4 U.S. dollar against RMB (Hong Kong) futures transactions summarized

Month	Trading days	Contract volume		Outstanding contracts
		The average daily	Total	
09.2012	10	217	2,172	1,076
10.2012	20	228	4,565	1,956
11.2012	22	294	6,465	3,551
12.2012	18	393	7,075	3,673
01.2013	22	550	12,089	4,847
02.2013	17	352	5,979	5,047
03.2013	20	349	6,986	4,791
04.2013	20	373	7,451	4,851
05.2013	21	879	18,455	6,685
06.2013	19	1,070	20,332	7,028
07.2013	22	414	9,104	7,904
08.2013	21	392	8,225	7,974
09.2013.	20	477	9,539	9,515
10.2013.	21	768	16,134	13,067
11.2013	21	601	12,626	16,863
12.2013	20	589	11,788	18,701

Source: HKEx

Domestic RMB derivatives market has been continuously growing

In the domestic market, the RMB derivatives trading mechanism has been improved in 2013. Regarding products from the inter-bank market, there were each one turnover for bond forwards and forward interest rate transaction, the notional principal amount of which were 101 million yuan and 050 million yuan, respectively. There were more than 24,206 transactions in RMB interest rate swap market transactions with notional principal amount of 2.710218 trillion yuan. Floating RMB interest rate swap transaction ends reference rate including Shibor, 7-day fixing Repo rate and the benchmark interest rate announced by the People's Bank of China. Linked with rates mentioned above, the notional principal interest rate swap transactions accounted for 33.45 percent, 65.14 percent, and 1.41 percent. Compared with 2012, the proportion of swap transactions regarding Shibor floating rate as reference decreased significantly (Table 2.5).

China Financial Futures Exchange officially launched the CSI 300 stock index futures in April 2010. Through the use of stock index futures, the Chinese stock market investors can make better risk hedging. CSI 300 stock index futures are currently becoming more active. In 2013, the annual turnover reached 140.700232 trillion yuan, representing an increase of 85.52 percent compared with 2012. In addition, the government bond futures market, having been closed since 1995, officially restarted in September 2013. By the end of 2013, the turnover was 306.389 billion yuan. Futures market functions well in price discovery. Especially, the launch of bond futures has extremely important implications for China's interest rate reform (Table 2.6).

RQFII has been expanded to all foreign institutions

With RMB settlement in cross-border trade area expanding and the development of RMB cross-border direct investment and offshore RMB business in Hong Kong, the demand for the return of RMB funds is getting increasingly strong.

Box 2.1 Shanghai Intends to Launch RMB-denominated Oil Futures

China has overtaken the United States to become the world's largest net importer of crude oil. As the largest consumer of crude oil imports, China needs to have a matching oil prices bargaining power.

Currently there are four world's major crude oil futures: light low-sulfur crude oil futures contract (WTI) on the New York Stock Exchange and high-sulfur crude oil futures contract; Brent crude futures in London's International Petroleum Exchange; and the Dubai acidic crude oil futures contracts on the Singapore Exchange, among which WTI crude oil contract is the benchmark for crude oil pricing in the world.

Asphalt futures listed and transacted on the Shanghai Futures Exchange on October 9, 2013, is considered to be one stepping stone of domestic crude oil futures. Highly active transacted bitumen crude futures laid the foundation for the launch of crude oil futures. The market expects that the underlying Chinese version of crude oil futures trading is the quality of sour crude oil, and the denominated currency is RMB.

On November 22, 2013, Shanghai International Energy Trading Center was officially inaugurated, marking the crude oil futures trading platform as basically completed. As a platform to promote international transactions of crude oil futures and other energy derivatives, the Shanghai International Energy Trading Center was registered in the Shanghai Free Trade Zone and funded by the Shanghai Futures Exchange with the registered capital of 5 billion yuan, which made it the largest enterprise regarding registered

continued ...

Table 2.5 Turnovers on major inter-bank markets 2012–2013 (in hundred million yuan)

	2012				2013			
	Season 1	Season 2	Season 3	Season 4	Season 1	Season 2	Season 3	Season 4
Interest rate swaps	4908.46	6821.21	8010.28	9276.26	7375.83	7960	5697.8	6068.55
Forward rate	0	1	0	1	0	0	0.5	0
Bond forward	144.57	15.86	5.7	0	1.01	0	0	0

Source: China Foreign Exchange Trading Center

Table 2.6 2012–2013 stock index futures and bonds transactions (in hundred million yuan)

	2012				2013			
	Season 1	Season 2	Season 3	Season 4	Season 1	Season 2	Season 3	Season 4
CSI 300 index	155837.09	157897.85	195679.28	248992.56	348705.50	331666.14	402066.87	324563.82
Treasury futures	0	0	0	0	0	0	1443.83	1620.05

Source: China Financial Futures Exchange

Box 2.1 continued

capital in the Shanghai Free Trade Zone. The business of Shanghai International Energy Trading Center includes organizing derivatives with underlying crude oil, natural gas, petrochemicals, and other energy products listing and trading, clearing and settlement, developing business management rules, implementing self-management, publishing market information, providing technological venues and facilities services.

Once China launches RMB-denominated oil futures contracts, it will strengthen China's power to speak on crude oil pricing and help to promote the internationalization process of RMB.

RMB Qualified Foreign Institutional Investors (RQFII) business came into being as a pilot system in capital market liberalization. On March 1, 2013, the China Securities Regulatory Commission announced the "Provisions on 'RMB qualified foreign institutional investors in securities investment pilot approach' implementation" to further regulate the behavior of RQFII on securities investment in the territory and expand the types of RQFII institutions and loss restrictions on the scope of RQFII investment. Within the limits specified in the approval, RQFII may invest in RMB financial instruments including stock trading or transfer of stocks, bonds, and warrants; fixed income products in the inter-bank bond market transactions securities investment funds; stock index futures; and other financial instruments permitted by the China Securities Regulatory Commission. RQFII can also participate in the IPO, convertible bond issuance, equity issuance, and allotment of purchase.

RQFII business learned the experience from qualified foreign institutional investors (QFII) system; however, there are a few changes. Firstly, investment capital needs to be raised in RMB instead of foreign exchange; secondly, RQFII institutions are limited to: domestic fund management companies and securities companies' subsidiaries in HK or financial institutions whose registered offices and principal places of business are in Hong Kong (in July 2013, the China Securities Regulatory Commission further expanded the scope of the pilot to Singapore and London); thirdly, the scope of investment would be expanded from RMB financial instruments on the exchange market to the inter-bank bond market; fourthly, under the premise of improving statistical monitoring, to simplify and facilitate the RQFII investment quota and cross-border capital expenditure management as far as possible. The implementation of the RQFII system helped to promote cross-border RMB business, expand offshore RMB investment channels for holders and directly promote the development of HK's offshore RMB market.

In 2013, the China Securities Regulatory Commission approved twenty-nine RQFIIs. At the end of 2013, the total number of RQFII institutions was fifty-two. The State Administration of Foreign Exchange's cumulative approval amount for RQFII reached 157.5 billion yuan. Through the significantly increasing use of RMB in domestic inter-bank bond markets by overseas institutions in three types (offshore RMB clearing bank, offshore RMB trade settlement participating banks, foreign central banks or monetary authorities), the RMB financial assets are becoming an important choice for global investors to build portfolios.

RMB overseas credit market

RMB overseas loans in domestic financial institutions

By the end of 2013, the amount of RMB overseas loans in domestic financial institutions had reached 187.376 billion yuan, an increase of 3.57 percent. The amount of 2013 new loans reached 6.465 billion yuan, a comparative decrease to 2012. RMB overseas loans accounted for 0.26 percent of the total loans, which rose slightly from 2012 (Figure 2.12). In 2013, the growth of Chinese overseas loans declined, and the ratio of overseas loans to total loans did not exceed 0.3 percent. According to the Bank of International Settlements, the USD, EUR, JPY, and GBP overseas loans accounted for 20 percent to 40 percent of their domestic loans, so the overseas credit market of RMB needed to be vigorously developed.

One important reason for the slow development of RMB overseas loans is the international expectations of a relatively strong appreciation of the RMB, which lowers the enterprise's desire to borrow RMB.

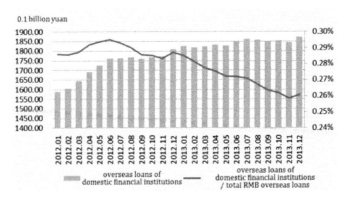

Figure 2.12   2012–2013 RMB overseas loans and the ratio of domestic financial institutions

Source: The People's Bank of China

Offshore RMB loans

Hong Kong is the main offshore RMB loan market. By the end of 2013, HK offshore RMB deposits had grown to 860.472 billion yuan, an increase of 257.476 billion yuan, accounting for 42.7 percent. In the same period, RMB loan in HK had reached 115.611 billion yuan, an increase of 36.595 billion yuan, accounting for 46.3 percent. Compared to RMB deposit market, the scale of RMB loans is smaller (Figure 2.13).

Shenzhen is a neighborhood in HK, with a natural geographical advantage. Under the framework of CEPA, Qianhai enterprises can obtain loans from bank institutions in HK. On January 28, 2013, Qianhai Holdings, Tencent, Konka, ZTE, SF Express, and fifteen other enterprises had the first taste of cross-border RMB loans. With eight Chinese bank HK branches and seven foreign banks, they signed a 2.62 billion agreement on RMB cross-border loans. Combined with the signed 6 billion loans between Shenzhen Petrochemical Exchange and Agricultural bank HK branch, a total of 8.62 billion yuan had been reached.

Within the free trade zone in Shanghai, based on Opinions issued on December 2, 2013, by the People's Bank of China, the zone allows foreign companies to borrow from overseas RMB funds. On the basis of the original foreign enterprises who borrow foreign investment, the financing subjects will be expanded to Chinese enterprises, which can help enterprises to reduce financial cost and broaden the financing channels.

RMB in global foreign exchange reserves

RMB has become an official reserve of more and more countries

According to the IMF, global official foreign exchange reserves comprise allocated reserves and unallocated reserves. By the fourth quarter of 2013,

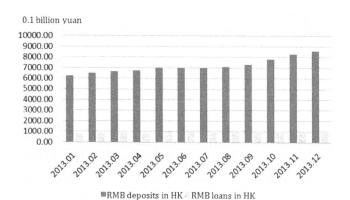

Figure 2.13 Development of RMB deposits and loans in Hong Kong

Sources: The People's Bank of China; Hong Kong Monetary Authority

Box 2.2 Innovative practice of RMB cross-border financing service in the Bank of Communications

1. Create "Rongyuantong" Brand, and Improve Cross-border Financing Service

The "customer-centered" mechanism is the constant innovation of BOCOM. Based on the strengths of close relationship to the market and close relationship to the main body, BOCOM did a comprehensive analysis in recent years to know customers' cross-border, cross-combination, cross-market, cross-platform, and cross-border financial demand in the process of RMB internationalization. Based on the cross-border trade supply chain, integrated cross-border investment and financing management of the trade market and financing market for customers, BOCOM introduced the entire level of cross-border RMB financial product – Rongyuantong. The brand of organic combination of six categories of nineteen products, including the important products, such as Huiduitong, Rongmaoda, Yuandai, and new products and the NRA account financing, RMB cross-border back-to-back financing. Rich and effective products provide customers with settlement, trade financing, investment and financing, wealth management, and such a package of financial solutions to meet the diverse needs of the enterprises to carry out RMB cross-border businesses. By printing the Yuanrongtong-RMB cross-border financing products brochures, BOCOM exported their cross-border products and service advantages to customers, which could help them know and use RMB cross-border products.

All branches take the Yuanrongtong brand as a chance to further detail and extend local services that are the exclusively specific services for customers combining local developing characters. Guangdong branch played to the location advantage, using the cross-border trade finance services of supply chain to drive the development of RMB cross-border trade businesses of both Hong Kong and Guangdong province. Shanghai branch caught the construction of Shanghai double center and multiple policy opportunities of FTZ, developing direct investment on capital fund, cross-border capital financing, external guarantees, RQFII and the like, and used a rich product line to meet the requirement of enterprise service trade and RMB cross-border business under capital requirements. Hubei branch worked on structured products and linkage combination products, taking the integrated and combined trade financing product as a flagship product. Bocom's landing services brought by "melting yuan tong" brand of RMB cross-border financial products service had provided enterprises with a solution to deal with the problems about cross-border settlement and financing and risk control.

2. Develop New Channels of Cross-border Financing Services

In order to improve the level of whole cross-border financing services, BOCOM strengthens the cooperation work of domestic and overseas branches in policy research, customer marketing, projects design, survey, group credit, loans, and laws and regulations. Considering the boundaries of internationalization strategy and the guidance of domestic and overseas linkage credit loans, BOCOM explores new ways to develop RMB cross-border loans from credit model, linkage benefit, and other factors. The branch, Jiangsu branch, for example, dug a new way from the existing policies, which was that it helps a large Sino-foreign joint venture car company successfully process a loan under the RMB financing guarantee within cross-currency loan businesses, an amount of nearly 700 million yuan. Shenzhen Branch had a flexible use of the new policy that, with a joint HK branch, by using the policy of foreign domestic enterprises to provide the guarantee, successfully designed a global credit new pattern for a large container group company. At the same time, having resorted to the cross-border RMB shareholder loan settlement channels, in the framework of two-way cross-border loans between affiliate companies, accompanying financing services of assets, debts, and other flexible mechanisms, BOCOM innovatively launched a global RMB fund pool for cross-border companies and helped them to reduce cost and realize the centralized management of the global RMB fund.

In the past 2 years, high-quality domestic companies all issued RMB bonds overseas. BOCOM actively used their investment banking business resources, with the advantage of linkage, to provide customers with foreign debt, raising capital flow and other one-stop services. The Beijing branch and the HK branch helped a large state-owned enterprise issue RMB bonds in HK. After the regulatory approval, the company became the first domestic institution that successfully implemented the RMB bond oversea, reaching the amount of RMB 1.5 billion.

3. Keep a Balance of Transverse and Longitudinal Development, and Better Improve Financial Services Experience

RMB cross-border businesses sustainably develop based on the close cooperation between banks and enterprises. BOCOM pays special attention to keeping a balance between transverse and longitudinal development, creating excellent service, and improving customers' cross-border financial services experience. On one hand, in providing a single customer (group) with the transverse, BOCOM practices the service concept of "One Bank, One Customer" based on cross-border renminbi,

continued ...

Box 2.2 continued

comprehensively considering the diversified demands of customers in local and foreign currencies and integrated cross-border settlement, combining other service projects of credit financing, foreign debt, the NRA account linkage with auxiliary technologies like electronic network, mobile, and integration, BOCOM helps enterprises to conduct global operations and capital management. On the other hand, in terms of the clients who get vertical RMB cross-border services, BOCOM provides the concept of classified services, emphasizing efficiency and utility.

For high-end customers, BOCOM provides exclusive service through a "one-to-one" model, highlighting the characteristics and enhancing cooperation viscosity. For medium-size customers, with standardized products, structured products, and linkage products as the main service content, BOCOM highlights the ease of cross-border renminbi and advantages of exchange rate risk management advantages. In view of the small micro-enterprises, guided by the "chain" marketing, BOCOM provides them with RMB cross-border settlement and trade finance products. For trade customers, BOCOM develops cooperation with them to conduct agency issuing, collection, remittance, insurance, and other businesses to deepen RMB cross-border businesses. For foreign central banks, foreign joint banks and other licensed institutions, based on mature experience, BOCOM facilitates the cooperation between the two sides in the agent of RMB bond-trading business. Taking RMB cross-border finance service as the detailed practice of realizing its internationalization and comprehensive development strategy, BOCOM continuously meets the financing requirements of customers, which are all-directional, richly connotative, and better experienced.

allocated reserves stood at $6.22 trillion, accounting for 53.29 percent of total reserves, and unallocated reserves stood at $5.45 trillion, accounting for 46.71 percent of total reserves. At present, RMB has not been ranked in allocated reserves, so it seems unable to reach the accurate statistics.

According to a public report, in March, 2013, the central bank of Bolivia published that they would increase the purchased volume of RMB in order to enhance its ability to maintain the value of international reserves and to diversify its foreign exchange assets. On November, 2013, the South African Reserve Bank announced its plan to invest around $1.5 billion in buying China's bonds, which accounted for 3 percent of its reserve assets. Nearly twenty countries have reported to IMF that they hold a certain amount of RMB in their foreign exchange reserve. With the gradual recognition of RMB abroad and the development of China's comprehensive economic strength, the RMB will become step-by-step a regional reserve currency.

By the end of 2013, the People's Bank of China had signed currency swap contracts with monetary authorities in twenty-three countries and regions; the total amount of currency swap reached 2.57 trillion yuan. In 2012, Brazil, the United Kingdom, Hungary, and Europe were the four countries or regions that were newly added to the list of currency swap contract; as a result, the total amount of currency swap increased by 0.90 trillion yuan. In the contract renewed with Singapore, the currency swap scale has expanded from 150 billion yuan to 300 billion yuan. The increase in the number of countries who have signed the swap contract and the expansion of the currency swap scale has provided necessary RMB liquidity to the market as well as material foundation for using RMB in trade settlement between China and these countries/regions or for the money creation of the other countries.

RMB has made breakthrough in obtaining official recognition from main developed countries. In order to support the development of the RMB offshore business in London, in June 2013, the People's Bank of China established a bilateral local currency swap contract with the Bank of England; the amount of currency swap was 200 billion yuan, which could offer adequate and timely liquidity support for the further development of the London RMB market. At the meeting of the Bank for International Settlements in September 2013, Zhou Xiaochuan, governor of the People's Bank of China, and Mr. Draghi, president of the European Central Bank, reached an agreement on the relevant arrangements; on October 9, both sides formally signed a currency swap contract after completing relevant approval progress, with a currency swap amount of 350 billion yuan.

The signing of the euro-China bilateral local currency swap contract marked the progress that the People's Bank of China and European Central Bank achieved by cooperating in monetary and financial aspects, and in turn, the RMB was officially recognized by a vast majority of developed countries (Table 2.7; Figure 2.14).

New trend in international reserve diversification

Due to the recent high volatility of international currency value, currencies have a trend of depreciation under quantitative easing, which has prompted governments to choose other currencies for official reserves. According to the IMF COFER data in *Currency Composition of Official Foreign Exchange Reserves*, in the fourth quarter of 2012, the Canadian dollar and Australian dollar were classified into "allocated reserves"; the number of world's reserve currency has increased to seven.

USD remains the most important reserve currency. By the end of the fourth quarter of 2013, the USD reserve stood at $3.81 trillion, 61.18 percent of the total allocated reserves; the euro at $1.52 trillion, 24.45 percent of the total; the British pound stood at $0.25 trillion, 4.01 percent of the total; the Japanese yen at $0.24 trillion, 3.94 percent of the total; the Swiss franc at $12.575 billion, 0.20 percent of the total; the Canadian dollar at $0.11 trillion, 1.74 percent of the total; and the Australian dollar at $0.10 trillion, 1.61 percent of the total (Table 2.8).

Table 2.7 The scale of currency swaps (billion RMB) between the People's Bank of China and other monetary authorities

Signing date	Monetary authorities	Duration	Amount
December 12, 2008	South Korea	3	180.0
January 20, 2009	Hong Kong, China	3	200.0
February 8, 2009	Malaysia	3	80.0
March 11, 2009	Belarus	3	20.0
March 23, 2009	Indonesia	3	100.0
April 2, 2009	Argentina	3	70.0
June 9, 2010	Iceland	3	3.5
July 23, 2010	Singapore	3	150.0
April 18, 2011	New Zealand	3	25.0
April 19, 2011	Uzbekistan	3	0.7
May 6, 2011	Mongolia	3	5.0
June 13, 2011	Kazakhstan	3	7.0
October 26, 2011	South Korea★	3	360.0
November 22, 2011	Hong Kong, China★	3	400.0
December 22, 2011	Thailand	3	70.0
December 23, 2011	Pakistan	3	10.0
January 17, 2012	United Arab Emirates	3	35.0
February 8, 2012	Malaysia★	3	180.0
February 21, 2012	Turkey	3	10.0
March 20, 2012	Mongolia★	3	10.0
March 22, 2012	Australia	3	200.0
June 26, 2012	Ukraine	3	15.0
March 7, 2013	Singapore★	3	300.0
March 26, 2013	Brazil	3	190.0
June 22, 2013	England	3	200.0
September 9, 2013	Hungary	3	10.0
September 12, 2013	Albania	3	2.0
September 30, 2013	Iceland★	3	3.5
Octorber 10, 2013	Europe	3	350.0

Source: The People's Bank of China.

Note: ★ The People's Bank of China has renewed the contract with other countries or regions

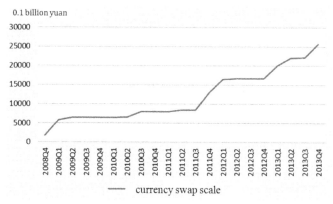

0.1 billion yuan

—— currency swap scale

Figure 2.14   The currency swap scale of the People's Bank of China

Source: The People's Bank of China

Box 2.3 IMF will add Canadian dollar and Australian dollar to the foreign exchange reserve currency statistics

On August 28, 2012, the 2012 data review released by the IMF showed that they would add the Canadian dollar and the Australian dollar to the tracking system of reserve currency. In the report, the IMF claimed that, except for the five main reserve currencies, the amount of central banks who have added the Canadian dollar and Australian dollar to their foreign exchange reserves were more than two. Therefore, the Canadian dollar and Australian dollar should be brought into the COFER tracking report and be calculated separately. This marked that the IMF would for the first time incorporate new reserve currency into the system since the euro was born in 1999.

According to the COFER report published on November 14, 2012, recent demands for the Canadian dollar and Australian dollar as foreign exchange reserves continued to rise in each central bank, although these two currencies had always been included in "other currencies" before then.

Early in 2009, central banks of countries like Russia and Switzerland began to add Canadian dollars to their foreign exchange reserve assets; in 2010, the central bank of Russia doubled its Canadian dollar reserves; the central bank of Switzerland brought the Canadian dollar and Australian dollar into its reserve system; in June 2012, the central bank of Germany expressed that they would buy Australian dollars for adjusting the foreign exchange reserve.

On March 6, 2013, a spokesman of the IMF confirmed that the amount of Canadian dollars and Australian dollars held by each central bank would be published since 2013.

The reason why the IMF has included Canadian dollars and Australian dollars into reserve currency is that, compared with the world's largest developed economy, Australia's and Canada's economic performance remained stable during the financial crisis. At the same time, the deficit-to-GDP ratio of Canada and Australia was less than 5 percent in 2012, while the United States, the United Kingdom, and Japan were faced with rising domestic debt burden, and the proportion had a tendency to shrink further.

Table 2.8 Percentages of currencies in global FER 2013 (%)

	2012				2013			
	Q1	Q2	Q3	Q4	Q1	Q2	Q3	Q4
Global reserves	100	100	100	100	100	100	100	100
Allocated reserves	54.71	55.51	55.77	55.56	54.85	54.58	54.11	53.29
US dollar	61.54	61.48	61.21	61.31	62.02	62.02	61.71	61.18
Euro	24.80	24.97	24.21	24.23	23.59	23.88	24.10	24.45
Japanese yen	3.85	3.95	4.27	4.09	3.94	3.90	3.88	3.94
British pound	4.02	3.84	4.12	4.04	3.89	3.84	3.94	4.01
Swiss franc	0.24	0.23	0.30	0.21	0.19	0.19	0.20	0.20
Canadian dollar				1.43	1.51	1.74	1.75	1.74
Australian dollar				1.45	1.61	1.65	1.63	1.61
Others	5.55	5.52	5.89	3.24	3.24	2.77	2.79	2.87
Unallocated reserves	45.29	44.49	44.23	44.44	45.15	45.42	45.89	46.71
Developed economies	32.98	33.68	33.89	33.76	33.18	33.02	32.97	32.70
Emerging economies and developing countries	67.02	66.32	66.11	66.24	66.82	66.98	67.03	67.30

Source: IMF COFER Database, International Financial Statistics released by IMF

Notes:
Data of allocated reserves come from IMF COFER database; proportion of each currency is the ratio of the amount of reserves denominated by this currency to the amount of total allocated reserves.
The amount of unallocated reserves is equal to the difference between that of global reserves and allocated reserves.

Foreign exchange market and offshore market

The foreign exchange market

According to the report of the Bank for International Settlements, from 2010 to 2010, the volume of RMB used in global foreign exchange trade increased by three times, the proportion rose from 0.9 percent to 2.2 percent, and its world ranking jumped from the seventeenth to ninth, ahead of the Swedish krona, the New Zealand dollar, and the HK dollar.

The direct trades of RMB to other currencies were further widened. On April 10, 2013, China's and Australia's interbank exchange markets launched at the same time RMB traded to the Australian dollar directly, forming the direct exchange rate of RMB to Australian dollar. The bid-ask spread of the interbank market and the bank counter has narrowed since then, which promotes the use of RMB and Australian dollars in bilateral trade and investment; the scale of RMB annual transactions reached 149.6 billion yuan. Meanwhile, the trade amount for RMB to main currencies increased significantly compared with last year (Table 2.9).

From the derivatives market, RMB foreign exchange derivatives were mainly composed of swaps. The scale of RMB foreign exchange swaps in 2013 was $3.4 trillion, increasing by 35 percent from 2012. Among them, the amount of overnight dollar swap reached $1.8 trillion, accounting for 52.2 percent of the total turnover of swaps. The main reason for sharp spikes in swap transaction volume was that enterprises used RMB to swap in foreign exchange in their wealth management business; the swap transaction has showed its outstanding function in financing local and foreign currency. After the lower limit of the cash basis was canceled in April 2012, demand for forward transaction continued to decline: the scale of RMB foreign exchange forward market was $32.37 billion, falling by 62.6 percent

Table 2.9 The trade amount of RMB to main currencies in interbank foreign exchange spot transactions market 2013 (billion RMB)

Currency	Trade amount	Growing rate on year-on-year basis
USD	23164.62	14.80%
EUR	274.82	183.80%
JPY	1273.74	67.80%
HKD	145.55	6.90%
GBP	17.16	360.10%
AUD	149.60	2166.70%
CAD	0.85	97.70%
MYR	1.14	4.60%
RUB	5.44	15.00%
THB	0.54	−70.30%

Source: China Foreign Exchange Trade System

from 2012; the scale of option transactions in interbank foreign exchange market in the first half of 2013 was $3.9 billion, which exceeded the total volume of 2012. As the RMB exchange rate became more flexible, the option's ability to manage the two-way volatility risk of exchange rate has been further revealed (Figure 2.15).

In addition, the subjects of the foreign exchange market were further expanded. By the end of 2013, the amount of members in the spot market had reached 405, with the number of members in forward market, foreign exchange swap market, currency swap market, and options market coming, respectively, to 88, 87, 80, and 33. The quantity of market makers in the spot market was thirty-one, which was twenty-seven in the forward and swap market.

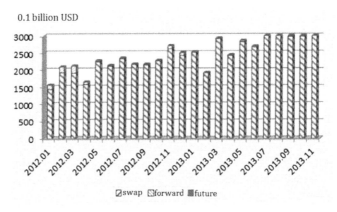

Figure 2.15   The development of RMB foreign exchange derivatives market 2012–2013

Source: China Foreign Exchange Trade System

Box 2.4 The new global conflict of exchange rate

Facing the soaring debt burden, central banks of developed economies started one after another the unprecedented quantitative easing of competition in recent stages, constantly challenging the base line of the monetary policy. The Federal Reserve launched the fourth round of quantitative easing, Jean-Claude Juncker, chairman of the euro group, warned that the euro exchange rate was confronted with high risk; the Bank of Japan released an unlimited easing measure. The unceasing "self belittling" of developed economies has caused the new conflict of exchange war.

On January 25, 2013, the Bank of Japan announced at the policy meeting that the Japanese government would start a limitless bond-buying plan, with the inflation target being raised to 2 percent, in order to stimulate economic growth, weaken its currency, and extricate itself from a difficult position of the 20-year-long deflation. What the Bank of Japan had done would undoubtedly provoke a new conflict of exchange rate. Multinational central banks cut their interest rates to take up the gloves. On May 2, the European central bank declared that they would cut the main refinancing rate by 25 basis points to 0.50 percent and cut the marginal lending interest rates by 50 basis points to 1.0 percent; this was the European central bank's initial rate cut after 10 months in 2013. On May 7, Australia's central bank announced that the benchmark interest rate would be cut by 25 basis points to 2.75 percent; this was the lowest interest rate level of Australia's central bank. On May 9, South Korea's central bank proclaimed that the benchmark interest rate would be cut by 25 basis points to 2. 5 percent, the first rate cut for 7 months. On May 13, the central bank of Israel announced that the interest rate would be cut by 0.25 percent to 1.5 percent.

To avoid the negative impact of the external shocks, several emerging economies took action in succession. On May 3, India's central bank announced that the benchmark interest rate would be cut by 25 basis points to 7.25 percent and this was the third time that they had cut interest rates. On May 8, the central bank of Poland declared their new plan to cut the benchmark interest rate by 25 basis points to 3.0 percent, which reached the lowest interest rate level in the history of the Polish central bank, near to the historically low rates of the country after the international financial crisis. The central bank of countries such as Vietnam, Sri Lanka, Kenya, and Georgia also announced that they would lower their interest rates.

Major economies expected to boost export growth by currency devaluation, so as to create more jobs. Under the background of global economic recovery, the competitive devaluation of the exchange rate was difficult to resolve since it concerned whether the national economy could get over the crisis as soon as possible. What was behind the currency war was trade protectionism and financial unilateralism; especially when the global long-term aggregate demand was insufficient, the potential economic growth had the downward trend; consumption-driven economies such as the United States and Europe began to look for the change to export-driven economy and use the exchange tool to balance the economy as well as to give up the responsibility as "anchor currency," which can increase export and promote employment. In this way, some of the major currencies might face the competitive devaluation like "benefiting oneself at others' expense," and it would become greater than the world economy could stand.

Historically, the conflict of exchange rate will cause the turbulence of the foreign exchange market, and it is likely to cause tit-for-tat protectionism and lead to the situation of "losing a lot," the result that is often against the original intention.

The offshore market

According to the UBS, by the end of 2013, the scale of global offshore fund had been around 1.2 trillion yuan. The numbers of the offshore market escalated in Asia, as Taiwan and Singapore have built the RMB clearing system; the RMB offshore business was carried out not only in HK but in a wider range of areas. In Europe, London, Luxembourg, Paris, and Frankfurt competed for becoming the European center of RMB offshore business.

Hong Kong is the first RMB offshore business center in Asia. In 2013, the breadth and depth of the RMB market were continuously upgraded in HK, the RMB products became increasingly abundant, and the complete spot product series had been formed to serve RMB bonds, foreign exchange, currency, and stock markets. The constant innovation in terms of RMB derivatives had been realized. On February 6, 2013, the cross-strait currencies no longer needed a third type of settlement currency to settle accounts; the Taipei branch of the Bank of China became the RMB clearing bank in Taiwan; RMB business in Taiwan was comprehensively conducted; Taiwan's RMB offshore market offered a range of services including cross-border RMB trade settlement, cash sales, remittances, deposits, loans, financial products, the discovery of ETF, Formosa bonds and trading, interbank lending, foreign exchange, RMB insurance policy guarantee slip, RMB traveler's checks, bond buy-back deal, and so on. As Asia's largest foreign exchange trading center, on April 2, 2013, Singapore's RMB clearing bank service launched. By the end of 2013, ICBC's branch in Singapore started all kinds of RMB business, including cross-border trade settlement, local remittance and clearing, offshore settlement between Singapore and Hong Kong markets, interbank cash transfers, fixed time deposit, RMB buy and sale, and lending and settlement for the issuance of RMB bonds, which met the demand for local RMB clearing services.

In Europe, London is the world's largest foreign exchange trading center. It has it's natural advantage in developing RMB business, since London can trade with both American and Asian markets on the same day. The signing of the Sino-British currency swap contract and the expansion of the RQFII scope contributed to the development of RMB business in London. Compared with London, Paris locates within the euro zone and has established a close relationship with the African, which can help the cross-border use of RMB. At present, the RMB foreign exchange products in Paris are various, including foreign exchange spot, non-deliverable forwards, deliverable forwards, currency swaps, currency options, and the like. Germany is the European country with the best real economy development; using the real economy to drive the development of RMB business is Frankfurt's greatest advantage for developing RMB offshore business. However, the RMB stock in Frankfurt is still on a small scale; the variety of RMB products is relatively limited, mainly focusing on the savings and loan, remittances, and inter-bank clearing services. In 2013, Luxembourg received great attention from the whole industry with its large RMB fund pool, RMB fund management scale, and bond issuance volume. As a rising star, Luxembourg has become the largest RMB fund pool of the euro-zone and has outstanding performance in RMB investment product innovation, channels of distribution, wealth management, and so on. In October 2013, CCB's European headquarters settled in Luxembourg. The purpose of Chinese-funded banks to settle their European headquarters in Luxembourg is to serve the clients of the large and medium enterprises who have gone abroad as well as European multinational companies in China that have a close business relationship with these clients. Loans, trade finance, international settlement, and RMB cross-border are the main businesses that have been given priority to develop. In addition, Luxembourg is Europe's largest RMB securities settlement center; the Clear stream is the first international central securities depository institution to fully support full-function RMB settlement. The clearing and settlement of bonds that are issued or sold by international financial center proceed in Luxembourg.

RMB exchange rate

RMB exchange rate regime

In 1994, China carried out its foreign exchange regime reform and established a market-based, single, managed floating exchange rate system. During this period, in order to cope with the volatile international financial environment and ensure the Chinese economy's orderly and gradual open-up, China had strict management of RMB exchange rate and the exchange rate fluctuation to a small extent. It was defined as a pegged exchange rate system by the IMF. In 2005, in the context of China's accession to the WTO in order to balance the international payments, China carried out the reform of the RMB exchange rate formation mechanism, which implemented market supply and demand as basis with reference to a basket of currencies. It was a managed floating exchange rate system.

In 2008, the international financial crisis broke out, and the RMB exchange rate stayed basically stable through the dollar peg. With the changes in domestic and international economic and financial situation, in June 2010, the People's Bank of China decided to further promote the reform of the RMB exchange rate formation mechanism to enhance the RMB exchange rate flexibility, achieve the normalization of exchange rate fluctuations, and put the periodic dollar peg policy to an end. In 2011, RMB enlarged its scale in the use of cross-border trade and investment, and the convertible scope of RMB under capital account was further broadened, which consolidated the market basis of the RMB exchange rate formation mechanism and made the exchange rate regime more flexible.

In 2012, strengthening RMB's flexibility in both directions became the key point of the RMB exchange rate regime reform. Since April 16, 2012, the floating range of the trading price of the RMB against the U.S. dollar in the inter-bank spot foreign exchange market had expanded from 0.5 percent to 1 percent. On June 1, 2012, the China Foreign Exchange Trading Center improved the RMB against the yen trading form in the inter-bank foreign exchange market and developed direct trading of the RMB against the yen. The RMB exchange rate against the yen formed according to the supply and demand of the market, which greatly promoted the trading scale.

In the last year, the RMB exchange rate regime had made useful progress, which could be listed as the following aspects.

Market-oriented reforms of the interest rate increased the exchange rate flexibility

On July 20, 2013, the People's Bank of China announced the cancellation of the floor on lending rates, and the price of RMB funds would be more determined by market supply and demand. In the background of an increasingly open capital market, according to the interest rate parity principle, RMB interest rate changes will inevitably pass to RMB exchange rate quickly, thereby increasing the frequency and amplitude of RMB exchange rate fluctuation.

Direct exchange of RMB with the Australian dollar, which made the direct exchange currency of RMB to three

Until April 8, 2013, the People's Bank of China approved ANZ and Westpac, the RMB direct exchange with the Australian dollar, which meant the RMB exchange rate against the Australian dollar was calculated without the U.S. dollar. Then, the Australian dollar became the third-straight RMB convertible currency after the U.S. dollar and the yen. The Australian dollar is currently the world's fifth-largest trading currency. In 2012, Australia's exports to China accounted for nearly 30 percent of its total exports. China is Australia's largest trading partner, and Australia is China's sixth-largest importer. The direct exchange of these two currencies can reduce trade settlement cost and help business companies to lower the risk of foreign exchange losses.

The increase of derivative varieties promoted the exchange rate liberalization

The currency derivative market in China began in 1997, when the State Administration of Foreign Exchange approved Bank of China to launch the forward Forex Sale and Purchase business foreign exchange rate pilot. After July 2005, the People's Bank of China expanded the range of forward foreign exchange settlement business, and in the meantime it promoted commercial banks to carry out the swap business of RMB to foreign currencies. In Chinese territory, the RMB derivatives market is not very active, and the RMB derivatives in foreign offshore markets is relatively abundant, including the off-board NDF, non-deliverable option swaps, RMB futures and options, and the like. The derivative market has promoted price discovery of the RMB exchange rate and has positive effects on the marketization of the RMB exchange rate.

There are still some basic problems in China's current RMB exchange rate regime, such as regulatory fragmentation and limbo, the thin and highly monopolized market, small flexibility, one-way appreciation, and so on. Only with fully understanding the complexity as well as importance of the RMB exchange rate regime can we effectively carry on the independent, progressive and controlled principle in the exchange rate reform, which will help to further promote the marketization of the RMB exchange rate regime and effectively promote RMB's internationalization process.

RMB exchange rate level

Nominal exchange rate

In 2013, apart from the pound sterling, RMB appreciated versus the eight other major currencies to varying degrees. The middle rate of RMB against the U.S. dollar had risen by up to 3 percent, which was mainly due to the United States' continued quantitative easing in 2013, while the overall U.S. economic growth remained weak and the Chinese economy adjusted its economic structure, maintained a high rate of development, and pushed the pace of internationalization of the RMB. As a result, the interest rate and exchange rate of RMB spirally rose. Thanks to the peg of Hong Kong dollar versus the U.S. dollar, the RMB against HKD and RMB against the U.S. dollar exchange rate movements are almost identical.

As the European debt crisis continued and economic recovery in Europe remained slow, in 2013, RMB against the euro achieved 1.18 percent appreciation in volatility. However, in the context of the U.K. economic recovery and tightening of quantitative easing, the British pound against RMB achieved a 1.37 percent appreciation.

In 2013, RMB's appreciation versus the Australian dollar was the largest among the major currencies, which was up to 17.03 percent. The main reason is that the Reserve Bank of Australia had long been supporting the depreciation of the Australian dollar, hoping to improve the declining terms of trade. This in turn contributed to the devaluation of the Australian dollar against the RMB. Although in July the Australian dollar had a slight rebound, it was mainly because the Australian central bank's annunciation of July's meeting summary in mid-July to keep interest rates at a record low of 2.75 percent unchanged, which spurred the Australian dollar rebound slightly. However, the Reserve Bank of Australia's further policy on cutting interest rates caused the Australian dollar to fall quickly.

In addition, in 2013, the RMB's appreciation against the yen reached 16.03 percent, second only to the appreciation of the Australian dollar. Since Abe took office in Japan, the depreciation of the yen became its promotion of economic recovery. The continued loose monetary policy is the main cause of the sharp depreciation of the yen.

In 2013, on the ringgit, the ruble, and the Canadian dollar was not a small margin of RMB appreciation, reaching 9.72 percent, 12.05 percent, and 8.59 percent, respectively. Although all of them rose with varying degrees of volatility, they did not form a clear trend of reversal, and the RMB remained an appreciation trend. This is mainly because of China's effects of the steady growth measures. With the steady economic recovery in China, RMB maintained its appreciation trend versus these countries' currencies. On the other hand, continued weakness in the performance of the U.S. dollar resulted in the capital flows to emerging market countries to restart and further enhanced the international community's confidence and acceptance of the RMB, such as Malaysia and other Southeast Asian countries. All these facts promoted the appreciation of RMB in 2013.

The appreciation of RMB in 2013 is mainly because of the confidence in China to maintain a high growth rate and the continued weakness of the U.S. dollar, which is also the main reason for appreciation of RMB in recent years.

Nominal effective exchange rate

According to data from the Bank for International Settlements, in the last 2 years since January 2012, the nominal effective exchange rate of RMB has appreciated up to 8.57 percent.

With the stable appreciation of the RMB nominal effective exchange rate, except for the yen, the other major international currencies have shown varying degrees of appreciation. In the last 2 years, the euro's, the pound's, and the U.S. dollar's nominal effective exchange rate have all appreciated, respectively: 7.34 percent, 4.03 percent, and 2.05 percent, while the yen suffered from 26.24 percent devaluation (Figures 2.16 , 2.17, 2.18).

According to statistics from the Bank for International Settlements, in the past 2 years after January 2012, the RMB real effective exchange rate rose significantly, reaching a total of 8.51 percent. The RMB real effective exchange rate appreciation coupled with weak external demand and enhanced trade protectionism in developed countries made China's exports in 2013 bear enormous pressure, but it was also the only way for China's economic restructuring (Figure 2.19).

This is similar to the nominal effective exchange rate: between 2012 and 2013, the euro, the pound, and the dollar as the main currency, respectively, achieved a 6.98 percent, 5.37 percent, and 0.59 percent appreciation while the yen suffered a depreciation of 28.23 percent (Figure 2.20).

The exchange rate of RMB NDF

In exchange-controlled countries, currencies usually cannot be freely converted. In order to avoid the risk of exchange rate fluctuations, in the 1990s there appeared non-deliverable forward as NDF in emerging market currencies such as RMB, VND, the Indian rupee, the Philippine peso, and so on.

In 2013, RMB NDF with different terms did not continue the slight depreciation trend at the end of 2012; instead, a shock of adjustment appeared in the first quarter. Then it headed into a V-shaped decline in the second quarter and, in mid-to-late June, it approached 6.24, showing a shape of the crest. In the second half of the year, due to the strong appreciation trend of RMB, the foreign

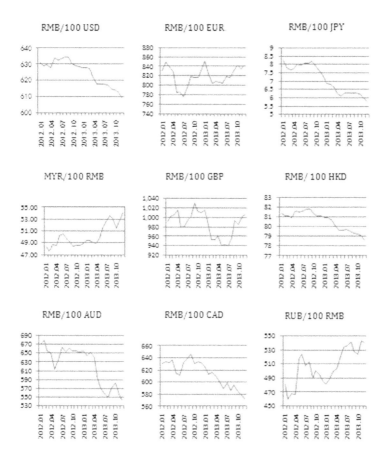

Figure 2.16 Central parity rate movements of RMB 2012–2013

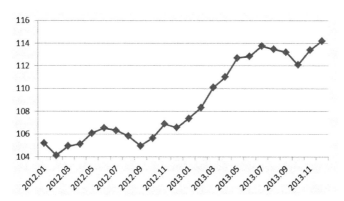

Figure 2.17 The nominal effective exchange rate movements of RMB 2012–2013

Source: BIS
Note: Monthly average, the index 2010 = 100

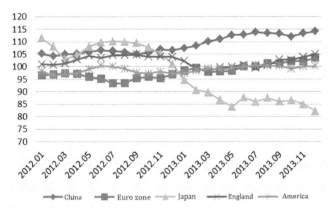

Figure 2.18 The nominal effective exchange rate movement of five economies' currencies 2012–2013

Source: BIS
Note: Monthly average, the index 2010 = 100

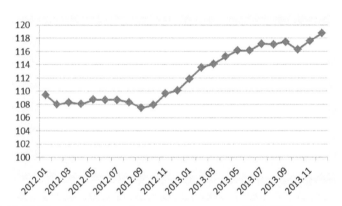

Figure 2.19   RMB real effective exchange rate movements 2012–2013

Source BIS
Note: Monthly average, the index 2010 = 100

investors had a stronger and stronger appreciation expectation on RMB. NDF rates stepped into the downstream channel as a whole, which showed obvious appreciation expectation (Figure 2.21).

On March 17, 2014, the People's Bank of China announced the expansion of a two-way floating range of RMB exchange rate. In the meantime, the continuing rising of RMB exchange rate against the U.S. dollar since 2014 has broken the RMB one-way appreciation expectations, and this has a good effect on forming a healthy marketization mechanism of the RMB exchange rate. Continuous appreciation of RMB is a "double-edged sword" for its internationalization. If a currency becomes an international currency only for one-way appreciation

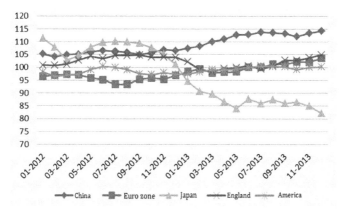

Figure 2.20 The real effective exchange rate movement of five economies' currencies 2012–2013

Source: BIS
Note: Monthly average, the index 2010 = 100

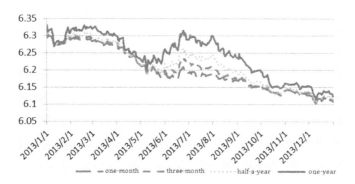

Figure 2.21 Daily closing price of RMB NDF 2013

Source: Bloomberg

expectation, its functions will be weakened as an international currency and are more likely to become a speculation object of the international money market, leading to sharp fluctuations in exchange rate. Therefore, a flexible and stable exchange rate plays an important role in promoting the internationalization of RMB. As for the long term, China's economic development and foreign exchange reserves are able to support the RMB to keep stable, and the yuan still has a certain space of appreciation, which is beneficial to boost the confidence of investors in RMB assets and expands the possibility of the RMB becoming an international reserve currency. It has a positive meaning on the promotion of RMB internationalization.

Current situation of China's capital account openness

In the "Annual Report on Exchange Arrangements and Exchange Restrictions" (AREAER) issued by the IMF, capital account transactions are divided into seven categories, further subdivided into eleven items, and then again into forty sub-items when assessing the capital controls status of its member states.

This report, first of all, measured China's capital openness in 2012 according to the AREAER 2013, then compared each item of China's capital account in 2012 with 2011 and listed the specific items changed in details.

Measurement of China's capital account openness

Epstein and Schor (1992) first proposed that AREAER could be used to measure the degree of capital control, and Cottarelli and Giannini (1997) quantified the capital controls information in AREAER as binary variables[2] and used the arithmetic mean to calculate the capital account openness. Due to its rough approximation, the credibility of the conclusion was doubted by many. We now use the mainstream capital openness measure method—the four constraints— to measure the degree of openness of China's nominal capital account.

According to the description of China's capital account control of 2012 in "AREAER 2013," three items were banned in China's 2012 capital account, mainly focusing on the nonresidents' participation in domestic money market and on the sale and issue of collective investment securities and derivatives. Compared with the four completely banned items in 2011, one of them gradually relaxing, large changes appeared. Partly banned items mainly concentrated in the deal of bond market, stock market, real estate, personal capital, and the like. Using the four-constraints method, considering the nuances at the same time, and comprehensively quantifying the description in "AREAER 2013," the degree of openness of China's capital scored 0.5815 (Table 2.10).

Notes

1 It refers to a dummy variable that equals 1 if there is capital account control, 0 otherwise.
2 We use the following formula:

$$open = \sum_{i}^{n} p(i) / n$$

where *open* denotes the degree of capital account openness, equal to a number between 0 and 1, a lower value means a stricter capital account control. n denotes the number of capital transaction items concerned, here the 40 sub-items; $p(i)$ denotes the degree of openness of sub-item i. If $p(i)$ equals 1, there is no constraint on this sub-item; if $p(i)$ equals 1/3, it means there is much constraint; 2/3 means little constraint; 0 means completely controlled, no transaction is allowed legally or practically. In addition, those sub-items included in AREAER but with only a few details are assigned 1/2.

Table 2.10 Current situation in 2012 of China's capital account control defined by the IMF

1 Control over securities transaction in capital market

A Trading of stocks and other equity securities

(1) Domestic purchase by nonresidents
QFIIs invested in A shares have to meet the following rules: (1) share of foreign individual investors should not exceed 10% of total share, share of all the foreign investors should not exceed 30% of total share of one company; (2) the investments by QFIIs are limited to 80 billions dollars; (3) the lock-up period of pension funds, insurance funds, mutual funds, and other long-term capital initiated by QFIIs is 3 months.
Foreign investors can buy the B shares valued by dollars or Hong Kong dollars and listed on the stock exchanges.

(2) Domestic sale or issue by nonresidents
Non-residents are allowed to sell A shares or B shares, there is no constraint on nonresidents issuing A shares or B shares, but there are no A shares or B shares issued by non- residents currently.

(3) Overseas purchase by residents
Overseas investment by an insurance company should not exceed 15% of its total assets of the preceding quarter, this ratio including all the foreign investors, such as stocks, bonds, and funds, etc.
Investments, including domestic and overseas stocks and stock fund, should not exceed 20% of its total assets of the preceding quarter.

(4) Overseas sale or issue by residents
Foreign-invested limited liability companies issuing overseas stocks needCSRC's approval and register in SAFE.

B Trading of bonds

(5) Domestic purchase by nonresidents
QFIIs are allowed to invest in RMB-denominated financial instruments: (1) stocks, bonds, and warrants transacted or transferred in Exchanges; (2) interbank fixed income products; (3) securities investment funds; (4) stock index futures; (5) other instruments allowed by CSRC.
RQFIIs and joint-venture foreign institutional investors are allowed to invest interbank bonds.

(6) Domestic sale or issue by nonresidents
International development agencies are allowed to issue RMB-denominated bonds with the approval of the Ministry of Finance, NDRC, and PBC. Now, there are no precedents for the locally issuing of the bonds by the nonresident. The foreign companies in China can also issue bonds.

(7) Overseas purchase by residents
QDIIs include banks, funds, securities, and insurance companies; they are allowed to buy foreign bonds within their own foreign exchange quota and within the allowance of related laws.
Investments in domestic and foreign unsecured enterprise (company) bonds and domestic and foreign securities investment funds should not exceed 50% and 15%.

(8) Overseas sale or issue by residents
If the application due date of issuing of the overseas bonds recorded on NDRC exceeds one year, NDRC have to review the application with the related departments. To request to apply for overseas foreign currency, bonds must be submitted to the State Council for approval.

2 Control over monetary market instruments

(9) Domestic purchase by nonresidents
QFIIs are allowed to purchase monetary market funds under the minimum lock-up period, but not to enter the interbank foreign exchange market directly. The lock-up period is a period of the investors' remittance being banned.

(10) Domestic sale or issue by nonresidents
Completely forbidden.

(11) Overseas purchase by residents
QDIIs can buy monetary market instruments within their own foreign exchange quota and under the restrictions of related laws.Overseas investment by an insurance company should not exceed 15% of its total assets of the preceding quarter. This ratio is applicable to all types and foreign investment tools, such as stocks, bonds, and funds.

(12) Overseas sale or issue by residents
Residents can issue monetary market instruments with the approval of SAFE, and their terms should be more than 1 year.

3 Control over collective investment securities

(13) Domestic purchase by nonresidents
QFIIs are allowed to invest in domestic close-ended and open-ended funds.

(14) Domestic sale or issue by nonresidents
Completely forbidden.

(15) Overseas purchase by residents
QDIIs can buy collective investment securities within their own foreign exchange quota and under allowance of related laws. Overseas investment by an insurance company should not be more than 15% of its total assets of the preceding quarter. This ratio is applicable to all types and foreign investment tools, such as stocks, bonds, and funds.

(16) Overseas sale or issue by residents
Residents can issue collective investment securities at the approval of SAFE.

4 Control over derivatives and other financial instruments

(17) Domestic purchase by nonresidents
If the transaction is to keep value, QFIIs are allowed to invest in domestic stock index futures under allowance of related laws.

(18) Domestic sale or issue by nonresidents
Completely forbidden.

(19) Overseas purchase by residents
Financial institutions are allowed to purchase and sell foreign derivatives for the following purposes: (1) hedge inherent balance sheet risks, (2) gain profits, (3) provide derivatives trading services for clients (including financial institutions).

(20) Overseas sale or issue by residents
Purchase application needs to conform to the laws and regulations.

5 Control over commercial credit

(21) Residents provision to nonresidents
Under some certain conditions,residents are allowed to expand trade credit
(including the delay payment and advance payment) to nonresidents. Data related
must be in the SAFE for the record.

(22) Non-residents provision to residents
Under some certain conditions, nonresidents are allowed to expand trade credit
(including the delay payment and advance payment) to residents. Data related must
be in the SAFE for the record.

6 Control over financial credit

(23) Residents provision to nonresidents
Domestic branch of a multinational company can provide loans to associated
companies abroad through domestic banks' loan with the approval of SAFE. Financial
institutions such as banks can provide foreign loans in accord with its business scope,
meeting the relevant instructions of bank regulators.

(24) Non-residents provision to residents
Ine-year international commercial loans should be approved by NDRC. Financial
institutions and China joint-equity enterprises authorized to engage in foreign
borrowing can develop one year or short-term foreign borrowing under the quota
approved by SAFE. All the foreign borrowing must be registered with SAFE.

7 Control over guarantee, insurance, and backup credit support

(25) Residents provision to non- residents
Domestic banks providing foreign financial guarantee must be approved by SAFE
except personal trading. Domestic banks providing foreign non-financial guarantee
need no approval. Domestic banks providing foreign financial guarantee must be
recorded on SAFE. Non-bank financial institutions and companies can provide
foreign financial and non-financial guarantee under the control of SAFE.

(26) Non-residents provision to residents
Those foreign companies(including but not limited to exclusively foreign-owned
enterprise, Sino-foreign equity joint venture, Chinese-foreign cooperative enterprise,
etc.) gained the approval of the Ministry of Commerce by the law related foreign
investment can accept the guarantee from the foreign institutions when borrowing
from domestic financial institutions.

8 Control over direct investments

(27) Overseas direct investment
There is no limit to the foreign exchange when domestic companies investing
overseas, they are allowed to buy foreign exchange and invest overseas directly.

(28) Domestic direct investment
Nonresidents can invest in China in line with laws and regulations related with
foreign investments, and investments must be approved by the Ministry of
Commerce.

(29) Control over clearing of direct investments
Early settlement before operating period needs original examination and the approval
of the authority or must be based on judicial decisions.

10 Control over real estate transaction

(30) Overseas purchase by residents
Domestic institutions buying foreign real estate should comply with the same rule in overseas direct investment: investment amount of an insurance company should not exceed 15% of its total asset.

(31) Domestic purchase by nonresidents
Nonresidents buying domestic real estate should comply with certain rules: actual needs and self-use principle, in order to pay the seller for buildings, converting foreign exchange at a designated bank.

(32) Domestic sale by nonresidents
On December 17, 2012, for the approval of SAFE, nonresidents can transfer the foreign exchange income from sale of real estate. Approval procedures about foreign exchange have been cancelled.

11 Control over individual capital transfer

Loans

(33) Residents provision to nonresidents
There are certain restrictions.

(34) Non-residents provision to residents
There are certain restrictions.

Gifts, donations, bequests, and heritage

(35) Residents provision to nonresidents
Residents with valid personal identification can buy foreign exchange in bank to aid and help the lineal relatives overseas, no more than 50,000 USD a year. For larger amounts, the individual must provide personal valid identity certificate to the bank and the relevant departments or the lineal relatives' material issued by the notary organization.

(36) Non-residents provision to residents
With personal valid documents, the individual's income from endowments, receiving gifts and bequests for no more than 50,000 USD can be done at the bank. More than this amount needs personal identity and the related proof and payment vouchers.

(37) Domestic debt settlement by emigrants
—

Assets transfer

(38) Transfer by emigrants
Pension fund can be remitted abroad. Natural person to emigrate or to live in Hong Kong, Macao, can clear the legal property within the territory of China and buy foreign exchange and remit abroad before getting their immigration status.

(39) Transfer by immigrants
There is no applicable law.

(40) Transfer of income—from the lottery and other winnings
There is no applicable law.

Degree of capital openness
0.5815

3 Public opinions and observations

Views of economists

Shanghai free trade zone: avoid "prisoner's dilemma" of capital account liberalization

In 2013, RMB internationalization rapidly progressed, bringing challenges to China's international balance of payments management system, forcing down the reform, and creating new opportunities for the reform. We can separate RMB capital account liberalization and capital account convertibility, and treat them separately. According to the IMF standards, there are forty-three capital subjects related to the balance of payments, and the majority of Chinese subjects have already opened or substantially opened. There are only three subjects related to capital controls, but they are centered on designed capital actor subjects. They are foreign direct investments which need review and approval; Chinese residents cannot have external liabilities in principle, and there is strict scale debt management; and Chinese capital markets cannot open to foreign investment in principle, and foreign investment needs specific permission to get into China's capital markets (i.e., QFII). Increasingly widespread international use of RMB makes China continue to maintain the above restrictions on foreign currencies while opening the local currency policy (i.e., RMB FDI). Chinese residents can have the external liabilities in the form of RMB, and the Chinese capital market is open to RMB overseas. The implication is that, while the currency is not fully convertible because of limited conditions, the local currency capital account liberalization can be realized. Through the opening up of the local currency by the currency capital projects, conditions for full convertibility can be created. In fact, the Chinese government sensitively seized this opportunity to avoid the "prisoner's dilemma" of the emerging market countries, which is that capital account liberalization must be dependent on full convertibility of the local currency, and open a fresh route different from the above traditional route. This is why the government established a free trade zone in Shanghai in 2013. According to the FTA program and relevant arrangements of People's Bank of China, FTA was set up through a special account which is different from general accounts. Firstly, achieve the opening of capital account when conditions are ripe; in these specific foreign currency accounts, currency inter-converting could be achieved, and then extended to the general account. This arrangement can be understood as, under the capital projects in the international balance of payments, the RMB first canceled the utility control and then gradually moved the conditions of using foreign currency closer to that of RMB within the control of three subjects. The conclusion is obvious that once the conditions of use of foreign currency and RMB capital account conditions are both abandoned, the RMB convertible under capital accounts would be achieved. This is different from the traditional route of fresh roadmap to make RMB fully convertible and operable. Predictably, we think in the next 2 years, the basic capital account convertibility can be realized. In this process, the exchange rate formation mechanism will be market-oriented, thereby enabling the interest rate market to deepen, especially in promoting the diversity products that are represented by fixed-income financial product, namely, the development of financial markets. In turn, it further promotes wider international use of the RMB. Shanghai financial currency center will become an international financial center.

In view of this, we believe that RMB internationalization will move to a new level in 2013, indicating that the internationalization of RMB will enter a new phase. If we say that in the past 5 years the internationalization of RMB just had bilateral use, then, in the future, RMB internationalization will enter the era of multilateral use, which is the true sense of the internationalization of the RMB. Indeed, this trend has appeared especially in the use in East Asia. Under the background of 2013, the original currency sin of developing countries, which was exposed sixteen years ago during the Asian financial crisis, re-emerged in 2013 because of the national currency turmoil, embodied in the currency mismatch, maturity mismatch, and structural fault coupled with a profound reaction of lack of local regional financial markets paid by local currency. The soultion to this problem is also clear: the currency-localization of regional monetary and financial cooperation. In 2013, Global National Bank, Bank of Shanghai Cooperation Organization Initiative, and the Asian infrastructure investment banks frequently proposed—and all suggestions were centered in—the localization of currency. As the Chinese economy is the world's second-largest economy and the largest trade body, the currency localization of renminbi in this process is destined to play an important role, so that RMB internationalization will enter a new stage of multilateral use.

—Cao Yuanzheng
Chief economist of Bank of China

Chinese-funded banks need to focus on the development of offshore business

RMB internationalization and the international development of Chinese financial institutions are complementary and mutually reinforcing. The faster the pace of internationalization of the RMB, the stronger the ability of domestic financial institutions' entering into other country's finance activities, and the pace of financial institutions and their international business development will also be accelerated. Meanwhile, the development of commercial banks and their business institutions overseas expansion can further promote the use of cross-border RMB. Chinese banks overseas institutions can use offshore RMB business to help improve the vitality of offshore RMB markets and accelerate the worldwide acceptance of RMB assets, thus promoting the internationalization of RMB.

On the one hand, in the early stage of internationalization of RMB, the RMB has not been fully realized as freely convertible. When the central bank clearing system has not been established or has just entered into the stage of test, Chinese commercial bank's own clearing system will support the development of RMB cross-border business and greatly strengthen the construction of the offshore RMB clearing and settlement markets. On the other hand, most operations of Chinese banks to carry out businesses outside will follow the "going out" strategy of Chinese enterprises. By giving clients a package of solutions, including trade finance, project loans, clearing, and financing, the international businesses can promote the RMB output and expand the scope of use.

Chinese banks can focus on the development of the following four categories of offshore RMB business to be profitable and to promote the internationalization of RMB. Firstly, offshore RMB deposits and loans: Offshore RMB deposit and loan business are the foundations of offshore RMB financial business and the initial platform and necessary conditions of the internationalization of RMB. The foreign institutions of Chinese banks should carry it out as a basic service. Secondly, offshore RMB bond-related business: Offshore RMB bonds provide high-quality investment channels for offshore RMB funds. Chinese banks should actively participate in underwriting bond issues from subscription and other related businesses to invest and expand the influence of the offshore RMB market. Thirdly, exchange rate and interest rate derivative business: With the internationalization of RMB to further promote, the hedging demand of market participants holding RMB assets is increasingly intense. Actively carrying out offshore RMB exchange rate and interest rate derivatives, businesses can meet the market demand and activate the offshore RMB market. Fourth, RMB Asset Management business: Chinese banks further expand offshore RMB insurance, funds, and other asset management business, which can broaden the investment channels for offshore RMB and enrich the offshore RMB market product line.

—Lian Ping
Chief economist of BOCOM

Strategies to promote RMB as a world reserve currency

Given the current positioning of the RMB in the path toward a status of world reserve currency and the past experience of major economies, it is good to keep two main lessons in mind. The world reserve currency status will lead to a weakening of the exchange rate channel of the economic policy. The associated opening of the capital account is a source of imbalance, born from an overly aggressive monetary and fiscal policy for compensating the competitive disadvantages of a structural over-appreciation of the currency and a source

Box 3.1 BOCOM'S experience in an innovative area of RMB cross-border trade settlement

1. Respond quickly, and steadily push the innovative business of Horgos Cooperation Center

On January 6, 2014, BOCOM Horgos International Border Cooperation Center Branch officially opened. China-kazakhstan Huoerguos International Border Cooperation Center is the innovation cooperation platform for China to develop Westward and keep a close relationship with Western countries in Asia and Europe. BOCOM Horgos international border cooperation center branch features RMB cross-border business by relying on innovation cooperation platforms to provide the NRA RMN cross-border settlement, RMB cross-border financing guarantee, RMB cross-border financial services for the enterprises in the park, personal, and offshore customers, which is an important window of BOCOM to develop Westward. On the one hand, BOCOM puts efforts into the account financial services. One is, for the registration of Chinese enterprises in the park, to open a special RMB financing account overseas, dedicated to receiving RMB funds from abroad used in project construction of the center, project construction abroad, and the trade with nonresidents. Secondly, it opens the NRA account for overseas institutions, carrying out innovation businesses, such as the cash deposit and withdrawal, the cross-border financing, RMB cross-border guarantees, the RMB deposit, and so on. Thirdly, it opens RMB trade settlement accounts for oversea banks to handle with RMB fund settlement with oversea banks, absorbs RMB trade deposits, and provides deposit service. On the other hand, the bank will focus on advancing the loan financing business. Putting low-cost RMB funds into the market through channels of RMB cross-border oversea borrowing settlement, the NRA account, and developing financing loans and guarantee business, it supports the project construction, enterprise's "going out," cross-border trade financing, and other activities.

2. Serve first, and create a new cross-border financing cooperation pattern of Suzhou Industrial Park, and Kunshan Cooperation Zone

Suzhou Industrial Park pilot policy supports Singapore bank institutions to issue loans to eligible enterprises in the park or projects; Kunshan Cooperation Zone develops RMB two-way loans and individual business pilot in the Taiwan-owned enterprises. BOCOM Suzhou branch lets the innovative financial service mode focus on RMB cross-border credit financing business. On the one hand, after the People's Bank of China, Nanjing Branch's release of cross-border RMB business innovation pilot management interim measures of Suzhou Industrial Park, Singapore branch and Suzhou branch jointly issued 47 million cross-border RMB loans to China-Singapore Suzhou Industrial Park Public Utility Development Company, Ltd., which was the first RMB cross-border loan issued by banks in Singapore on the park, expanding a new channel of funds. BOCOM Suzhou branch, Taipei branch, on the other hand, jointly set up channels for RNB lending businesses between Taiwan-owned enterprises groups, and provide financing services for two-way loans between Taiwan-owned enterprise branches and Taiwan linkage companies, reducing the cost of raising RMB.

3. Innovate positively and expand the RMB cross-border use in Shanghai free trade zone

BOCOM positively first tries to expand the RMB cross-border related businesses in FTZ, getting a number of starting businesses. One is signing on the first borrowing business of overseas non-bank financial institutions. BOCOM leased and BOCOM Singapore branch signed an RMB cross-border loan agreement. Second, it successfully signed the first batch of Chinese enterprises overseas borrowing. BOCOM free trade zone branch signed a contract with a Shanghai e-commerce company to borrow RMB debt by the mode of overseas direct loan to operate the cross-border e-commerce platform for the company. Third, the linkage between the Hong Kong branch and free trade zone branch successfully deals with RMB cross-border borrowing for one group in FTZ. Fourth, FTZ branch becomes the first bank to deal with the first commercial factoring settlement service and commercial RMB foreign debt for wholly foreign-owned commercial factoring business companies. Fifth, FTZ branch started the first single plane and ship leasing business with a certain express and a shipping group. Sixth, BOCOM positively joins the market construction of FTZ financing, makes schemes of RMB fund transferring for the international energy trading center, expands the scope of RMB cross-border utility, and pushes forward the development of FTZ financial market.

of inequalities. The current cautious approach of the Chinese government regarding the opening of its capital account is well adapted.

Following the experience of the USD in its accession to the status of world reserve currency, we can identify four categories of imbalances, each of which requires economic policies to get prepared in advance.

First, the industrial policy has to combat the loss of competitiveness associated with the over-appreciation of the currency once the status of reserve currency is reached. It produced an accumulation of trade deficits in the USD case. The industrial policy has to reduce the sensitiveness to price-competitiveness for avoiding the accumulation of trade account deficits. The status of a reserve currency is more adapted to an economy where consumption or service activities have a dominant position, as the over-appreciation of the currency is favorable to the domestic demand via lower import prices. Besides, service activities are more isolated from international competition. An over-appreciation of the currency will therefore have fewer damaging effects in an economy where service activities represent a large share of the GDP. The accession to the status of international currency for the RMB has therefore to be put in parallel with the structural reforms of the Chinese economy targeted by the new administration. The targeted promotion of consumption and service activities are consistent with a progressive accession of the RMB to a status of world reserve currency. The Chinese government also has to promote the technologic content of Chinese products via the support of R&D activities, encourage the development of services and non-tradable goods, and increase the average quality of products. These orientations are in line with the objectives of the new administration and will reduce China's dependence on price competitiveness. It should therefore lower the impact of RMB appreciation in its process of internationalization.

Second, the fiscal policy has to be vigilant and not misuse the seigniorage benefits linked to the status of foreign currency reserve in accumulating public debt. The fiscal policy has to avoid the accumulation of public debt as the status of world reserve currency fosters moral hazard strategies. The structural demand for USD-denominated assets has encouraged the U.S. government to increase the level of public debt due to particularly favorable funding conditions. The global supply of Chinese bonds has to be promoted but also carefully monitored, as the inflow of hot money could be destabilizing. In this regard, the reining in of local government debt, its access to the bond market, and its monitoring, targeted by the current administration, seems to be a necessity.

Third, the monetary policy has to monitor and prevent the formation of bubbles inherent to the weakening of external performances of the economy. The monetary policy has to prevent the formation of bubbles. Institutional reforms are necessary over the long-term for keeping the control of financial activities, especially capital repatriation movements, which can be destabilizing for the whole economy. We have seen that the weakening of the exchange rate channel could incite the central bank to implement an over-expansionary monetary policy. To avoid such a pitfall, the status of the PBOC probably has to be reformed for a higher degree of transparency and for a larger importance of market mechanisms in the determination of interest rates. The supervision of financial markets has to be reinforced.

Fourth, the social policy must be prepared to face increasing inequalities linked to the opening of the capital account. The social policy has to organize the sharing of gains linked to the opening of the capital account for reducing inequalities. The fight against the increase of inequalities becomes more difficult, as the opening of the capital account and the attraction of foreign capital imply a low level of tax and therefore a low capacity of redistribution.

The free circulation of capital will be favorable for a minority and, at the same time, generate new fiscal revenues. The reduction of inequalities represents a clear priority for the current government.

—Yifan Hu,
Chief economist of Haitong International

The internationalization of the RMB will not be accomplished at one stroke

The strong economic strength does not mean that a country's currency can become an international currency. Some argue that China's economic strength will surpass the United States in predictable time, which can support the RMB to be an international currency for the relevant time period. In fact, America's GDP jumped to the world's first place in 1894; its industrial output was equivalent to the sum of the British, French, and German industrial output in 1913. Until the Bretton Woods Agreement was signed in 1944, the United States established finally the dollar's core status of international currency. It took 50 years for the United States to accomplish the above process. Obviously, without regard to the conditions of the internationalization of other currencies, China's economic aggregate is still far from the world's first; the internationalization of RMB is more impossible to be achieved in a short time.

The "double surpluses" phenomenon of the balance of payments determines that China cannot provide sufficient RMB to the world in the short term. For a long time, China's consumption is insufficient, the growth of GDP mainly relies on the investment, and a large number of goods and services created by the investment can't be completely absorbed in domestic, they must be transported to other countries through the export, which has led to the current account surplus. At the same time, as the main emerging market country, China is facing the access of the international direct investment and financial capital; surplus of capital inflows has also appeared under the capital account. Since 1994, China's international balance of payments has been all along in the situation of "double surplus," and it will be hard to reverse the tide in a long period of time. In the prevailing circumstance, the monetary authorities can only use currency swap or expand the RMB outflows under capital account, in order to deliver RMB to the international market by reducing the scale of capital account surplus, but these methods can be applicable only in a short time.

RMB cannot become the major international reserve currency for a long time. On one hand, China's comprehensive economic strength is still not enough to support RMB to be chosen as an international reserve currency by important economies. On the other hand, China's financial market is far from sane; the market's capacity and depth are not sufficient. These two aspects may explain why central banks of various countries have to possess a large number of dollar assets.

Since the financial market capacity is insufficient, the capital account cannot be fully opened without consideration. For China, the fully open capital account means that the domestic financial market will be completely exposed to the free shocks of the global capital; if the capacity is not enough, the financial markets will be hard to resist the impact from global capital. Especially when the bond market is short of capacity, the inflow and outflow of large quantities of money will cause a sharp increase or decrease in interest rates and bond prices, which results in direct damage to the real economy. Compare the capacity of the dollar and RMB local financial market: The scale of the United States' fixed-income market (less risky) reached $38 trillion in 2012, accounting for 240 percent of America's GDP; by the end of October 2013, the total amount of China's bond market had been only $4.86 trillion. Due to the vast difference between the market capacity, under the same circumstance, the impact of an equivalent amount of international capital flow to the market is completely different.

Serving as a currency of price is the RMB's greatest weakness during the internationalization of the RMB. The international valuation function of RMB refers that RMB could undertake functions such as value measure and tally for private or official use at the international level. Relative to the RMB's function of international settlement, the current international valuation function of RMB faced a severe hysteresis phenomenon. For example, although our country has gradually become a country with large consumption of staple commodity and trade, the import quantity of various commodities has taken the world's first place; the pricing power of global staple commodity is still mainly under the control of developed economies like Europe and the United States, which has formed several commodity-pricing centers, such as CBOT (Chicago Board of Trade) for agricultural products; NYMEX (New York Stock Exchange) for energy; and the LME (London Metal Exchange) for non-ferrous metals. These pricing centers have launched a dollar-based commodity-pricing mechanism and the price of staple commodity based on the historical inertia, the accepted degree of sides, the path and the capacity of hedging, theoretical model and the complete degree of hardware auxiliary system.

Generally, whether a particular currency can serve as an international currency of price is mainly related to the following factors: one is the inflation; the currency with low inflation rate and stable value is more likely to be chosen as a currency of price in trade; the second is the volatility of the exchange rate: Both sides of import and export will be more inclined to choose the currency of the country with stable monetary and exchange rate policy; the third is the development degree of the financial market. Both sides of import and export are more willing to choose the currency that can be generally accepted by traders of other countries and with the lowest conversion costs; this requires the currency-issuing country to possess developed monetary market, capital market, foreign exchange market, and perfect instruments in the money market; the fourth is the convertible degree of the currency: If a currency has not become a convertible currency, the risk and cost of holding currency abroad may be relatively high; the currency will be at a disadvantage in the valuation competition with other convertible currencies. From these aspects, RMB still has a long way to go to become an international currency of price.

—Huang Zhiling,
Chief economist of CCB

Can RMB become the top three of the international monetary?

Currently, the IMF believed that only four currencies can be regarded as widely used and widely internationally traded currencies: USD, EUR, JPY, and GBP. These four currencies make up the currency basket of IMF Special Drawing Rights (SDR). Several indicators were used to assess whether a currency is widely used in the world and is widely traded in the principal exchange markets. These indicators include the following.

Currency composition of official reserves: More and more central banks from all over the world have said they had added RMB to their foreign exchange reserves, but the statistics of the RMB in the global foreign exchange reserves are not yet available for use. However, the RMB's share of global reserves may still be tiny. According to the latest data from the International Monetary Fund, currency reserves named by "other currencies" (including RMB) at the end of the third quarter of 2013 accounted for 3 percent of the total "distributable reserves." USD still dominates the market, and the ratio is 61 percent; EUR followed, accounting for 24 percent; while JPY and GBP each accounted for 4 percent. Available data indicate that with the central banks turning to the diversification of foreign currency holdings, although "other currencies" share has risen in recent years, the degree of diversification is still very limited.

An additional indicator of the use of RMB as a reserve currency is the amount of currency held by central banks. One survey for reserve managers showed that 15 percent of respondents hold the RMB (Royal Bank of Scotland, 2013). For some reserve managers, the lack of convertibility of RMB is generally considered to hinder investment. However, 37 percent of respondents said that in the next 5 to 10 years they would consider investing in RMB.

Currencies of international banking liabilities and international bonds: BIS data on international debt outstanding loans reflect the dominance of the USD and EUR in the medium- to long-term international financial transactions. These two currencies broadly held the range of 75 percent to 80 percent of the total share. JPY and GBP were far behind in third and fourth. Although the share of RMB did not make a separate report, it was included in the "other currencies" item, by the end of September 2013 reaching 7 percent.

In the foreign exchange market trading volume: The triennial central bank survey of Bank for International Settlements showed that, in 2013, RMB had become the ninth of most actively traded currencies. The survey pointed out that the role of the RMB in the global foreign exchange transactions increased, mainly due to a significant expansion of offshore RMB transactions. From 2010, RMB trading volume had soared from $34 billion to $120 billion in 2013. However, there was only 2.2 percent of global foreign exchange RMB trading volume, but USD accounted for 87 percent, EUR for 33 percent, JYP for 23 percent, and GBP for 12 percent.

Overall, based on the scale of China's economic growth potential and trade links, the internationalization of RMB is imperative. However, modernization and deepening of China's financial industry, the gradual opening of the capital account, are at advancing stages; although as a trade settlement currency, RMB has a place, which still has a certain gap to those currencies meeting the standard of being "widely used" and "widely traded" during the international financial transactions.

I believe that the RMB has great potential to become an international currency. To promote the internationalization of the RMB, the main challenge for the future is to open capital account in support of financial market liberalization, develop deep and liquid financial markets, liberalize interest rates and exchange rate, and strengthen the supervision and regulatory framework. The pace and sequence of these reforms are equally challenging. The experience shows that the recent financial crisis tends to occur at the time of underdeveloped countries with weak regulatory framework opening the capital account. These reforms have been the core of China's reform agenda. The Third Plenary Session of Eighteenth announced plans to accelerate reforms. If reform can proceed smoothly, I think RMB must be included in the IMF SDR "currency basket" and "The International Monetary freely usable" in 2020.

—Zeng Songhua,
Former deputy director of the IMF Asian and Pacific Bureau

How to select the path of RMB internationalization?

There are three big changes in the global financial market. The first big change is the malignant expansion of the virtual economy and the virtual economy's increasing deviation from the real economy. It has been not only one of the most obvious features of the global economy over the past 40 years but one of the most confusing and interesting phenomena of the global economy. Proportion of global financial assets to GDP in 1980 was 1:1; however, the proportion was eleven times the global GDP in 2012. The second big change is that the global monetary and financial structure has been changed by the quantitative easing monetary policy. Quantitative easing monetary policy led by the U.S. Federal Reserve has deteriorated the virtual economy's departure from the real economy, which has become a major threat to the stability of global economy and finance. The U.S. Federal Reserve is planning to exit quantitative easing in 2014; however, if the speed of the exit is too fast, the exchange rates of BRIC countries, except China, will devaluate dramatically, and even the dilemma of the Asian financial crisis in 1977 may occur. The third big change: Dollar hegemony continued to improve. The global financial crisis has not weakened U.S. dollar hegemony. What is more, it has strengthened the dollar hegemony from many lateral sides. After the global financial crisis in 2008, the amount of dollar reserves was more than 8 trillion. Such a large foreign exchange reserve has further consolidated the international role of the U.S. dollar. China was the largest creditor in the world, so it would not reduce large holdings of U.S. dollar assets because it was not willing to shoot itself.

Which path of RMB internationalization should China choose in the end? I think there are three basic paths of currency internationalization. The first one is the trade route: the way from trade settlement to the financial settlement and then to the reserve currency. The classic examples are Japan and Germany. The second one is the monetary and financial path, establishing a totally financial center, such as Luxembourg, Zurich, and Hong Kong. The last one is a classic route building a manufacturing center, a trade center, and a financial center simultaneously. The processes of internationalization of dollar and pound are the typical classic route. The United States and the United Kingdom had already been the world's manufacturing center, trade center, and financial center during their currency internationalization. China is the largest trading country currently but not a power of manufacturing, nor is it a financial center. It even has no right to speak in the financial market. Which path should RMB choose is the core problem today when there are huge changes in the structure of global economy and global power. With the hope of developing Hong Kong offshore market though the channel of trade settlement, the People's Bank of China chooses the first path—trade route—to achieve internationalization of RMB. Will the path be successful? Maybe the examples of Japan and Germany prove that this path is not correct. In addition, the United States is vigorously promoting the TPP to subvert the WTO. Will a new structure of trade rules be formed soon? Trade rules will have a direct effect on the financial transactions and settlement, so their changes will have an obvious impact on monetary and financial rules inevitably. Does the trade route of RMB internationalization work under the new trade rules? What is the real relationship between virtual economy and real economy in the end? Does the real economy lead virtual economy or virtual economy lead the real economy? And what is the relationship between monetary center and financial center? Based on these issues, I believe that the global capitalist economy has entered the third stage. The first stage is the stage of commercial capitalism, the second one is the stage of industrial capitalism, and the third is the stage of financial capitalism. Because the global capitalist economy has entered the third stage, the traditional principals of economy based on the first two stages can no longer explain the current economic phenomenon effectively. The difficulty of the trade path is increasing under the background. There are some other problems hindering the development of RMB internationalization. For example, the degree of dollarization of China's monetary policy is deepening: namely, the influence of dollar and the monetary policy of U.S. Federal Reserve on the domestic monetary policy and supply of currency is so big that the independence of domestic monetary policy has disappeared partly or entirely. In addition, the construction of overseas branches of Chinese commercial banks is too slow, which is a big gap between the internationalization of RMB. The number of assets, market value, revenue, and profit of the Industrial and Commercial Bank of China are first in the world. However, it is not a global, systemically important bank. According to the regulation, a bank can be called a global systemically important bank only if its proportion of the overseas income to total income is up to 30 percent, drawn up by the Basel Committee on Banking Supervision, because its proportion is less than 5 percent.

Finally, "The Decision on Major Issues Concerning Comprehensively Deepening Reforms," released at the close of the Third Plenary Session of the

Eighteenth CPC Central Committee, has a significant role in promoting the internationalization of RMB. "The Decision" emphasizes explicitly the decisive role of the market for the first time and affirms that the market-oriented reform is the basic direction of deepening economic reform. Gradual marketization of financial markets is the core and key to financial reform. The following items are some specific policies that related to the RMB internationalization: (1) accelerate interest rate liberalization in the field of finance; (2) accelerate exchange rate liberalization (gradually); (3) promote reform toward a registration-based stock-issuing system and increase the proportion of direct financing; (4) develop and standardize the bond market; (5) improve market-based exchange rate formation mechanisms for the RMB, accelerate interest rate liberalization, and complete the Treasury yield curve which reflects a relationship between market supply and demand; (6) promote the two-way open of capital markets and orderly and financial transactions to improve cross-border capital convertibility; (7) accelerate capital-account convertibility of RMB; (8) the finance, education, culture, and medical sectors will enjoy an orderly opening-up to market access; (9) enterprises and individuals will be encouraged to invest overseas and undertake contract and labor cooperation projects at their own risk, through green field investment, mergers and acquisitions, equities, and joint investment. Investment treaty negotiations with other countries and regions will be expedited. Enterprises and individuals in China will bring a new round of overseas investment boom with the function of "The Decision."

—Xiang Songzuo,
Chief economist of the Agricultural Bank of China

The strategic thinking, "internal and external interaction," is needed in RMB internationalization

With the rapid development in recent years, the path of RMB internationalization is becoming clearer.

However, some deep problems are also gradually exposed with this process. Under the circumstance of limited liberalization of capital account currently, one of the main challenges for enhancing the international status of RMB is how to ensure and constantly develop the liquidity of RMB offshore markets and increase the attraction of RMB to foreign holders effectively. Positive interaction of RMB offshore market and domestic RMB business is helpful for solving the problem above. The strategic thinking, "internal and external interaction," needs to walk on two legs: one is establishing a mode of offshore financial center that is separated from the domestic financial centers, and the other one is extending the domestic advantages of RMB business to the outside by promoting the international development of Chinese banks.

First of all, the establishment of various forms of RMB offshore markets can promote increasing demand and use of RMB all over the world. Learning from the experience of Japan and Singapore, China can establish an offshore financial center that is separated from the domestic financial centers. First, Hong Kong

(HK) and other RMB offshore centers should be supported to get greater development. After HK, RMB offshore centers can be established in Singapore, London, Tokyo, and other international financial centers. In addition, Dubai of the Middle East, Johannesburg of South Africa, Moscow of Russia, New York, and São Paulo are also potential RMB offshore markets. We should provide the rapid development of RMB offshore markets with all kinds of soft and hard conditions by further supplementing the mechanism of RMB offshore clearing; enriching the system of RMB overseas products; playing the role of Chinese banks; strengthening the regulation, cooperation, and integration between onshore and offshore markets; and preventing and controlling the risks of offshore canters. Second, the internationalization of RMB should be accelerated by means of extending cross-border use of RMB in Shanghai Pilot Free Trade Zone. Shanghai Pilot Free Trade Zone will be built not only into an RMB offshore financial center but a settlement and clearing center of RMB products all over the world as well. At the same time, along with the increasing number of domestic pilot free trade zones, it is considered that with the opening of RMB offshore business in other potential pilot free trade zones, more competent Chinese banks will be allowed to open offshore financial business within the territory of China. Third, the cooperation between the RMB offshore market and domestic market should be strengthened. In the future, the offshore market needs to define their respective development position; the relative monetary authorities, regulatory authorities, and financial institutions should adhere to the concept of "win-win," and they should also maintain a close cooperation and develop RMB offshore business together. The RMB offshore markets should be opened to one another for ensuring convenient liquidity among the markets. Flowing free contributes to the formation of a same price among the offshore markets, which reduces the management and transaction cost of participants in RMB markets and increases attractions of overseas use of RMB.

Meanwhile, the development of RMB cross-border business also provides new ideas and opportunities for the internationalization of Chinese financial institutions. Globally, international financial institutions are important carriers of the internationalization of domestic currency. On the one hand, greater progress in the overseas use of RMB has to be supported by the internationalization of Chinese banks. On the other hand, Chinese banks as the main service providers in the RMB business can extend domestic advantages of RMB business to the world market with RMB cross-border business for promoting the internationalization. Chinese banks should continue to supplement the network of RMB clearing, accelerate the financial product innovation of RMB offshore, support enterprises to "go out," and actively participate in the process of internationalization of the RMB. In terms of regulation policy, RMB internationalization, as a part of highest level of financial strategies in China, especially needs a good top-level design. Meanwhile, attention should be paid to considering the internationalization of RMB, enterprises' "going out," and internationalization of Chinese financial institutions together and developing them together.

—Zhan Xiangyang,
Director of financial research of ICBC

Analysis on the public sentiment of RMB internationalization

The extent of RMB internationalization can be measured in two ways in two different perspectives: One is using the RII indicator, in the perspective of international monetary function; the other is examining the public sentiment about RMB to indirectly reflect the acceptance of RMB worldwide, in the perspective of media attention.

Analysis methods and techniques on international public sentiment

With the accelerating process of RMB internationalization, the share of RMB in international trade, direct investment, and international credit gradually increases, ranking among the top ten trading currencies. RMB-denominated settlement, changes in RMB exchange rate, and monetary policy have an impact on the economic interests of a growing number of countries whose companies and individuals are linked to RMB more or less. Hence, the degree of national media coverage and attention to the RMB deepens. There is no doubt that the attention itself embodies the internationalization of the RMB.

The miscellaneous international public sentiment includes both the mainstream media and non-mainstream media coverage, and motives involved with the specific content of RMB are quite different, not necessarily related to the internationalization of the RMB. Therefore, we need to design a scientific program to tap the intrinsic link between the international public sentiment and the internationalization of RMB by following the three steps.

First, use the Delphi method to invite experts on global monetary issues to select the world's major news media. According to these experts, we got the final English Media Directory (101 media in Table 3.1) and took their English website database for the study. Considering that the regional distribution of these media is uniform and they are typical of print media and able to represent the mainstream media, using them to study the internationalization of RMB is relatively credible and reliable.

Second, take the time period 2001, when China joined the WTO, to the end of 2013 to tap the international mainstream media attention to RMB. Given that the major news media on RMB had been really rare before 2008 (for example, there is no report on RMB in 2003), we merger the statistics in and before 2008, accounting for "2008 and before."

Third, study these media and their focuses. Searching for news containing words like 'RENMINBI," RMB, CNY, and then "Internationalization" and "International use" on their English websites found out that there were a lot of international media reports about the RMB in recent years, but a relatively smaller number of reports about "Internationalization" and "International use." As the "RMB internationalization" is a domestic academic term and "the RMB cross-border use" is an official term of Chinese government, the two terms are rarely used in international reports. Hence, we amended the technical path to analyze the public sentiment and identified RMB as searching object. Directly

Table 3.1 The regional distribution of media researching on public sentiment of RMB internationalization

Countries and region[1]	The numbers of media
North America	15
Including: United States	11
Canada	4
South America	9
Including: Brazil	3
Mexico	4
Argentina	2
Asia	25
Including: East Asia(Japan, Korea)	5 respectively
Southeast Asia (Indonesia)	4
South Asia (India)	7
West Asia (Saudi Arabia)	4
Europe[2]	36
Including: European Union	7
United Kingdom	8
Germany	5
France	5
Italy	2
Russia	6
Turkey	3
Australia	4
Africa (South Africa)	13

Notes
1. The data WSJ website cannot be acquired, hence this paper didn't use it.
2. The European Union refers to the media that can represent European Union.

search news containing "RENMINBI," RMB, CNY news and then tap the high-frequency words in the text database that these news combined, forming the outcome of follow-up research.

Public sentiment analysis mainly uses the regular expression (Regular Expression):1, LDA modeling, and 2, general text-mining techniques.

Characteristics of the public sentiment toward RMB

The research on the public sentiment of RMB mainly focuses on two aspects: one is the longitudinal study on the evolution of international media attention to RMB, and the other is the horizontal comparison between the economic activities of different countries and regions that concern RMB. Table 3.2 gives statistics about reports that were involved with RMB. According to the table and charts derived from it, we summarize some characteristics of international public sentiment.

First, RMB attracts more and more attention from the mainstream media. Prior to 2008, there were accumulatively 259 pieces of reports about RMB selected from the 101 mainstream media. Along with a comprehensive start-up internationalization of the RMB, there was a sharp rise in the extent of global media attention to RMB, the number of reports increasing to 552 in 2010. And it doubled to 1,334 in 2013. The annual average number of articles per media was more than ten. In the global mainstream media, measured by the number of reports, the United Kingdom, India, Canada, and Australia were the top four countries that give most attention to RMB (Figure 3.1).

Second, media attention varies greatly in different regions and nations, with Europeans as tops. Before 2008, reports about RMB existed only in Europe, precisely, only in the UK's mainstream media. The media coverage extended to Asia, Africa, Latin America, and Oceania, and the number of reports doubled and doubled in the next 3 years. European media were the main force; RMB-related reports from them accounted for more than half of the world-related reports. It is worthwhile to note that reports from the United Kingdom accounted for more than 80 percent of Europeans reports, indicating that as the world's largest financial center, the United Kingdom was more involved with RMB, and London paid more attention to the prospect of RMB as international currency. In addition, unexpectedly, Turkey paid more attention to RMB than Germany, France, and other traditional large EU countries did, indicating that there might be a new breakthrough in economy and trade between China and Turkey. In addition, since 2010, as China participated in the European sovereign debt crisis mitigation plans and increased direct investment in the EU, media

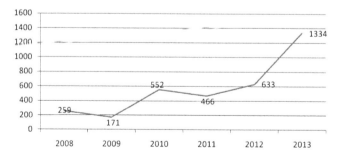

Figure 3.1 The number of reports on RMB by the mainstream media around the world

Table 3.2 The number of reports on RMB by the mainstream media around the world (2008–2013)

Country	Year						
	2008	*2009*	*2010*	*2011*	*2012*	*2013*	*Total*
Africa					4	2	6
Asia			66	92	169	181	508
East Asia			21	27	67	25	140
South Asia			20	37	67	116	240
Southeast Asia			23	24	29	23	99
West Asia			2	4	6	17	29
Europe	259	168	422	296	325	1,041	2,511
European Union			17	4	5	24	50
France			5	2	1	9	17
Germany			10	10	3	1	24
Russia				1	2	1	4
Turkey			23	35	38	13	109
UK	259	168	367	244	276	993	2,307
North America		3	39	41	88	67	238
Canada			37	38	46	30	151
USA		3	2	3	42	37	87
Oceania (Australia)			24	36	47	43	150
South America			1	1			2
Argentina				1			1
Mexico			1				1
Total	259	171	552	466	633	1334	3415

in Germany and France, the two core countries in the EU, had showed great interest in RMB. There is a significant increase in the number of reports, and the coverage density of Germany is much higher than that of France, which shows a positive correlation to the growing trade and investment between the Chinese and Germans (Figure 3.2).

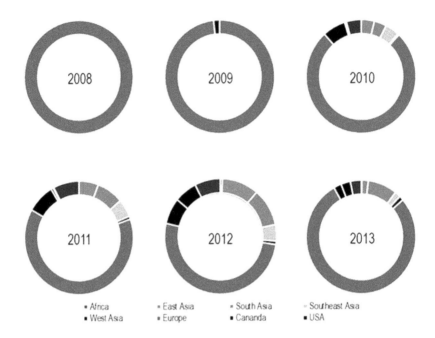

Figure 3.2 The comparison of the number of reports on RMB by the mainstream media in different regions and nations (2009–2013)

Third, the Asian media is giving more attention to RMB. The number of reports showed a gradual increase in East Asia, Southeast Asia, and South Asia since 2010, peaking at 163 pieces in 2012. In addition to the European media, the number of reports involving RMB from Asia media accounted for more than half of remaining reports, and India from South Asia had the highest frequency, with a total of 240 articles from 2009 to 2013. Particularly, in 2013, when the attention to RMB declined globally, the number of reports soared by 73 percent to 113 pieces in India. This showed that financial cooperation mechanisms among BRIC countries, international monetary system reform, and the RMB internationalization attracted much concern in India. What is more, in 2013, the number of reports about RMB increased from 6 to seventeen in Saudi Arabia in 1 year (Figure 3.3).

Fourth, North America showed a strong interest in RMB in the recent 2 years. Although the cross-border use of RMB mainly happens in peripheral areas of China and Asia, it has a great shock in North America. In 2012 and 2013, there was a significant rise in the number of reports on RMB in the United States and Canada, about forty pieces reported annually. Overall, having a closer economic relationship with China, the United States has fewer reports on RMB than India, which is only eighty-seven pieces.

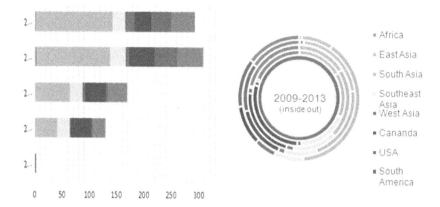

Figure 3.3 The comparison of reports on RMB by mainstream media in different regions excluding Europe (2009–2013)

Comparison about focuses on RMB in international public sentiment

Through mining and analyzing high-frequency words from the 101 selected media databases, we found out that the international community's focus on RMB is mainly involved with economy and trade. From 2013 onward, reports about RMB has been more involved with finance, such as foreign exchange, securities, investment, and so on. Media focus varies continentally, but most are concerned about bilateral economic and financial transactions with local characteristics.

The international public sentiment focuses on trade and finance

Analysis on the use of high-frequency words associated with RMB in media coverage can accurately reflect the focus on public opinion. Figure 3.4 shows the first twenty-five high-frequency words from reports between 2010 and 2013, with "Economy," "Bank," "Market," "Finance," and "Trade" ranking the top five. RMB exchange rate ranked ninth in terms of frequency, attracting widespread concern.

In fact, the international use of the RMB has also drawn a lot of media coverage, linking RMB and the world economy, globalization, and the international community. In these reports on RMB, "Global," "World," and "International" frequently appeared, ranking seventh, tenth, and seventeenth, respectively. It is worth mentioning that "London" as a place ranked twenty-fifth among high-frequency words, suggesting that the United Kingdom was very sensitive to the internationalization of the RMB with intense social concern.

RMB internationalization is a product of the 2008 international financial crisis, embodying the international monetary system reform. It is also fully reflected in international public opinion. In RMB-related reports, "dollar," "Crisis," "debt,"

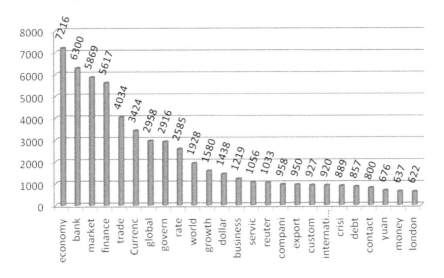

Figure 3.4 The number of high-frequency words associated with RMB around the world

and "currency" ranked twelfth, twentieth, twenty-first, and twenty-fourth, respectively, in the high-frequency words. Quite a number of news reports analyze the financial crisis and debt analysis in the U.S. dollar-dominated international monetary system, suggesting that RMB internationalization is an inevitable trend.

Second, the focus of international public opinion varies with the international economic and financial situation.

The international financial crisis forced the world to a painful readjustment of economic structure, leading to a dramatic change in international political, economic, and monetary situation accordingly. This change will, undoubtedly, be reflected among media coverage for the first time, as we can see it from the different focuses of reports (Figure 3.5).

Changes in high-frequency words show that as time went on, "finance" and the "bank" are getting more and more attention; the ranking of "bank" increased year by year, from fourth in 2010 to third in 2011, and ranked second in 2012 and 2013. "Finance" has not yet been in the top ten before 2010, ranking seventh and eighth in 2011 and 2012 and first in 2013. On the contrary, "trade" retreated from second in 2010 to fourth in 2011 and 2012, then eighth in 2013. In fact, this change is highly consistent with the process of RMB internationalization. RMB internationalization started from RMB-denominated trade settlement, but its development relies on promotion of the banking and financial transactions.

Third, the focuses of the continents are with local characteristics.

China is the world's largest trading nation; the cons and pros in RMB-denominated settlement are quite different. Analyzing their focuses is conducive to grasping the channels through countries to know, accept, and recognize RMB, which is beneficial to extend the use of RMB.

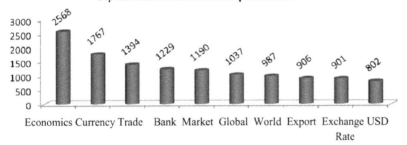

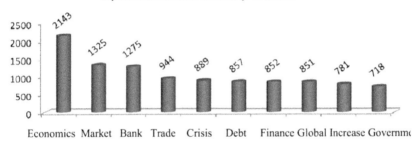

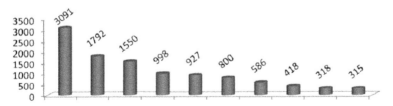

Figure 3.5 Focuses in RMB-related reports during (2010–2013)

The focuses on RMB vary greatly in different years, and countries and regions pay more attention to the affairs that they are involved with. Ranking the words in terms of frequency in different years and continents, we can see the general changes in public opinion (Table 3.3).

Public sentiment analysis shows that European countries are concerned more about the macro-areas involved with RMB, such as the markets, trade, banking, finance, government control, crisis, and economic growth. Their focus transfers to finance and banking in the recent 2 years.

North American media focus on the U.S. dollar, deficit, foreign exchange reserves, income, trade, and other issues, while the United States is more concerned about the high-tech exported to China. In addition, in 2009, the North American countries were very concerned about specific issues about optical glass, attention to finance and reserves, and investment significantly increased in 2010.

Because the dollar is the dominant currency today and RMB internationalization will affect the dollar to some extent, so the U.S. attitude toward the RMB is very complex. Thus, public sentiment in the United States is worthy of a separate analysis. The United States is a very pragmatic country. Before 2012, there were few reports about RMB in the United States, with relatively divergent topics and low frequency of high-frequency words. For example, in all reports that mentioned RMB in 2011, "Apple" was the word with the highest frequency, and its main products—iPhone, iPad—were also ranking among the top in high-frequency words, suggesting that American concern for the RMB is due to the Chinese heat for Apple products. After 2012, there was a surge in the number of reports on RMB and also in high-frequency words, indicating that the U.S. mainstream media began to focus on the impact of the internationalization of the RMB. Trade, markets, banks, funds, investments, and bonds are the focuses of American on RMB.

Research on South American news media includes those of Brazil and Argentina. Due to the economic structure, trade patterns, and geographic distance and other reasons about South America, they paid less attention to RMB. In all those reports from 2004 to 2013, there was only one piece involved with RMB in Brazil in 2010 and in Argentina in 2011. And related reports focused on the import, export, trade, inflation, and agriculture.

Asian countries have extensive and complex links with China in politics, economy, military, and finance. The goal of RMB internationalization in the first phase is to become a regional currency area in Asia. As China has signed free trade agreements with some East Asian and Southeast Asian countries, China has built close economic relations with them. Relatively speaking, the trade scale is smaller between China and South Asia and West Asia. In order to deeply study the Asian focus on public opinion, we divide Asia into four regions—East Asia, South Asia, Southeast Asia, West Asia:

1   The reports mentioning RMB in Japan and South Korea focus on economy, finance, bank, bond, international reserves, the relationship between the yen, and RMB. From the specific content of high-frequency words, we can

see that they showed greater interest in universities and research than in economy. Focuses of 2012 also include Taiwan and islands, reflecting the impact of the political situation on concerns about RMB.

2   Choose India as the representative of South Asian countries: There has been a growing number of reports on RMB since 2010, peaking in 2013. India's concern about RMB is directly related to currency internationalization, since the reports on RMB are always associated with "currency," "Russian ruble," "dollar," and other words. In the Indian view, as denominated currency in trade or investment, there exists competition between RMB and the U.S. dollar or the Russian ruble. In addition, India's concern about RMB also includes banking, trade, economy growth, governance, and infrastructure.

3   Southeast Asia's focus on RMS is much more straightforward. The most relevant word with RMB is "currency," followed by "trading" and "market." and then by "finance" and "bank." With the increase in the scale of authorized issue of RMB, funds, bonds, and investment became the focus in reports. Compared to other regions, Southeast Asia may pay the most attention to the internationalization of RMB, with "international" and "global" among high-frequency words. Not only that, "dollar" is also closely related to the frequency of RMB, suggesting that RMB internationalization does impact U.S. dollar.

4   Saudi media represent West Asia. In Saudi reports on RMB, "dollar" and "Islam" appear frequently as well as "Japan." Since Saudi Arabia is an oil-exporting country and the United States and Japan are the main oil-importing countries, the U.S. dollar is the dominated currency in export, indicating that Saudi Arabia is concerned about the impact of RMB internationalization on oil export revenues. In addition, 2013 IMF reform is also a high-frequency word in Saudi reports.

5   As the representative of Oceania, Australian media were most concerned with network and browser before 2012 and focused on wine in 2013. One brand of wine is "Penfold," in China called "benfu," being very popular in the mainland market and hotspot of media. Like other regions, the focus of Australian media turned to investment banking, trade, finance, and globalization.

6   There were no relevant reports on RMB in Africa before 2012. After that, reports focused on the economy and finance. "Trade" tops in the 2 years as the focus of reports, followed by foreign exchange, banking, finance, economy, bonds, and so on.

Observation: The internationalization of renminbi

Investigation and research of renminbi cross-border business in Qianhai

On August 26, 2010, the State Council officially replied "Overall Planning for the Development of the Qianhai Shenzhen-Hong Kong Modern Service Industry Cooperation Zone." Supporting Qianhai being a pioneer in financial

Table 3.3 The change of the focuses to RMB in different regions and nations over the years

	Before 2009	2010	2011	2012	2013
Africa				Trade, bond, proprietary, client, income, revenue, equity	Specular, system, tax, transact, trillion
East Asia		University, professor, faculty, science, economy, growth, rate, invest, export, corporation, demand	Fund, Japan, invest, company, bond, exchange	Taiwan, island, state, Japanese, dollar	University, Waseda professor, faculty, science, reserve, Hong Kong, corporate
South Asia		India, reserve, deficit, rupee export	India, trade, Singapore, global, power, rupee, infrastructure	Trade, nation, Indian, foreign, growth, invest	Offense, agree, rupee, recommend, disagree
Southeast Asia		Police, Indonesia, fund, export, invest, trade, exchange, industrial, capital, dollar, nation	Hong Kong, Indonesia, intern, ASEAN, region	North, dollar, Indonesia, state, region	Bond, Indonesian, inflate, increase, plan
West Asia		Brand, trade, blond, export, fashion	Malaysia, Islam, fund, capital, ICM, offer, product, service	Billion, Islam, issuance, sector, industry, manage, plus, continue	Hong Kong, yen, growth, Japan, IMF, monetary, value
Europe	Currency, market, dollar, economy, trade, rate, company, one, turn, price	Currency, economy, world, market, global, one, last, export, policy, dollar	Crisis, debt, photography, finance, growth, trade, Europe	London, need, now, Chinese, time, growth	Continue, custom, seen, without, try, contact, describe

Region				
Canada (North America)	Canada, dollar, percent, business, reserve, global, trade, bond, today, right, last	Reserve, trade, intern, interpret	Fur, reserve, invest	Digit, reserve, main, investor
USA	Dollar, hold, policy, trade, currency, deficit, dunk, fiberglass	Dollar, company, exchange, value, cost, custom, factory, foreign, job, mobile	Apple Store, debt, iPhone, Asia, iPad, buy, Obama	Dollar, billion, growth, rate, invest, fund	Dollar, billion, investor, export
South America			Inflate, agriculture, export, devalue		
Oceania		Google, Chrome	Euro, global, intern, trade, dollar, monetary	Wine, Penfolds, drinker	Invest, dollar, fund, growth

reform and innovation, building itself as an exemplary window for the opening up of China's financial industry, and "eight items about finance"[1] are pointed clearly in "Reply of the State Council on the Relevant Policies Supporting the Development and Opening-up of the Qianhai Shenzhen-Hong Kong Modern Service Industry Cooperation Zone," which was released on June 27, 2012.

The RMB internationalization research team of the International Monetary Institute of RUC went to Shenzhen for the special investigation of RMB internationalization. The research objects include Shenzhen Center Sub-branch of the People's Bank of China; Management Committee of the Qianhai Shenzhen-Hong Kong Modern Service Industry Cooperation Zone; Management Committee of Qianhai Bonded Port and other policy-making bodies and regulators; Bank of China; China Construction Bank; Ping An Bank; local banking institutions such as China Development Bank and China Merchants Bank; local securities institutions such as China International Trust and Investment Company; Guosen Securities; China Merchants Securities; Ping An Securities; China Southern Fund; Bosera Asset Management; and representative enterprises such as ZTE Corporation and Tencent. Experts have put forward their own opinions about the development of RMB cross-border business that are based on the practical development of Qianhai of Shenzhen.

The positive significance of innovation of RMB cross-border business

Innovation of RMB cross-border business has a positive significance not only on internationalization of RMB but on import and export trade in China. The key of international society acceptance and use of RMB is to solve the problem of the narrow investment channels. If there is no entry, there is no exit. Only if appropriate channels of reflux are established can the RMB internationalization go farther.

Freedom and innovation are the life and vitality of Shenzhen. Emancipating the mind, greater reforms and breaking some obstacles of system and policy are encouraged in Qianhai. At the same time, relying on the communication with HK RMB offshore market, Qianhai is trying to build the perfect channels, and it has already attained certain achievements. At present, the cross-border RMB loan policies that are in "eight items about finance" have basically been implemented, and it has gotten a good response from the market. Financial institutions have been paying close attention to the development of Qianhai, and they have been cooperating with one another and doing some innovation work. Equity exchange, petrochemical exchange, climate exchange, and other markets of factors exchange are booming in Qianhai.

The problems of RMB cross-border business

The channels of RMB reflux are not smooth.

Currently, there is an obvious phenomenon that is encouraging exit and preventing entry in the RMB cross-border business. However, the blocked channels of reflux will have a negative impact on RMB internationalization. In addition, some existing cross-border RMB businesses have put excessive emphases on the risk control, which reduces market capacity and vitality. For instance, the policies of cross-border loan in Qianhai before were limited only to use in the zone by the enterprises. In fact, body or projects of many enterprises are not in Qianhai although they are registered there. Therefore, the demand of financing is inadequate, and massive bank lending is difficult to digest and use. In the aspect of cross-border bond financing, although the green channel has been opened, it is difficult for enterprises to obtain the qualification of issuing bonds, and the demand and motivation of financing of enterprises that have gotten that qualification are inadequate, because of the requirement of three years of operation and complicated policy approval, except for the problem of the main location of enterprises.

The cost of offshore RMB is high

In the aspect of nominal interest rate, the price of the offshore RMB is lower by 3 percent than the domestic one, so that attraction of the former one should be big. However, in cross-border RMB financing, the regulations such as housing risk-weighted assets in off-balance sheet to guarantees and banks push up the cost of capital, and large enterprises are polarized with the small and medium-size enterprises. Although the large enterprises with better credit can use bonds financing, their demand and motivation of financing are inadequate because of the high tax that almost offsets the advantage of low financing cost overseas; the small and medium-sized enterprises have a strong financing demand, but the difficulty of financing is big, and the cost of financing is high for them, because measures of increasing credit are needed for obtaining external loans, and it is difficult to mortgage the domestic land and real estate.

The amount of overseas RMB is insufficient

In recent years, the People's Bank of China has signed a series of bilateral currency exchange agreements with many national central banks, which injected a large amount of liquidity. However, the amount of RMB is still limited relative to the potential of RMB. Worries of RMB liquidity risks hinder the use of oversea RMB to some extent. Because the offshore RMB mainly gathered in HK and the amount of RMB stocked in Europe and the United States is relatively small, price of foreign currency is much better than that of RMB, which hits the willingness of RMB use of European and American enterprises. Therefore, it is difficult for RMB cross-border business to increase its scale.

The construction of policy and law lag behind.

While its advantages of policy were obvious in the early days of construction of Qianhai, the implementation of police, finalizing the details, and other aspects lag behind. Policy making involves the People's Bank, foreign exchange bureau, Ministry of Commerce, the National Development and Reform Commission, and many other departments. It is relatively sensitive to deal with the tax work of RMB reflux. At the same time, the support of policy of the Land Bureau, the Trade and Industry Bureau, and other departments is needed on guarantees, counter-guarantees, and other aspects. In the practical work of cross-border RMB business, many policies and regulations should be refined and coordinated because they are vague and conflictive. Meanwhile, there are some problems that the law of HK does not match with domestic regulations, which exist in the linking process of cross-border business between Qianhai and HK off-shore markets. Lack of consistent interpretation brings barriers of policy and regulation for working of cross-border RMB business.

The directions and recommendations in the future of RMB internationalization

The further breakthroughs in the traditional framework, cooperation of Shenzhen and HK, and achieving innovations and growth are needed for the development of RMB cross-border business in Qianhai.

SPECIFY THE POSITION OF FUNCTIONS.

The channels of RMB reflux in Qianhai should be dredged as soon as possible so that the vitality of the HK offshore market can be released and global capital can be attracted into Shenzhen and HK. The cooperation of Shenzhen and HK implies linking the policies of Shenzhen and HK. Continually expanding the use of cross-border RMB loans is needed after dredging the loan route. Accelerate the liberalization of investment channels and release the enterprises' overseas investment demand; improve the RMB cross-border business of financial institutions in Qianhai continuously. In addition, the relationship between Qianhai and Shanghai on the RMB cross-border business is complementary. As an international financial center, Shanghai is supporting RMB to go out and open up the channels of foreign investment capital; Qianhai is opening up the channels of RMB reflux, relying on HK's offshore RMB market. In the condition that capital account has not yet liberalized fully, Shanghai and Qianhai can try to build RMB internationalization circle and promote the process of internationalization of the RMB together.

LINK THE POLICIES OF SHENZHEN AND HONG KONG

In the preliminary stage of development of RMB internalization, policies and rules of RMB cross-border business are changing and updating so rapidly. Qianhai should enhance the communication with HK and other major RMB offshore markets or settlement areas, which can ensure timely acquiring of regulatory requirements and direction of policy in mainland China. HK is a stock-trading center, and it is important for the growth of amount of RMB offshore stocked that issuing and trading shares in HK. Combined with the HK capital market and adopting HK standards it allows enterprises in Qianhai to be listed in HK, it tries to isolate the start-up board from the Shenzhen Stock Exchange and merge it into that in HK, and gradually decrease the policy restrictions.

EXPAND THE CHANNELS OF INVESTMENT AND FINANCING OF CROSS-BORDER RMB

With the internationalization of the RMB, the RMB offshore market is booming. The cooperation areas of Qianhai RMB cross-border business should not be limited in HK, and it should include Taiwan, Singapore, and other countries and regions gradually. Meanwhile, the gradual liberalization of scales of the RMB investments and financing can reduce the threshold of RMB investment and financing, which can further broaden the channels of cross-border RMB investment and financing. First, promote the differential account management between the domestic and overseas business in Qianhai's financial institutions, and allow the large financial institutions to launch a pilot project of mixed operation. Second, achieve the overall amount management of settlement of exchange in Qianhai's enterprises, replace the approval system with the record-keeping system in the appropriate scopes, and gradually cancel the limit of amount of settlement of exchange to Qianhai's enterprises in the long run. Third, further reduce the threshold of overseas issuing RMB bonds of Shenzhen's enterprises, allow Qianhai's registered stock broker to issue RMB, achieve free reflux and use of RMB under the effective regulation, increase the space of activity and innovation, promote the issuing of RMB funds overseas that raise money, and further broaden the scale of investment. Finally, promote the construction of fortune management centers to import financial products overseas into China, allocate global resources, and promote the development of RMB cross-border business.

IMPROVE THE CONSTRUCTION OF SUPPORTING MECHANISMS

Complete the laws and regulations and enhance the spirit of laws. Regarding applicable law as a key of breakthrough, develop international arbitration greatly and allow the subjects of commerce to choose the legal system by themselves. Deepen the reform of regulations of fiscal taxation and business in Qianhai to adapt to the international situation. Pay attention to the policies of talented person for increasing Qianhai's ability of sustainable development. What is more significant, enhancing propaganda of media and public relations associations or promoting the development of RMB cross-border business in Qianhai.

Research on Hong Kong's offshore RMB market

Hong Kong is the world's largest offshore RMB market. With the process of internationalization of the RMB, the RMB offshore market in HK has expanded rapidly in recent years, achieving self-improvement cycle. Among them, the scale of dim sum bonds in HK continues to expand, and the scale of issuance of RMB bonds maintains more than 30 percent annual growth. The price discovery function of RMB has emerged, as well as the clearing systems and other facilities gradually have been improved. Hong Kong has become a hub for offshore RMB trading and provided favorable conditions for the future progress of RMB internationalization.

The International Monetary Institute, Renmin University of China research team investigated the RMB internationalization process and the development of HK's offshore market. The research objects included the institute of global economics and finance of Chinese University of Hong Kong, Hong Kong Monetary Authority, JP Morgan Chase, BOC Hong Kong, HSBC, Hong Kong Branch of Bank of Communications, Fitch, and other departments in academic and industrial sectors. Based in HK's offshore market, experts gave valuable suggestions on the future development of the internationalization of RMB.

THE IMPORTANCE OF THE DEVELOPMENT OF HONG KONG'S OFFSHORE RMB MARKET

The construction of the offshore market is not prerequisite since there are multiple paths for RMB internationalization. However, under the condition that the current Chinese capital accounts are not yet fully open, the construction of RMB offshore markets is an optimal way in reality. RMB offshore market developed from trade and financial needs and is market-oriented to fully reflect the price discovery function while reflecting the RMB real exchange rate and interest rates, which will help to enhance the attractiveness of RMB assets, to serve the global needs of the residents, and to accelerate the process of internationalization of RMB.

Hong Kong is the world's largest offshore RMB center. Compared with other offshore RMB markets, HK's market has obvious advantages. First of all, the close connections in economic and trade exchanges between HK and mainland China result in a large stock of RMB funds to serve the financial needs of the domestic economy, thus, preferential policies exist significantly. Second, Hong Kong's RMB offshore market basically opened up channels for two-way flow of RMB loans, RQFII, the inter-bank bond market, the RMB direct investment, dim sum bonds, and the like. Issuance of RMB bonds in HK maintains a high growth of 30 percent per year, and the regulatory approval process has been simplified. Market behavior is driven significantly to enhance the attractiveness of RMB assets. In fact, HK has become the overseas RMB lending center. Then, the HK offshore RMB market basically has formed a complete financial ecology. Interest rates and exchange rates can conduct rapidly, and price discovery function of RMB has emerged; meanwhile, the market can help to guide the price of RMB in other markets such as London, Singapore, and so on. Fourth, HK's RMB clearing system has been improved, and it connects with the central bank system and foreign bonds system, which makes clearing and settlement become more convenient. What is more, 15 hours' trading partially covers the trading time of the United States and Europe, making the market an offshore RMB trading hub. Finally, institutions, policies, and laws in Hong Kong are in accordance with international standards, receiving high recognition all around the world.

PROBLEMS IN THE CONSTRUCTION OF HONG KONG'S OFFSHORE RMB MARKET

Hong Kong's offshore RMB market accumulated a lot of practical experience due to its fast-growing development. The process of internationalization of the RMB has played an important role in the promotion; however, the market is also facing some problems during its development:

Weak liquidity risk supervision

Substantial investment and arbitrage on RMB assets make the liquidity risk management in the HK area become challenging, resulting in big fluctuations on interest rates, exchange rates, and other prices. At present, the liquidity of RMB is mainly managed by BOC International. Compared with the Fed's management of offshore dollar liquidity, the central bank has not yet fully fulfilled the role of managing offshore RMB; thus, there is still a lot of weaknesses existing in liquidity risk supervision.

A strong dependence on the expectation of RMB appreciation

In recent years, the RMB internationalization process has gone through trade and financial settlement, two stages as China's economic growth: liberalization of the financial market channel, and the rapid increase in the trading volume of offshore RMB. From the perspective of RMB financial transactions, the RMB appreciation and the expectation of appreciation of the market are expected to be the main driving forces behind the development of the offshore RMB market. Countries outside Asia know little about RMB financial. More efforts should be spent on the promotion. Currently, there is more short-term arbitrager than long-term investors on the RMB offshore market, which means the structure of investors is unreasonable. Stagnation of HK's offshore RMB market will appear once there is a reversal of RMB appreciation trend.

Imperfect products of RMB funds pool

Financial product innovation and an improved product system play a crucial role for the internationalization of the RMB and RMB offshore market development. Currently, the leading products on HK's RMB offshore market are RMB certificates of deposit, private wealth management products. Thus, products of RMB funds pool are not diversified enough. Also, compared with the U.S. dollar and other major international currencies, the RMB product system is not sound. The problems mentioned above constrained the HK offshore RMB market from attracting mainstream international institutional investors. From this perspective, the products system of RMB funds pool needs to be further improved.

Lack of effective linkage between the onshore and offshore markets

Financial reform in China lags. Both financial markets and financial institutions have a lower degree of internationalization. RMB market regulations and policy system have many differences with that of international market and RMB onshore market on law, taxation, and accounting standards, which hinders the formation of an effective linkage between the onshore and offshore markets.

Rating system needs to be improved

The dim sum bond market is an important part of HK's RMB offshore market. Sixty percent of companies from mainland China did not conduct ratings, although many of them issued RMB bonds in HK, resulting in lower recognition of foreign investors as well as a bad influence on the expanding of the dim sum bond market.

PROPOSALS FOR RMB OFFSHORE MARKET DEVELOPMENT

The construction of Hong Kong's offshore RMB market has a positive role in promoting internationalization of the currency. The construction process must be market-oriented to better serve the real economy.

Fostering the internationalization of the real economy

The basis of currency internationalization is a powerful economic entity. From the national strategic point of view, China should strengthen the cultivation of the process of real economy internationalization, improve the international competitiveness of the real economy, and switch the RMB speculation in cross-border use into real investment behavior. Bigger and stronger Chinese industrial entities are essential if China wants to consolidate the foundation for the development of offshore RMB market and steadily promote the internationalization of the RMB.

Reforming the financial system steadily

Hong Kong's offshore RMB market interest rates are lower than that of mainland onshore market. The big spread indicates that there is more serious financial repression in China's financial market presence, and factor mobility is restricted. Therefore, China's financial system should transform the financial repression into financial freedom by promoting interest rate liberalization, reducing the cost of capital, and adjusting the financial structure to ensure that finance serves real entity economy.

The open level of capital account is one of the determinants of internationalization of the RMB. Before China's capital account is fully open, the HK RMB offshore market should play a role in promoting a two-way flow of offshore and onshore RMB transaction and the role of trade hub, achieving effective interaction between offshore and onshore market.

Realizing the internationalization of RMB financial products

RMB internationalization is actually the process of providing Chinese credit to the world, prompting the international market acceptance and the use of the RMB. The designing of RMB financial products requires accordance with the international standards and the international legal framework, reducing legal risks. Chinese-funded institutions should not be limited to the issuance of RMB bonds but trying to issue dual-currency bonds such as the U.S. dollar bonds to reduce foreign-funded enterprises' customer concerns. China institutions also should recommend that RMB bonds' attractiveness should be enhanced worldwide and stably to ensure the international RMB bond investment, improve services, and focus on long-term cooperation with the investor community through global network. And all of the above should be in consideration of investment preferences of the major international fund asset pools.

Special investigation of RMB internationalization by foreign specialists

RMB internationalization needs to reach a necessary consensus worldwide. China and neighboring countries' awareness of the internationalization of the RMB is relatively high, for the reason that the RMB internationalization is associated with their vital interests, while such feelings do not appear to happen in European countries. In order to reflect the views of the international community fully and accurately and prevent us from generalization errors, we designed a questionnaire specialized for economists in European and American central banks, international organizations, and research institutions to know their prospects for the internationalization of the RMB, the RMB offshore market opportunities and challenges, as well as opinions on other aspects. Officials of IMF's Asia-Pacific bureau, senior correspondent of Reuters, a senior adviser of the Swiss bank, and researchers of the Bank of England took part in our questionnaire program. Through this survey, we found out that foreign experts believe that the offshore market could overcome the current obstacles to the free movement of RMB to some extent, which would help to boost the internationalization of RMB. The key to the future internationalization of RMB lies in the current progressive reforming opening up of the capital account, the deepening of the financial market, as well as internal and external policy coordination.

The role and risk of offshore markets

An offshore RMB market can help expand the RMB oversea use and circulation

Interviewed experts believe that the development of an offshore center is not necessary in the internationalization of the currency, but it can help RMB with certain obstacles caused by the unopened capital accounts. In this way, the establishment and development of an offshore market become a necessary objective need in the process of RMB internationalization. Construction and development of the RMB offshore market will certainly help with RMB's internationalization, but it still depends on the government's target, whether to internationalize the use of RMB or promote RMB as a reserve currency. Offshore markets will complement one another with the open capital accounts, and they can increase mobility and accessibility of the currency, broaden the scope of access, expand a financial innovation basis, and so on. The offshore market and Shanghai FTA, which is currently under construction, are both aimed to promote the use of RMB in international trade and investment in the context of the limitation of capital free flow.

Offshore markets can help expand the RMB oversea use and circulation, especially before the Chinese capital items fully open up. The development of RMB offshore markets is of great significance to broaden the oversea investment channels of RMB, expand the use of RMB, and promote a deeper development of RMB internationalization. Circulation and settlement of RMB in the world is the basis of RMB internationalization, which means that RMB is becoming the worldwide recognized invoicing and settlement currency and even reserve currency of other countries. There will be a large number of foreign enterprises, institutions, and individuals holding RMB assets oversea. This requires a convenient, safe, and low-cost financial market environment for payment, settlement, exchange, investing, and financing activities. Offshore market transactions are subject to less restrictive market regulations and taxation, and it has complete financial infrastructure and advantages such as various financial products, legal transparency, political stability, and the like. Its higher efficiency is conducive to price discovery and efficient allocation of resources, which are able to create conditions for circulation and exchange rate proof as well as appreciation.

The offshore market's risk lies in the coordination of internal and external macro-economic policy goals

The majority of experts interviewed agreed that for the Chinese government and the People's Bank of China, accounts numbers and the number of HK's RMB's increasing can help boost liquidity in HK offshore RMB transactions. However, the risk of developing the offshore market is that the gradual increase of the offshore pool of assets will affect and interfere with the domestic interest rate benchmark. From the macro-economic point of view, we need to confirm that there is no conflict between the domestic and foreign monetary policies and fiscal policies. Meanwhile, the development of the offshore market requires the improvement of transparency in decision making and information and the deepening of the financial markets. All these practices would bring some unexpected risks.

A deeper level of risk is that China has not yet established the necessary institutional infrastructure, independent and honest legal system, as well as a deep-seated, liquid financial market. Why did the USD quickly become an international currency? It owes to politicians' carrying out a series of policies to promote the internationalization of the U.S. dollar during World War I, including the establishment of the Federal Reserve, establishment of the commercial paper market in New York, allowing U.S. banks to establish branches oversea, and so on. And the more important reason is that the United States has established the necessary system foundation, such as the independent and faithful legal system as well as the deep-seated and liquid financial markets. However, in the past few decades, China has not yet completed the above steps.

The ongoing internationalization of RMB is unprecedented. In the late 1950s and early 1960s, the development of the Eurodollar market was to circumvent some of the regulatory policies from the U.S. government, and by the time that Eurodollar market became a pure offshore market, the U.S. dollar had been a key reserve currency. This process and the promoting construction of offshore RMB market are essentially different.

Opportunities and challenges of the offshore market

Opportunities and challenges

In the context of the underdeveloped financial markets and not-yet-fully-open capital accounts in Chinese territory, the development of the offshore RMB market can open up investment channels so that foreign enterprises, institutions, and individuals are more willing to hold RMB, which can help expand the international use of RMB as well as isolate the international financial risk relatively. At present, the RMB offshore market's breadth and depth are still insufficient, and it has great development space and potential.

When it comes to the opportunities and challenges brought by offshore centers, interviewed experts made a very apt analogy. Establishing an offshore RMB center for trade services instead of allowing nontrade free capital flows to get into China is just like training a child riding a bicycle with rear stabilizers. We can give her or him a helmet and protective clothing and a hand on the shoulder to protect him or her at the beginning, but at some point we have to let go to let the child become independent. Experts interviewed agreed that China will need to finally abandon capital controls, and when faced with the problem of how to match up the capital account opening with domestic economic development issues, the answer is full of uncertainty. China needs reforms in the banking and financial sector and to continue to make the exchange rate more flexible.

Determinants of offshore centers' choices

According to the functions of offshore centers, interviewed experts believe that the decisive factors in choosing an offshore RMB center can be listed as follows. The first consideration is whether China has jurisdiction on it, such as HK. As China's administrative region, Hong Kong has the most intimate dealings with China. It has a long history of offshore RMB business and has been by far the most efficient offshore RMB business center in the world. The second consideration is whether the local language and culture are similar to China's, such as Singapore and Malaysia. The third is whether there is a close trade with China, such as Taiwan. Cities holding a close trade relationship with China, trading ports, and transit cities are more likely to become an offshore center. The fourth consideration is whether there are deep-seated financial markets as well as deeper and more abundant financial market products, such as London, Paris, and New York. The fifth consideration is whether it is in the same time zone with China, such as London. Trading time in the same time zone is similar to facilitate the transactions.

The prospect of RMB internationalization

The future of RMB internationalization

International experience shows that the process of internationalization as well as becoming a reserve tool of a currency will be influenced by some important factors, such as: economies of scale and extensive trade network which can promote the need for the currency as a measuring unit and exchange media; macroeconomic stability, low inflation and sustainable development of public debt which can enhance the credibility and attractiveness of the currency in terms of store of value; capital account convertibility which can keep good liquidity of the currency in international financial markets; depth and liquidity of the domestic financial market (along with currency convertibility) which can enable global investors to borrow various financial instruments in their own currencies for investment and storage value.

Interviewed experts agreed that the RMB internationalization will be realized in the future, and the trade scale as well as economic importance of China both show that RMB will eventually become the currency widely used in international trade and investment. However, on the issue of whether RMB will become a reserve currency, experts interviewed are at sixes and sevens. Some experts believe it may take 20 years for RMB to exceed the share of the yen and the British pound as a reserve currency, and it will take longer for RMB to match the euro. Some experts argue that the proportion of RMB as a reserve currency will still be very low by 2030, and how many shares it can get depends on whether RMB can earn the confidence of foreign investors as a store of value.

Three challenges in RMB internationalization

Although in the past decade China has achieved remarkable economic growth and its economy scale as well as trade shares are one of the world's top, what is more is that China's financial sector reforms have also made good progress. However, the breadth, depth, and liquidity of China's financial system still have a considerable gap with those reserve currency countries. The open extent of China's capital account is still insufficient. When asked about the three most important challenges in the process of RMB internationalization, interviewed experts have different opinions. Some experts believe that the key lies in the government. Some experts believe that the three major challenges are financial reform, the exchange rate reform, and government reform, while some other experts believe that the three major challenges are domestic political compatibility, international acceptance, and China's choices in the face of the current account deficit and willingness to give up capital controls as well as other aspects.

The financial sector reform program proposed by the Third Plenary Session of the Eighteenth has received the praise of many experts at home and abroad, and it has a comprehensive and far-reaching significance including strengthening financial regulation, interest rate liberalization, a deposit insurance system introduction, a market-based exchange rate regime, and economic policies. With the full implementation of these reforms, China will usher in a more efficient and market-based financial system. The interviewed experts believe that these measures are incremental, and the important policy challenges China is going to face are uncertain. The main challenges include whether to slow down the speed of credit creation in order to avoid the accumulation of non-performing loan, when to stop the non-market "rigid payment," and how to slow down the accumulation of foreign exchange reserves. The prospect of RMB internationalization depends on the proper handling of credit management policies and the conflict between the interest rate and capital account liberalization so that the expected effect of financial reform can come out.

Notes

1 (1) Qianhai is allowed to explore for broadening the channels for repatriation of overseas RMB capital, coordinate and support the development of the offshore RMB business in HK, and position itself as an innovative and experimental hub for cross-border RMB-based business. (2) Banking institutions established in Qianhai are encouraged to grant RMB loans for offshore projects; proactive studies are encouraged for the granting of RMB loans by Hong Kong-based banking institutions to enterprises established in Qianhai within the framework of the Mainland/Hong Kong Closer Economic Partnership Arrangement ("CEPA"). (3) Qualified enterprises and financial institutions registered in Qianhai are encouraged to issue renminbi bonds in HK within the amount approved by the State Council for the development and construction of Qianhai. (4) Establishing an equity fund of funds in Qianhai is supported; the innovative development of foreign (including Hong Kong)-funded equity investment funds in Qianhai is supported, and new modes of capital settlement of foreign exchange, investment, fund management, and others of those will be actively explored. (5) The opening-

up of Qianhai financial market to Hong Kong will be further promoted. (6) Lowering of access conditions of setting up institutions and engaging in financial business for HK financial enterprises are supported under the framework of CEPA. (7) According to the State's general plan and requirements for regulated development, various innovation-based financial institutions beneficial to market functions in Qianhai are encouraged to be established, a transaction platform of new elements will be promoted exploringly, and reforms of mechanism of financial system and innovation of business modes, which are focusing on the real economy, are supported to carry out. (8) Hong Kong financial institutions and other overseas financial institutions are encouraged to set up international or national management headquarters and business operation headquarters in Qianhai in order to accelerate the improvement of financial internationalization level and promote the cluster development of finance and headquarters economy in Qianhai.

4 Currency internationalization and offshore market

Historical implications

Offshore market is an inevitable consequence of the development of international trade and international financial market

Production and trade are two perpetual topics in the development of the world economy. With the development of economy, the cross-border commodity trade among nations requires the financial service to become worldwide, such as currency exchanges, international settlement, and trade financing. Thus, the emergence and development of offshore financial markets is one indispensable result of the development of the world economy.

Financing in international trade drives the emergence of offshore financial market

Trade-financing activities in the form of export credit and so on benefit the expanding scope of international trade. International trade business developed dramatically after World War II, and the growth rate of global trade went far beyond that of the economy of any nation in the world. However, countries with a trade deficit would commonly constrain the outflow of domestic currency by adopting restrictive policies such as trade protection, protective financing, and control of foreign currencies. These policies would increase the demand for trade financing by foreign currencies in the market. In the meanwhile, countries with a trade surplus would tend to find currency exchanges that are convenient for deposit and withdrawal and of high required return, to invest their money surplus. When the gap between money demand and supply gets worse, financial institutions aimed at fund financing came into being in offshore financial markets. In 1951, when the pound crisis broke out, British authorities prohibited domestic commercial banks from providing any trade-financing services nominated by British pounds, so there emerged demands for trade-financing services nominated by non-British pounds. Then the British commercial banks in response issued loans to international traders by collecting American dollar deposits in the international financial market. As a consequence, the most basic banking business, such as European dollar and trade financing, emerged in European financial markets like London, and the American dollar offshore market hence came into existence.

Multinational corporations' demand for financial services promotes the development of offshore financial markets

Multinational corporations are important carriers of the deepening social division of labor. Centering on the home country, multinational corporations participate in the promotion of economic globalization through the establishment of a worldwide network of production operations throughout the northern and southern hemispheres or active engagement in direct investment activities. Multinational corporations not only conduct international production and sales business but also actively engage in international investment, financing, overseas mergers and acquisitions, and other financial activities. In addition to the basic business of payment, international settlement, and clearance, high-level demand for financial services such as asset management, risk hedging, and financial advisory services need to be satisfied by the international financial markets and international financial institutions.

With the intensification of market competition, multinationals generate special financial needs for confidentiality, tax avoidance (or tax evasion) in the business of mergers and acquisitions, or asset management. With a lot of confidentiality, avoidance featuring bookkeeping offshore financial centers has grown. To the Netherlands Antilles, for example, based on the strict secrecy law on local banks and tax treaties signed in 1948, the United States and the Netherlands (the Netherlands autonomous island region) local businesses can get very significant tax advantages from making investment in the United States. So Netherlands Antilles became the main source of investment in the United States in the twentieth century.

International financial institutions become the main driving force of the development of offshore financial markets

Financial institutions are important participants and intermediaries in the international financial markets and intermediaries. International operations of financial institutions promote the development of offshore financial markets and performance in the following aspects. First are the international parties involved in the transactions that have served both residents and nonresidents. The second aspect lies in the transnational branches of financial institutions. After the 1960s, large banks in European and American countries have set up branches or subsidiaries to expand business overseas. Wherever there lies a major international financial center also gathers international banks. Third is the variety of international business, with the rise of offshore banking business as well as increased cross-border capital financing, such as short-term interbank funding transactions carried out among offshore accounts, the European syndicated loans, negotiable certificates of deposit issued in foreign currencies, options, futures, and other foreign exchange transactions. Fourth, the international composition of financial assets: Offshore banking assets constitute a larger share of the global cross-border banking business. According to the statistics of 2013 Bank of International Settlements (BIS), although offshore banking since the 1990s has been reduced, the cross-border banking assets remained above 50 percent of the total assets of international banks. Fifth, international sources of revenue: Back in the 1970s, half of the profit growth in the thirteenth-largest U.S. multinational banks came from the European credit. Therefore, multinational banks pay more attention to overseas businesses, which can provide a steady stream of power for the development of the offshore market.

Offshore financial markets: A result of financial liberalization and ease of government control

Financial liberalization is the motive for the emergence and the development of offshore markets. Financial liberalization could be reflected in offshore financial markets back in the late 1950s. First, market access was less restrictive. For example, in London, the Bank of England took a more lenient policy for foreign domestic institutions to set up an offshore bank. Another example is in the Cayman Islands: a multinational bank with only $240,000 of the capital will be able to set up branches to meet the local minimum capital limit. Second, cost management requirements are lower. The vast majority of the offshore market regulatory authorities do not require the offshore financial institutions to pay the deposit reserves, and the tax incentives are also more favorable. Most bookkeeping offshore financial centers do not collect personal and corporate income tax, capital gains tax, interests tax, and dividend withholding tax. Third is the ease of supervision over institutional business market operation activities. Generally there is neither restriction to interest rate and exchange rate fluctuations nor do the restrictions on foreign exchange transactions and international capital flows. Basically, financial innovation activities are less regulated.

The globalization of economy and financial liberalization mean the free flow of a variety of economic and financial factors as well as the market opening, which is necessarily under the precondition about the government deregulation. The deregulation of government control of international economy and finance plays an important role on the formation and development of offshore financial markets. Second, some level of restriction is permitted on import and other items of residents. One of the measures in every country is to gradually increase the proportion of liberalization of imports of goods, that is, portion of the free import of total imports. By the end of 1958, the proportion of free import of Western Europe accounted for 90 percent of all imports in the region. Third is the deregulation of international mobility of capital. After the 1960s, the United Kingdom and other European countries generally relaxed restrictions on nonresident banks to accept foreign currency deposits, funds (mainly U.S. dollars) due to changes in interest rates and massive flows among countries. In the 1980s, as European countries canceled restrictions to capital inflows on the domestic market, the European bond markets have developed rapidly, so that the offshore financial market investment and financing activities become more active, and business types and size of the transaction have exhibited a rapidly expanding trend.

Significance of the development of offshore financial markets

The key difference between an offshore financial market and a domestic financial market, which distinguishes the former from traditional international financial markets, is the absolute freedom.

Features of offshore markets

Lax regulation and flexible operation

The traditional international financial markets must be bound by the policy of the act issued by the local government, but offshore financial markets are not subject to government regulation and taxation countries' limit. They get rid of management constraints under any government decree. On the one hand, the "supranational" capital market was formed to avoid the sovereign state intervention. Essentially, the currency-issuing country has no right to impose controls on the issue of national currency outside the country; on the other hand, in order to attract more European monetary funds to expand their lending business, governments in thriving markets usually adopt various preferential measures to try to create a relaxed management climate. Therefore, this market operates very freely, without any control, such as flexible borrowing conditions and free intention for the use of funds; offshore financial markets have strong competitive edges because the capital allocation is flexible, and the procedure is quite simple. Offshore financial market liquidity is very fast and flexible scheduling due to the little jurisdiction of these funds. Therefore, this market meets not only the needs of multinational companies for both importers and exporters but also of many Western countries and developing countries.

Low cost of capital

Not subject to statutory reserves and deposit rates to the ceiling, offshore financial market interest rates compared to the domestic financial market's are unique, as they feature on the small interest spread between deposit and withdraw. Put alternatively, the deposit interest rate is slightly higher than that of domestic financial markets, while the interest rate of an issued loan is slightly lower than the domestic financial markets. Deposit rates are higher, on the one hand, because of the larger risk of deposit in foreign countries than domestic deposits, so that depositors demand a higher risk premium to compensate. On the other hand, the interest spread between deposit and loan is not subject to statutory reserves and deposit rates to the ceiling. The loan interest rate is slightly lower, because European banks are duty-free and exempt from the country's reserve and other favorable conditions. This could explain the relatively low capital cost of the loan, which can lower lending rates to attract customers. Offshore financial market interest spread is small, typically 0.25 percent to 0.5 percent—pretty attractive to both lenders and borrowers.

A more open, deeper, and wider financial market than a domestic market

Offshore financial markets have an extremely large scale of fund pool. The offshore financial market has not only a wide range of funding sources around the world but also ample liquidity and all major convertible currencies with different period, different risks, and different uses of financial products and styles, which can meet various financial needs of the government, financial institutions, and multinational companies. In fact, the offshore financial market is a "wholesale market" for the most essential big customers. The amount of each financial transaction is large, typically ranging from a few hundred thousand dollars to hundreds of millions or even billions of dollars.

Lending relationship mainly built by nonresident parties

Lending relationships in international financial markets are mainly between foreign investors and foreign fund raisers; in other words, among nonresidents. There are typically three types of transactions on the international financial markets: first, transactions between foreign investors and domestic fund raisers, such as foreign direct investors in the stock market directly buying securities issued by the national fund raisers; second, transactions between domestic investors and foreign fund raisers, such as domestic investors purchasing securities issued by foreign fund raisers on the stock market; and third, transactions between foreign investors and foreign fund raisers, such as foreign investors providing funds to foreign fund raisers through an intermediary bank or the stock market. The first and second trading are transactions between residents and nonresidents; the formation of the relationship of such a transaction is the traditional lending relationship in international financial markets. At present, most of China's cross-border RMB business belongs to this type. The third type of transactions, between nonresidents is also known as *transit* or *offshore transactions*. This trading relationship is the lending relationship in offshore financial markets.

Functions of offshore markets

Provide currency liquidity

Offshore financial markets have incomparably strong domestic markets for capital supply and high market openness. Competitive interest rate structure and freedom make governments, multinational corporations, and financial institutions willing to put money into offshore financial markets, which enhances the ability of the market to derive deposit formation independent from the domestic currency supply system, as the offshore market does not have any deposit reserve requirements. In theory, the market has unlimited ability to derive deposits. In the absence of a financial crisis or in normal circumstances, the offshore market liquidity is sufficient to meet the funding needs of various market players.

Provide facilitation for clearing and settlement

International offshore financial centers are distributed in several major time zones. Through the networking in different time zones, the offshore market could ensure the trader to trade 24 hours a day but can also radiate the impact to the world's major economies, enabling customers in various time zones normal foreign exchange transactions to be completed so as to meet international trade and financial transactions by clearing settlement demand for capital.

Provide an efficient, low-cost, and safe currency payment transaction platform

Offshore markets have several remarkable advantages: stable politics, transparent law procedure, high latitude, a comprehensive variety of financial products, and low transaction cost. Besides, due to the institutional advantages of low tax rate and good confidentiality, the offshore market is an ideal platform for international financial trade and settlement.

Provide a platform for national risk management

Country risk is the risk that needs management most and could cause the largest loss. A state government, through political, legal, tax, and protection of privacy and other coercive power within a given jurisdiction, impedes the use of funds and reduces the value of assets, which would directly harm the interests of investors. Offshore financial markets offer effective channels to circumvent coercive power of government issuing the currency and thus become an extremely popular national risk management platform among investors. The earliest offshore market in history is the U.S. dollar deposits of the former Soviet Union placed in London in case the U.S. government might freeze the assets. Currently, one of the main reasons why the top ten global offshore markets have attracted two-thirds of U.S. dollar deposits is to avoid the unpredictable national risk.

Of course, the practice of separating the currency risk from country risk derived from the problem of excessive concentration on infrastructure or operational risk if dollars were placed within one country. The September 11, 2001, terrorist attack in New York led to the U.S. Treasury destruction, "which allows central banks to realize the potential benefits of diversity that can bring to trading places." When the normal trading of the U.S. Treasury is suspended within the U.S. territory, the dollar securities deposited in European offshore market by the U.S. central government may still carry on, as the U.S. payment and settlement system continues to run, without impact on the payment activities of dollar clearing and settlement systems.[1]

Provide a third-party trading platform and consolidate the international currency status

The international currency often facilitates the economic exchanges between countries issuing non-international currencies. This is a phenomenon known as the use of international currency by the third party. Because third-party use of international currencies is independent of the domestic economy of the country, considering the convenience and security reasons, the transactions are mainly conducted in the offshore market instead of the domestic market of the country issuing currencies. In the offshore market, the higher the degree of use of international currencies by the third party, the higher the strength of the currency's international status. For example, the U.S. foreign trade accounted for about 10 percent of global trade, investment activities of U.S. residents to participate in the global investment accounted for about 20 percent to 50 percent, but the U.S. share of global foreign exchange trading was up to 42 percent; the dollar is widely used in third-party transactions, topping the list in the international monetary system.

The influence of offshore markets in the world

Improve the integration of international financial markets

Offshore financial markets largely break the isolated state of monetary and financial systems between countries. Development of the European market brings the financial market and foreign exchange market across the Atlantic Ocean together, thus contributing to international capital flows. Arbitrage activities engaged in a wide range of international banks makes the interest rate parity between the two international currencies valid so as to promote the integration of international financial markets, and improve the global financial efficiency.

Promote economic growth

Offshore markets establish a free-market mechanism that allows efficient flow of capital, which helps optimize the allocation of global resources and thus is an important power promoting the world economic growth. If there were no offshore financial markets, in the 1960s and 1970s, the "Asian Tigers" and "Latin American miracle" would not have appeared. Huge amounts of money provided by offshore financial markets in a large part helped the rapid economic recovery in western Europe and Japan from the rubble of World War II and created favorable conditions for developing countries to achieve "balance development" and get rid of the "Matthew effect," the vicious economic cycle.

Solve the international deficit problem

Offshore financial markets greatly facilitate short-term capital flows, especially promoting the petrodollars to flow back. According to IMF estimates, in the years between 1974 and 1981, the total deficit of countries in the current account of international balance of payments climbed up to $810 billion, but the total amount of funds raised through the international financial markets amounted to $753 billion, which largely eased the worldwide imbalance of international payments. During this period, deposits of oil-exporting countries in the offshore financial markets amounted to $133 billion, which played an important role in the prevention of international payments imbalances that may lead to a currency crisis.

Challenge the validity of domestic financial monitor and currency policy

Offshore markets are a parallel with the domestic national monetary system free from government regulation. If a country's business and financial activities of financial institutions put over-reliance on offshore markets, especially when hot money flows too frequently in large amounts, the amount of domestic currency, asset prices, and exchange rates will inevitably be disturbed. In addition, a strong currency derived from offshore markets may exacerbate international transfer of inflation, and the effect of monetary expansion will flow from major currency countries, resulting in failure of the countries' currency policy or expectancy. This presents new challenges for the country's macroeconomic management.

Inner logic of Chinese RMB internationalization and the construction of offshore markets

Construction of offshore markets is beneficial for the development of RMB

Construction of offshore markets benefit the basic function of markets

Because the reform of China's interest rate market and exchange rate market has not fully accomplished the presence of domestic and foreign financial markets dual pricing, arbitrage becomes one of the main reasons why there is a significant growth in RMB scale. By improving the construction of offshore RMB markets, on the one hand, it can play an exemplary role in guiding influence of behavior of market players to promote the interest rates and exchange market and create favorable market conditions for the RMB capital account convertibility. On the other hand, it may enhance the basic role of an "invisible hand" of RMB exchange rate and interest rates, reducing the space within the jacket arbitrage profits as well as reducing currency risks.

Construction of offshore markets could enlarge the body mass of RMB export

RMB internationalization means that the yuan will gradually become a third-party use of money, which requires a steady stream of export of yuan in the offshore renminbi market to maintain adequate liquidity. However, the current export of RMB relies more on trade channels; within the context of China's trade surplus, the yuan is difficult to export, and the size is very limited, unable to meet the huge demand in the international market potential for the renminbi, which restricts the yuan to perform international monetary functions. According to the estimation of Ma, Xu, et al., if you do not open the capital account, exporting the output of RMB through trade items would only restrain the degree of internationalization of the RMB at less than 10 percent of its true potential.[2]

The issuance of RMB bonds in the offshore market, loosening the RMB exchange limit for residents, and providing RMB loans and a series of measures and arrangements targeting an ease of capital control can effectively solve the problems of lack of RMB export. The offshore market and trade surplus enable the realization of the mode of renminbi's net export, which is conducive not only to maintaining stable growth of China's economy but also to ensuring the positive impact of export on economy growth. Also, it could avoid the Triffin dilemma induced by RMB internationalization achieved by trade surplus. In addition, the derivation function of offshore markets can play the role of amplifier, which produces several times as much as the liquidity of the original RMB deposits. In HK, under the 25 percent liquidity ratio requirement specified in the Hong Kong Monetary Authority, HK can derive 3 trillion yuan more of deposits (4 × multiplier) on the basis of the 1 trillion of "original RMB deposit" from the mainland. If these derived yuan are used by the third party (CPB), there will be an expansion to a larger multiple times the size of RMB as the original term of net output.

Sound financial service encourages international demand for RMB

With the expansion of cross-border RMB trade settlement, more and more RMB deposits happen overseas. The international community needs for RMB financial services have gone on, hoping to get a high-quality currency exchange, payment and settlement, trade finance, risk management, wealth management services, and so on. Under the current capital controls, if there is no such RMB offshore market with a rich variety of product and functions to meet these needs, it is difficult to establish the acceptance of the international community's and the confidence for use of the RMB, and the RMB internationalization process will inevitably encounter obstacles. Therefore, at this stage, the RMB offshore market has some special effects. In addition to the function of financing through offshore RMB market, it can also manage a variety of market risks through innovative RMB interest rate swaps, futures, options, and other financial derivatives, increasing the value of the asset and improving the confidence of overseas economic agents to hold the RMB. Of course, RQFII, the multinational pool of RMB funds and other institutional arrangements, establish a greater value-added space for the establishment of a modest channel of RMB flowing back, thus providing greater value-added space for overseas RMB holders, which is also conducive to improving the demand for the RMB in the international market.

Offshore markets could temporarily relieve the currency exchange obstruction before opening the capital account

RMB internationalization interactively promotes the reform of capital account

Capital account liberalization is a process of gradual relaxation of capital controls, allowing residents' and nonresidents' holdings of cross-border assets and engaging in cross-border asset transactions, aiming to achieve a freely convertible currency. Capital account liberalization of convertibility is not completely laissez-faire and cross-border capital flows. Instead, capital account liberalization in essence is a managed exchange and capital flow. Since December 1996, although China has maintained a mixed policy of "current account liberalization capital account controls," the capital account has been moving toward a goal of orderly, controlled release. At present, China has overall allowed long-term two-way direct investment and trade financing except for some relatively stringent controls on short-term capital flows, securities investment, cross-border lending, and derivatives transactions. In the background of significantly increasing global capital flows, endless practice of micro-market participants to circumvent capital controls has emerged. The cost and difficulty of capital control have also increased significantly. The Chinese government is now facing an embarrassment situation of "uncontrollable" to "poor regulation."

International experience shows that capital account liberalization is not a sufficient condition for an international currency, not even a necessary condition in the early stages of an international currency. For China, RMB internationalization and capital account reforms are implemented progressively, a process from simplicity to complexity, in which both can promote and complement each other.

On the one hand, the capital account reform pushes up the RMB internationalization index. According to the estimation of RMB internationalization Report (2013), in 2012 China's capital account openness was 0.5125 (0.5045 in 2011), at the middle level of openness in the international arena. With the continuing liberalized cross-border RMB policy over capital flows, the way of RMB outflow and reflux varies when the scale gradually expands, in 2012 making the RMB internationalization index reach 0.87, an increase of 49 percent in comparison with the prior year. Among them, the proportion of global RMB direct investment rose to 2.18 percent, becoming the fastest-growing area of international use of the RMB. In the promotion of capital account reforms, the internationalization of RMB have developed from the solely driven model of denomination function to the dual-way model (both the trade denomination and the financial denomination), a more reasonable and more stable pattern. Currently, some of the country's central bank and sovereign wealth funds have already held the RMB bonds and stocks through QFII channels. It is believed that as long as the country continues to allow AFII to expand the business scale or to loosen up trade restrictions, the gradual liberalization of the capital account would simultaneously enhance the international use of the RMB.

On the other hand, the internationalization of RMB put forward higher requirements for capital account reforms. In the promotion of cross-border trade in RMB clearing business to a global scale, the channel output and the return of the RMB under the trade items have already opened. With the establishment of China's largest trading position and the expanding trade settlement in RMB, nonresidents' demand for hedging and trading of RMB asset management is naturally induced, which objectively requires China to further open its capital account in order to achieve the free convertibility of the yuan, provide a wealth of RMB investment and financing tools, and create more level RMB backflow channels. Once the pace of RMB appreciation slows down, international payments tend to be balanced. Coupled with the accelerating pace of international financial institution development, the potential to promote RMB internationalization under trade items will be exhausted. In the long term, to become an important international currency and reserve currency, the RMB will not avoid being fully convertible. Therefore, we must reform the RMB capital account to create the conditions for its broader and deeper international use.

It is still premature to fully open the conversion of capital account

Capital flows promote the optimal allocation of resources in the world, with great benefit to both the countries with inflows and outflows, but capital flows themselves are a "double-edged sword" whose size and volatility tend to pose policy challenges. When a country's financial system and financial institutions have not yet been strong enough to cope with the impact of hot money on the temerity to open the capital account, it is likely to cause financial market instability and even a financial crisis. From China's specific national conditions, we think it is not the best time to completely liberalize capital account, at least not suitable in a radical way. The reasons are as follows.

First, from the perspective of international environment, under the influence of the QE monetary policy put forward by the major developed countries, international capital often flows in large amounts across emerging markets. In order to guard against systemic risk, restrictions on short-term arbitrage funds are necessary. Otherwise, the asset market bubble and the huge expansion of the financial risk will be inevitable. For example, in June 2013, the Fed issued a signal to exit quantitative ease in the second half of the year. The market reacted violently, within a week causing a lot of rapid withdrawal of international hot money from emerging markets. Russia, India, Brazil, and other emerging market countries stuck into a great panic of immediate liquidity shortage, and there also emerged precursors of financial distress such as economic downturn, rising interest rates, and currency devaluation.

Second, from the perspective of domestic macroeconomic environment, although China's national economy has maintained strong growth, ample foreign exchange reserves, and a more professional management of financial institutions (which seem to be in line with the required preconditions of liberalizing capital accounts, according to the experience in Western countries) it cannot be ignored there still remain many uncertainties because China is currently in a period of great reform and major adjustment where issues like price distortion or institutional inefficiencies are facing great changes. If the capital account is liberalized immediately, the international hot money may amplify the negative effect of these uncertainties, which is not conducive to China's financial stability. Besides, there are other economic dilemmas such as excessive real estate bubbles and debt of local government that could trigger another crisis. These factors remind us that special attention is needed when pondering the capital account policies.

Third, from the operation of financial markets, China's capital market interest rate for deposits and loans is much higher than the international market. Arbitrage opportunities attract large cross-border flows of short-term speculative funds. It is inappropriate to fully open capital accounts. Fully liberalizing capital accounts when the domestic interest rate maintains a high level is equivalent to an opening gate for large-scale domestic and foreign capital flows, which is bound to disrupt the normal order of domestic financial market. In addition, the one-way expectation of the appreciation of RMB is expected to lead many domestic enterprises to use settlements in the offshore market. Some scholars have pointed out that with all other factors unchanged, a completely open capital account may lead to net massive fund outflows of China.[3]

Foster offshore markets for RMB before liberalizing the capital account

Under the current conditions of the capital account controls, the development of offshore RMB markets is significantly positive to promote the internationalization of the RMB. Construction of the offshore RMB market has a degree of substitution effect on the capital account liberalization. For example, it is of the same nature as QFII operation to allow three types of overseas financial institutions to invest in domestic inter-bank bond market using the RMB that they finance from offshore markets. Companies can freely convert foreign currency through a branch in the HK offshore RMB market, which to some extent breaks the restriction of currency exchanges under capital items. Fostering RMB offshore markets in this phase of the Chinese economy is actually a transitional financial arrangement, equivalent to a completely open capital account that could take control of potential risk of capital flows within the scope of the offshore market, ensuring the stability of the domestic financial market environment. Meanwhile, it could boost capital account RMB internationalization under the disguised capital account liberalization. The financial arrangement in offshore markets is an essential variant to realize the capital account convertibility. The purpose is to regulate the size and structure of the offshore RMB market in a timely and orderly expansion of channels between the "offshore" and "onshore" market, so as to interactively promote the functional position of both capital account liberalization and internationalization of the RMB. It is a second-best choice to foster the RMB offshore market under the current conditions of capital account controls because it creates a valuable time window to leave enough time and space to deepen the capital account reform and lays a solid foundation for the smooth progress of RMB internationalization strategy.

Grab the current opportunity to promote RMB internationalization via offshore markets

Fully take advantage of the transformation of domestic economic structure to promote RMB internationalization via offshore markets

After the international financial crisis, the demand from Western countries was weakened, leading to our long-term export-oriented economic growth model which was unsustainable. To promote the internationalization of the RMB by building offshore markets could be an important starting point to adjust and optimize the economic structure. Because the internationalization of the RMB can play an important role in speeding up economic restructuring and promoting the coordinated development of economic autonomy, this improves the international status of RMB in the offshore market, encourages financial innovations of offshore RMB products and meets international market demands for increasing the value of the main asset of RMB. This is surely a shortcut to the promotion of cross-border trade settlement in RMB for greater acceptance. This is not only conducive to China's gradual change in U.S. dollar-based, passive accumulation of foreign exchange reserves but also can promote a more balanced measure in foreign trade of China to reduce the trade surplus. In addition, we can also build strong offshore RMB markets through foreign direct investment in RMB and RMB foreign lending to further broaden our residents' channel to conduct RMB investment. Through the improvement of the offshore RMB bond market as well as the offshore RMB financial derivatives market, Chinese enterprises under "going out" policy are to be provided with richer financial services and more convenient conditions.

Fully take advantage of the adjustment period of international offshore financial center to globally construct the offshore market of RMB

The current international offshore financial center is in the adjustment period in depth of business structure mainly in the following aspects. First, since the twenty-first century, under financial liberalization and a highly competitive environment, structural changes have occurred to offshore financial centers. The development of offshore financial centers relies more on the improvement of efficiency and quality such as market liquidity, depth, breadth, settlement, and other payment services rather than a variety of incentives. Therefore, offshore financial markets with a more sound financial base have developed rapidly, relying on the wave of financial globalization, while the number of offshore financial centers famous for tax havens such as the Caribbean island offshore financial centers shows a trend of business contraction, even gradual extinction. Second, the 2008 financial tsunami made the tax-based offshore centers widely criticized because they promised to provide confidentiality as well as tax incentives for many international funds that could thus drift outside the international regulatory system. At the same time, OECD, FSF, FATF, and other international organizations have repeatedly attached importance to transparency, cooperation, and information exchange. They also urge improving the conditions of the under-regulated offshore market through the establishment of a system of unified international norms measures. Under the pressure imposed by the international organizations, the offshore financial island centers have amended some necessary confidentiality policies and tax incentive regulations, which could be regarded as a start of integration to regulate the financial business structure of international offshore market. Third, after the financial crisis, under the international financial environment changes, the increasing competition among offshore financial centers and the slowing down of business revenue growth contribute to some mergers among large exchanges. Traditional offshore centers need to seek new profit growth opportunities.

We should make full use of the competition of the major offshore financial centers' adjustment period to rationally distribute the world's offshore RMB market. After the financial crisis, emerging markets, especially China, have become one of the main forces driving global economic growth. As the world's largest exporter and second-largest importer, the economic and trade relations between China and the rest of the world have become a major driving force of local economic development. With the steady increase of China's import and export trade as well as the amount of cross-border investment, driven by cross-border RMB trade settlement and central bank currency swap agreements, foreign stocks and trading volume of RMB are experiencing rapid growth. Once an offshore market becomes an offshore RMB center, naturally there will be more RMB trading volume, which would lead to more financial institutions entering and bringing in more innovative financial products, so as to stimulate the development of the local financial industry, which is a great appeal for any financial center. Because of this opportunity, after the establishment of the HK RMB offshore financial market, London, Singapore, Luxembourg, Paris, Frankfurt, Zurich, Geneva, Sydney, and Taipei have expressed willingness to develop offshore RMB centers. China should seize this historic opportunity to actively promote the layout of offshore RMB centers, giving full play to their respective advantages of offshore centers, rationally planning the function positioning. China should use the function of aggregation, circulation, and radiation effects of the offshore market to develop the offshore RMB financial services and business so as to expand the scope of overseas use of the yuan and to promote the internationalization of RMB.

Fully take advantage of the demand for currencies hedging risks in the international market, to provide more diversified financial services in offshore RMB business

The current recession in Western countries after the financial crisis and the period of unconventional monetary policy create a large liquidity injection into the international market. The value of the U.S. dollar, the euro, the yen, and other major reserve currencies fluctuates frequently. On the one hand, the

U.S. economic recovery is weak, and there arises a global risk aversion against the European debt crisis. The demand from the market for financial hedging instruments and safe-haven assets will continue to improve; on the other hand, paradoxically, the euro and the U.S. dollar that have been long considered to avoid currency risk are now suffering from a trust crisis due to the impact of unconventional monetary policy, which will force the market to choose a new safe haven currency from market varieties. A large number of hedge funds and profit-driven capital start looking for a new currency with stable value as means of settlement and investment. At the same time, the strong economic growth in emerging market countries encourages their currencies to be sought after at varying degrees by the international market. Especially after the start of yuan-denominated cross-border trade settlement pilot in China, the Southeast Asian countries as well as our neighboring markets form a strong market demand for the renminbi. In the current environment, the market demand would further promote the process of RMB internationalization through the cross-border trade coupled with the construction of an offshore yuan market.

Overall, this time window is staged. Once Europe and other major economies gradually recover from the crisis, it would get more difficult to promote the internationalization of the RMB. Therefore, it should be, in the current environment, better to grasp market demand on the basis of the steady development of China's economic environment and international trade as well as the stable value of RMB to promote third-party transactions via offshore RMB markets. In addition, importance should also be attached to RMB direct investment and offshore RMB futures products so that the function of measurement, investment intermediaries, and storage of RMB would be maximized, conducive to RMB internationalization.

Promote RMB internationalization on the basis of offshore markets: Theoretical and empirical analysis[4]

Factors influencing the distribution of international currency regions

Trade and the real economy

The scale of international trade is an important factor in determining the distribution of the international monetary regions. Rey (2001) pointed out that changes in the pattern of world trade at the beginning of the last century directly contributed to the rise of the dollar and the decline of the status of the pound and directly affected the distribution of the dollar and the pound in the world. In fact, if it is essential or of great weight for a country's international trade with a country issuing international currencies, then the latter's currency will be more attractive because the exporters and importers of the former country would have more opportunities to trade with the currency-issuing country, and thus the according international currency would be used more (Ding Yibing Zhong Yang, 2013). Therefore, if there is more international trade between currency-outflow countries and currency-inflow countries, the currency of the currency-outflow country will take a large weight in its global distribution. Bergsten (1997), Mckinnon (1998), and Mundell (1998) in empirical research also show the importance of international trade in determining the extent of currency internationalization. High volumes of foreign trade will generate a lot of currency trading, thus naturally making the currency of the economy become an integral part of the currency exchange market. At the same time, the existence of economies of scale reduces the marginal cost of the large number of transactions and also enhances the willingness of importers—exporters as well as foreign investors— to use international currency. In addition, along with a strong economy and the improvement of production efficiency, the expansion of foreign trade and high surplus of trade balance, the high trade surplus lays a solid economic foundation for the export of the currency, and the country's capital and financial account appears a large deficit. High trade surplus and a high capital and financial account deficit are the infant characteristics of the internationalization of a currency. From the historical point of view, similar patterns of currency internationalization were also identified in the United States and the United Kingdom experience.

However, trade volume is not the sole factor in determining the global distribution of a currency. The development of real economy of the currency-outflow country and the relative status of the international currency in the world monetary system also play an important role in the global distribution of the international currency. For example, in the internationalization of the yen, Japan's export trade was also developing rapidly. However, the main destination of Japan's exports are Europe and other developed countries, while the main goods imported by Japan are raw materials, such as oil, minerals, and other dollar-denominated commodities. Article Seiichi (2001) pointed out that high risk of the yen exchange rate, poor negotiation power of import and export business, and the selection tendencies in using foreign exchanges (inertia) are important reasons frustrating the yen internationalization. Therefore, from the experience of Japan, which is a typical "international trade country," the dilemma of the yen internationalization reflects the difficulties of "trade countries" in the current international economic and financial system (Li, 2005). In addition, after the economic bubble burst in the 1980s, Japan encountered a long period of recession. Due to the lack of a huge domestic market and economies of scale to support the process of internationalization of the yen, the yen internationalization eventually stagnated (Zhang Guoqing, Liu Junmin, 2009; Table 4.1, Table 4.2).

Capital and investment factors

In general, the flow of transnational capital can often improve the scope of use of the international currency in the currency-inflow countries, thereby reducing their transaction costs and conversion costs. Kindleberger (1967) pointed out that if an international currency can flow in a larger context, it will receive a higher demand, thereby reducing transaction costs. Krugman (1984) and Rey (2001) expanded the theory of Kindleberger, arguing that trade and investment can promote the use of international currency in the currency-inflow countries.

Table 4.1 Proportion of imported raw material over total import in Japan

Product	1980	1985	1990	1995	2000	2005	2009
Energy & Fuel	50.03%	43.75%	24.25%	16.09%	20.36%	25.64%	27.63%
Metal & Mine	9.99%	8.91%	9.05%	6.65%	5.57%	6.10%	6.35%
Agriculture	8.64 %	6.68 %	6.56%	5.56 %	3.09%	1.99 %	1.44 %

Source: World Development Indicators & Global Development Finance, World Bank Data

Table 4.2 Proportion of trade volumes of Japan in different export regions

Regions	1991	1994	1997	2000	2003	2006	2009
Developing	19.56%	23.19%	25.45%	22.63%	28.35%	32.01%	38.91%
Developed	80.44%	76.81%	74.55%	77.37%	71.65%	67.99%	61.09%

Source: World Development Indicators & Global Development Finance, World Bank Data

And Prasad et al. (2006) believe that the official capital flows (such as aid, foreign exchange reserves, and so on) would indirectly impact international currency transactions through international capital flows.

Second, the higher the degree of financial development of a country, the more transparent and less costly international currency transactions will be, and thereby it increases the local trade of international currency. Chen and Khan (1997) pointed out that the direction of capital flows were affected by the extent of the country's financial development and growth potential of the capital inflow countries. If a country has a more developed financial market, it is easier to attract capital inflows. In addition, the role of the international financial center in the currency internationalization is increasingly important. Despite the wide suspicion about the virtual economy after the global financial crisis, its role in promoting the development of the world economy is undeniable. This also means that if a currency is intended to become an international currency, it is inseparable from the international financial status of the country issuing the currency. This is because the developed financial market is not only beneficial to the international community to increase demand for the currency but also helps importers and exporters in the international trade with foreign exchange risk management. New York and London, for example, used to play an important role in promoting the U.S. dollar and the British pound to be the international currency. On the other hand, since the financial revolution in Japan was not radical, Tokyo has not developed into a major international financial center. According to statistics of 2013, from a global comparative look at forex trading, the proportion of forex trading in London and New York over global foreign exchange trading volumes was 40.9 percent and 18.9 percent, respectively, while only 5.6 percent in Tokyo, closer to that of Singapore and HK.

Accordingly, what can be learned from the development of the U.S. dollar and the British pound is that at least three areas should be addressed by developed financial markets to enhance the attractiveness of the domestic currency in the world, thereby expanding the distribution range of the international currency. First, the developed financial markets provide international market investors with an open stock market with good liquidity. Generally, investors will not solely hold the balance of international currency but will invest the majority of its international currencies in interest-earning assets with good liquidity in order to avoid capital losses. Second, the developed financial markets also provide investors with a range of quality services, such as financing or domestic currency investment or services to increase the value of international currencies. Third, a well-developed financial market can attract amounts of overseas business by attracting foreign companies of good quality to get listed there and invest.

Geographical factors

More and more studies show that geographical location has a significant influence on the transaction costs and using habit of a currency, thereby affecting the regional distribution of international currencies. Ghosh and Wolf (2000) believed that due to the geographical disadvantage, Africa and the western countries relative to other areas have more difficulty in obtaining capital inflows. Flandreau and Jobst (2009) in the empirical study on the process of the internationalization of the British pound in the nineteenth century found that geographical distance caused discrepancies in the level of use of international currencies through the varied transaction cost. However, due to the presence of network externalities of currency, the smaller the scope of an international currency used in the region, the higher the transaction costs are, which will further impede the local use of the international currency.

On the other hand, from the perspective of the assets, geographic factors could impact the asymmetric information problems in currency trading. In general, due to asymmetric information problems, investors prefer domestic assets, thereby reducing the willingness of domestic investors to use the international currencies (Gehrig, 1993; Kang and Stulz, 1997). Specifically, Tesar and Werner (1995) considered that the geographical barriers prevented some information collection from investors. The problem of asymmetric information is caused by factors such as language, institutions, laws, and the cost of access to foreign information. Coval and Moskowitz (1999) argued that the problem caused by geopolitical factors, such as ticket prices between the two countries and the number of telephone lines, exacerbated the problem of asymmetric information in the course of currency trading.

Political and cultural factors

To become a regional economic core or international currency, a currency will be involved in the process of cross-cultural cooperation and integration, including recognitions regarding social systems, life philosophy, and the market. And due to the large difference between Chinese economic developments, social systems, history, and culture with the West, the RMB—in order to form a comprehensive layout on a global scale—must undergo a relatively long period of time. The internationalization of the euro shows that within the common political or cultural context, the international development of a currency will be relatively smooth. Cohen (1997) pointed out that whether two countries were using a shared language had a very significant impact on the distribution of regional currencies. Hattari and Rajan (2011) believed similar cultural habits could increase the mutual identity of the two peoples, which helps to improve the use of the international currency in the country with currency inflows.

In addition, during the process of currency internationalization, political and other external factors cannot be ignored. In fact, currency internationalization is not simply a financial struggle but a comprehensive competition involving politics, military, technology, culture, and other aspects. For the United States and other countries enjoying the current international monetary seigniorage, they will not be willing to give up their market share. In addition, because of the contrast to the Western political system adopted by China, foreign investors appear more cautious about China's economic and political environment and the use of the yuan. Generally, factors like political stability and a sound system of institution have significant influence on the promotion of the local use of the international currency. This is because a stable political system and a sound legal system help to improve the social stability and the transparency of information and reduce the cost of information. Bergsten (1975) noted that the political factor in promoting the scope of use of the international currency included a stable social institution and good support from international cooperation, and Mundell (1983) believed that political stability and military forces had to consolidate the international status of the currency.

Institutional construction (offshore market construction)

From the view of currency internationalization, a country's currency in order to become a major international currency must have an offshore market in leading international financial centers, because it can improve the acceptance of the RMB among foreign importers and exporters (He and McCauley, 2010). From the internationalization experience of U.S. dollars, the development of the money market and bond market of the Eurodollar prompted foreign investors to a greater extent to use the U.S. dollar in the local transactions. The 2010 BIS report showed that approximately 80 percent of the U.S. dollar foreign exchange transactions (including spot and forwards, swaps, options, and other derivative instruments) occurred in the offshore markets outside the United States. Meanwhile, the rise of the volume of dollar transactions promoted the improvement of the dollar clearing and settlement systems, thereby reducing transaction costs of the U.S. dollar and further increasing the convenience of dollars in the local use, which in turn increased the proportion of the U.S. dollar in local trade. The internationalization of the euro was also accompanied by the development of the offshore market. Ma (2011) also pointed out that the internationalization of the RMB was inseparable from the construction of the offshore market. Those currencies without reliance on offshore market have little potential to become an international reserve currency. Instead, they are basically currencies of small economies for clearance and denomination, such as the currencies in regions like South Korea, Taiwan, and Singapore.

Therefore, the establishment of the RMB offshore market can improve the region's acceptance and frequency of use of the RMB to promote the rational distribution of the yuan in various regions of the world, which is a global monetary network. This is because the construction of the offshore market provides greater convenience for foreign investors, which could promote a large number of "third-party" transactions using RMB. From the experience of the development of the U.S. dollar, a large number of U.S. dollar foreign exchange transactions overseas are unrelated to the domestic economy of the United States but are mostly to meet the need of other countries dealing with the trade, investment, and foreign exchange reserves settlement. Therefore, if the RMB offshore market further expands into other regions, then it will be beneficial to exporters and investors in that region to deal with clearing and settlement in RMB, which can reduce transaction costs. Second, the construction of the offshore market can improve the security of RMB transactions, increasing investors' confidence in the region to use the yuan. From the perspective of the development path of dollars, the worldwide U.S. dollar offshore market ensures the 24-hour trading in U.S. dollars, which to some extent reduces the risk of U.S. dollar clearing and settlement and improves the exporters and investors' confidence in the use of the U.S. dollar. Finally, the construction of the offshore market can induce domestic residents and foreign residents to hold RMB assets.[5] When the RMB offshore market matures, funds having inflows into China may choose financial products traded in offshore markets measured in the RMB, which will increase the RMB overseas volume of transactions.

Empirical research on the factors influencing the distribution of currency

Data and variable

In order to measure the distribution in the various regions of the international monetary, we use the forex trading volume of the national currencies in each region as measurement. Transaction data of various international currencies were taken from BIS Triennial Central Bank Survey of Foreign Exchange and Derivatives Market Activity (hereinafter referred to as Triennial Survey). The Triennial Survey was published every 3 years by the BIS, from 1995 to date (seven times in total). The survey covers almost global foreign exchange trading, which is an important source for policy makers and market participants to understand the global foreign exchange.

Based on this investigation, this study selected the foreign exchange trading volume in the years 1995, 1998, 2001, 2004, 2007, 2010, and 2013 to analyze the distribution of international currency in different regions. Meanwhile, in order to maintain the consistency of the sample, this study selected twenty-six countries and regions,[6] the same as those reported in the 1995 Triennial Survey. According to the Chinn and Frankel (2008) study, this study selects seven major international currencies (dollar, pound, euro, Japanese yen, Swiss franc, Canadian dollar, and Australian dollar). It should be noted that, in view of the fact that the euro had not appeared until 1999, this study simulated the share of transactions of the euro in Eurozone countries and the European Monetary System currencies (EMC) prior to 1999 so as to maintain consistency.

This study defines country *i* as a currency-outflow country and country *j* as a currency-inflow country. Table 4.3 describes the main variables.

Table 4.4 reveals the proportion of the trade volumes of the seven international currencies over total trading volumes in different countries and regions.[7] According to the statistics, the international currencies are mainly concentrated in England, the United States, Japan, Singapore, and HK. However, the geographical distribution of a currency greatly differs from another. For instance, the proportion of trade for the euro in England (nearly 50 percent) is higher than that of other international currencies in England. However, the proportion of euro in regions like Japan, Singapore, and HK is lower than that of other currencies like the US dollar, British pound, and the Australian dollar.

Table 4.5 reports the statistical features of the main variables. It could be found that the trading proportion of international currencies differs greatly with every other. The maximum is approximately seventy times as much as the median, while the maximum of investment in log form is 1.5 times of the median, which implies the sharp difference of international trade in different countries. From the perspective of population and gross GDP, there is great difference among economic entities. Besides, it could be found from the average level that the political stability of the currency-inflow country is slightly better than that of the currency-outflow country, and there is a higher proportion of currency-inflow currencies practicing civil law than that of currency-outflow countries.

Empirical analysis

This study employs the method adopted by Martin and Rey (2004), who employ the gravity model to analyze the factors determining the distribution of the regions of international currencies. Four conclusions could be drawn upon the empirical results.

First, in terms of the influence on the distribution of international currency regions, of population, GDP per capita, bilateral trade, and capital communication, the empirical results reveal to us that the trading proportion of the international currency is positively affected by population and GDP per capita in currency-inflow countries (or regions). This suggests that the larger of the economic scale of the currency-inflow country, the greater is the demand of the international currency in local trade, and thereby expands the network for currency circulation and reduces the transaction costs. Meanwhile, the

Table 4.3 Definition of main variables

Variable	Definition
$share_{ijt}$	In year t, the proportion of transaction volumes of the international currency i over the total foreign transaction volume
$Investment_{ijt}$	In year t, log of the amount of the bilateral equity and bond investment between country i and j[1]
$trade_{it}$	In year t, the proportion of the trade volume between county i and country j over the total trade volume of country i[2]
$trade_{jt}$	In year t, the proportion of the trade volume between county i and country j over the total trade volume of country j
$lnpop_{it}$	In year t, log of the population of country j
$lnpop_{jt}$	In year t, log of the population of country i
$lngdp_{it}$	In year t, log of the GDP per capita of country i
$lngdp_{jt}$	In year t, log of the GDP per capita of country j
$center_{j}$	A dummy variable equal to one if country j is an offshore financial center, zero otherwise[3]
$civil_{i}$	A dummy variable equal to one if the legal system of country i is civil law, zero otherwise
$civil_{j}$	A dummy variable equal to one if the legal system of country j is civil law, zero otherwise
ps_{it}	In year t, the political stability of country i[4]
ps_{jt}	In year t, the political stability of country j
$lndist_{ij}$	Log of the distance between country i and country j
$comlang_{ij}$	A dummy variable equal to 1 if country i and j share the same language, zero otherwise

Notes
1 Data source: IMF Coordinated Portfolio Investment Survey
2 Data source: IMF International Trade Statistics
3 Data source: IMF Offshore Financial Centers Report
4 For detailed estimation of Kaufmann, please refer to "Governance Matters III" World Bank Policy Research Working Paper

empirical results also suggest that the bilateral trade and capital communications have a positive influence on the proportion of local trade over the foreign trade volumes of an international currency, which proves the first hypothesis right. Particularly, the higher proportion of the currency-inflow country's trading volumes from the currency-outflow country over the total trading volumes of the currency-outflow country, the higher is the proportion of that of this international currency in currency-inflow countries. In the real world, the great economic power of the United States, the Euro zone, and Japan grants

Table 4.4 Share of distribution of seven main international currencies in 26 countries and regions

Country	Currency inflow						
	USD	EUR	JPY	GBP	CHF	CAD	AUD
USA	–	22.54%	25.22%	38.33%	24.71%	35.54%	20.11%
England	40.24%	50.61%	40.22%	–	40.53%	37.30%	37.40%
Austria	0.58%	–	0.42%	0.45%	1.39%	0.16%	0.10%
Belgium	1.32%	–	0.60%	2.71%	0.75%	1.27%	0.68%
Denmark	2.17%	2.07%	0.52%	1.70%	3.07%	0.39%	0.27%
France	4.02%	–	2.56%	6.44%	4.44%	2.43%	1.78%
Germany	4.96%	–	2.84%	7.91%	6.86%	1.32%	1.44%
Italy	1.25%	–	0.67%	1.58%	0.76%	0.22%	0.23%
Luxembourg	1.11%	–	0.65%	1.69%	1.18%	0.49%	1.13%
Netherlands	1.79%	–	0.92%	3.42%	2.40%	0.61%	0.54%
Norway	0.76%	0.65%	0.14%	0.54%	0.18%	0.12%	0.31%
Sweden	1.16%	1.67%	0.29%	1.18%	0.71%	0.39%	0.18%
Switzerland	5.93%	7.76%	3.51%	9.45%	–	3.17%	2.37%
Canada	2.73%	1.00%	1.06%	2.40%	1.28%	–	0.91%
Japan	10.66%	4.90%	–	7.48%	1.76%	3.98%	9.41%
Finland	0.23%	–	0.03%	0.22%	0.57%	0.09%	0.02%
Greece	0.18%	–	0.51%	0.17%	0.22%	0.04%	0.05%
Ireland	0.39%	0.70%	0.32%	2.09%	0.23%	0.41%	0.14%
Portugal	0.13%	–	0.08%	0.28%	0.11%	0.04%	0.02%
Spain	0.85%	–	0.23%	1.50%	0.26%	0.14%	0.09%
Australia	4.55%	2.47%	3.49%	5.08%	1.52%	2.50%	–
New Zealand	0.43%	0.08%	0.19%	0.26%	0.05%	0.08%	2.06%
South Africa	0.59%	0.17%	0.11%	0.49%	0.07%	0.03%	0.05%
Bahrain	0.17%	0.13%	0.14%	0.33%	0.15%	0.04%	0.02%
Hong Kong	6.36%	1.66%	6.96%	7.68%	1.94%	2.61%	8.98%
Singapore	8.33%	4.43%	9.20%	9.92%	4.86%	6.63%	12.66%

Source: BIS, Triennial Central Bank Survey of Foreign Exchange and Derivatives Market Activity (1995, 1999, 2001, 2004, 2007, 2010, 2013)

Note:
– indicates no share is included in the distribution of the currency in this area.

Table 4.5 Descriptive summary

Variable	Mean	Sd.	Min	Max	Median
$share_{ijt}$	0.0433	0.0937	0.0000	0.5536	0.0080
$lninvestment_{ijt}$	9.8342	2.3857	0.0000	14.9060	10.0517
$trade_{it}$	0.0246	0.0510	0.0000	0.6825	0.0079
$trade_{jt}$	0.0590	0.0940	0.0004	0.6890	0.0259
$lnpop_{it}$	17.9409	1.3031	15.7605	19.6174	17.9026
$lnpop_{jt}$	16.5309	1.3507	13.1834	19.5646	16.1719
$lngdp_{it}$	10.8060	0.8935	9.8044	13.1835	10.5588
$lngdp_{jt}$	10.2408	0.5922	8.0130	11.5850	10.2876
$center_j$	0.4723	0.4994	0	1	0
$civil_{it}$	0.4286	0.4951	0	1	0
$civil_{jt}$	0.6571	0.4749	0	1	1.
ps_{it}	0.9397	0.3123	0.0496	1.4915	1.0021
ps_{jt}	0.8700	0.5459	−1.2169	1.6681	1.0132
$lndist_{ij}$	8.1562	1.0451	5.2883	9.3599	8.5265
$comlang_{ij}$	0.2866	0.4524	0.0000	1.0000	0.0000

them prerogative in negotiation. The advantage of being used for international clearance and settlement makes the currency of the country receive greater demand from currency-inflow currencies, thereby increasing the weight of the international currency in local trade.

Second, whether the currency-inflow country is an offshore financial center has a significant influence on the trading volumes of international currency in local trade. According to the record, 70 percent of the trade volume of the international currency lies in London, New York, and Japan, who have offshore financial centers. Generally speaking, since the offshore financial centers are large and historical with sound systems and facilities, there is great liquidity of the international currency in local trade and relatively low transaction cost. Meanwhile, the strong radiation effect of the offshore financial center has a significant influence on the network for expanding the currency circulation, which further increases the trading volumes of the currency in local trade. This suggests the great importance of the offshore financial center in promoting the internationalization level of a currency.

Third is the significant influence of political and legal systems. The empirical results show us that political stability could increase the use of international currencies in local trade. In addition, if the currency-inflow country has an Anglo-American legal system, it would positively influence the use of international currency in local trade, statistically significant at the level of 1 percent. In the real world, countries with an Anglo-American legal system (such as England, the United States, Singapore, and HK) have a higher extent of financial openness and freedom, which makes for an easier requirement for the local use of international currencies and larger trading scale and circulation of the international currency in local trade. In general, a good social institution would prompt the local use of the international currency.

Fourth, while language culture makes a difference, geographical distance does not. The empirical results show that the variable of common language (comlang) is statistically significant at the 5 percent level. Portes and Rey (2005) point out that if two countries share a common language, the currency-inflow country would have a higher recognition of the currency-outflow country, known as the "familiar effect," which in turn broadens the scale of asset transaction. For example, in regions like Australia, New Zealand, Singapore, and HK, the trading proportion of the British pound is greater than that of the Japanese yen and the Swiss franc. Therefore, this to some extent proves the importance of language culture in determining the geographical distribution of international currencies. As for geographic distance, even if it has a negative coefficient, the variable is not statistically significant at the 10 percent level. Different from trade, the currency trade does not require transportation; hence, there is little influence of geographical distance on the international trade of different currencies. Meanwhile, with the development of information technology, both the openness and renewal of information have developed further, and the transaction cost has decreased thanks to the Internet. Therefore, this study attempts to conclude that geographical distance is not one of the deciding factors of the geographical distribution of international currencies.

Simulation of the trading proportion of the RMB in the main international offshore financial centers

On the basis of the standard model, this study estimates the trading proportion of the RMB in the five main international offshore financial centers, in the year of 2001, 2004, 2007, 2010, and 2013. On the grounds that the internationalization of the RMB is still in the infant stage, it is assumed that the RMB is a relatively mature international currency before we start to simulate the distribution of the RMB in the main international offshore financial centers. Basically, the assumptions are as follows:

1   The RMB capital account is convertible, and the RMB could flow across the border.
2   The offshore market of the RMB develops very well where a great variety of financial product is denominated by the RMB.
3   A well-developed offshore clearance and settlement system of the RMB.
4   Approximately the same international recognition of the RMB as other international currencies.

This study estimates the trading proportion of the RMB in five regions—the United States, England, Japan, HK, and Singapore—by using the data of bilateral trade, capital communication, population, and GDP per capita in the years 2001, 2004, 2007, 2010, and 2013 (Figure 4.1).

It could be found in Figure 4.1 that the proportion of the RMB in these five offshore financial centers increases from 37.65 percent to more than 45 percent, consistent with the global transaction volumes of foreign currencies in these five offshore financial markets. However, there are still some discrepancies between estimation and reality. According to the estimation results, the RMB's trading proportion in the United States is higher than that in HK; similarly, the proportion in England and Japan is higher than that in Singapore. However, according to the record in June, 2013, the stock of the RMB in the international offshore market was approximately 900 billion yuan, of which 600 billion is in HK, 100 billion is in Singapore, and less in other regions.

In recent years, HK and Singapore have been playing an important role as the offshore financial centers of the RMB, the only two regions with the RMB clearance bank. Therefore, the convenience of clearance and settlement reduces the transaction cost of RMB trading in HK and Singapore. Meanwhile, due to the common language tradition between mainland China, Chinese HK, and Singapore, the RMB is well accepted by local residents. Hence, most of overseas business of the RMB takes place in HK and Singapore.

However, from the path of the internationalization of a currency, if the RMB is intended to become one of the international currencies, the RMB offshore financial market must be built in the main international financial centers. In fact, the trade and financial business between China and regions like England, the United States, and Japan is not necessarily less than that of HK and Singapore, and the population and economic scale is sharply greater than that of HK and Singapore. Therefore, in theory, the RMB would take a big share in these three regions. However, as the majority of the RMB offshore financial markets are distributed in HK and Singapore, most of the offshore business of the RMB takes place in these two areas. With regard to factors restraining the development of the RMB offshore market in the United States and England, the first is policy barriers. Capital control has not been fully freed, and the marketization of the RMB interest rate and exchange rate has not been fully completed. The second is the constraint applied by the market supply and demand. On the one hand, there lacks quality financial product from the suppliers' side in the offshore market; on the other hand, the lack of liquidity of the RMB and the product denominated by yuan inhibit the foreign demand for the RMB. The third is the lag of construction of the overseas clearance and settlement trading system. The current technology of the RMB clearance and settlement cannot meet every technique required by the clearance business in the U.S. and European zones. Therefore, the pertinent department of the authority should further promote the reform of the RMB's interest rate and exchange rate, enrich the variety of overseas financial product of the RMB and overseas RMB clearance and settlement, and thereby develop the RMB offshore financial market and

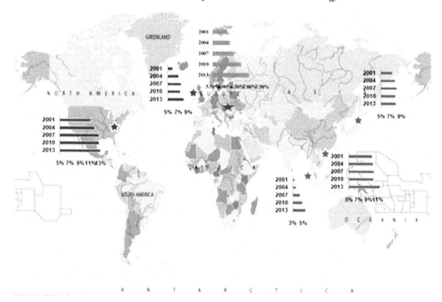

Figure 4.1 Distribution of the RMB trade in the main international offshore financial centers

Source: BIS, Triennial Central Bank Survey of Foreign Exchange and Derivatives Market Activity, processed by the author

improve the global distribution as well as internationalization of the RMB. In addition, China could also strengthen its foreign influence by promoting Confucius Institute to promote the recognition of foreign residents toward China in an attempt to increase the internationalization of the RMB.

To sum up, due to the network externality of the international currency and the asset nature in itself, the transaction cost and information cost make a great difference in the distribution of international currencies. To be more specific, the global distribution of an international currency is affected by the bilateral financial trade, the economic scale of the currency-inflow country, financial development, legal system, and language culture, but geographical distance makes little difference in the global distribution of a currency. Particularly, the trade and capital communication between the currency-outflow country and the currency-inflow country really matter because the international movement of a currency needs economic activities as media so as to expand the circulation and scale of use in local trade of the currency and realize the economic scale effect. Similarly, the higher the population and GDP per capita of the currency-inflow country, the higher is the demand of the international currency in currency-inflow countries, which benefits the economy of scale of the international currency's circulation. Financial development and legal systems would influence the transaction cost and information cost of the international currency in local use indirectly. Finally, common language culture would increase the recognition of the currency-inflow country to the international currency and the willingness of the residents of the currency-inflow country to hold the international currency, thereby increasing the share of the currency in local trade.

In the long run, the share of the RMB offshore financial services and its trading scale in the main international financial centers would be one of the most important criteria judging whether the RMB has become a main international currency. It should be seen that it would be a result of market selection whether or to what extent the RMB is accepted by these developed international financial centers. It is ultimately decided by the various parties on the local market. Therefore, in the future when we are building the RMB offshore market in developed countries like the United States and England, not only should Chinese enterprises cooperate with the internationalization of Chinese financial organizations, but also the monetary bureau should tackle the institutional barriers and technical problems of the global trade of the RMB asset. In addition, accordingly, the promotion of Chinese culture in developed countries would remarkably increase the worldwide recognition of the RMB, encourage the acceptance of the RMB asset in the main international financial centers, and ensure the achievement of the RMB internationalization.

Notes

1 Dong He and Robert McCauley. The offshore market of domestic currency: Issues on monetary and financial stability [J]. Comparison, 2010 (1).
2 Jun Ma and Jiangang Xu. The path of the RMB going out: The development of offshore market and capital account liberalization [M]. Beijing. Chinese Economy Press, 2012.
3 Tamim Bayoumi and Franziska Ohnsorge. Do inflows or outflows dominate? Global implications of capital account liberalization in China [WP]. IMF working paper WP13. 2013.
4 Limited by the coverage, detailed empirical process and the full reference are not included in this chapter. Readers with any interest could refer to the full version of text at http://imi-sf.ruc.edu.cn
5 In order to diversify risks, investors would choose to purchase in the offshore market assets denominated by this currency (He and McCauley, 2010).
6 The Triennial Survey in 1995 only included twenty-six countries and regions. In consideration for sample consistency, this study selected the same twenty-six countries and regions as the benchmark. In the meantime, 80 percent of the total transaction volumes were involved in these twenty-six countries and regions, which justify again the typicality of the sample selection of this study.
7 Given that this study focuses on the foreign distribution of a currency, the according share in domestic trade is excluded. (As for the euro, the trading proportion of euro in the European Union members is excluded.)

5 Current situation and the future of the offshore RMB market

Hong Kong offshore RMB market

Development process

From late 2003, the establishing process of the Hong Kong offshore RMB market can be divided into three stages in general: the embryonic stage (late 2003–late 2008), the formative stage (early 2009–July 2011), and the overall construction stage (August 2011–present). Meanwhile, because the Hong Kong offshore RMB financial business is gradually becoming more difficult, the process of establishing the Hong Kong offshore RMB market has experienced the development of a series of offshore RMB businesses such as offshore RMB personal business, offshore RMB bond business, offshore RMB deposits and loans business, and offshore RMB product innovation. Besides, the establishment and development of the Hong Kong offshore RMB market is closely related to our government's policies.

The embryonic stage

Hong Kong's offshore RMB market originated from an important intergovernmental system arrangement called *the Mainland and Hong Kong Closer Economic Partnership Arrangement (CEPA)* and an essential intergovernmental cooperative agreement called *The Memorandum* signed by the People's Bank of China and The Hong Kong Monetary Authority. The CEPA, which is the first bilateral economic and trade cooperative system arrangement signed by Chinese mainland and Hong Kong, was officially signed in Hong Kong on June 29, 2003, and came into effect on January 1, 2004. *The Memorandum* was signed in Beijing on November 19, 2003. The People's Bank of China began to provide clearing arrangements for the personal RMB deposits, foreign exchange, and remittance business in Hong Kong, with Bank of China (Hong Kong) serving as the clearing bank. *The Memorandum* signed by the People's Bank of China and The Hong Kong Monetary Authority has provided a significant condition for the development of offshore RMB deposits in Hong Kong.

Hong Kong offshore RMB personal business is considered as the beginning of offshore RMB business in Hong Kong. On February 24, 2004, Hong Kong–

licensed banks began to provide RMB personal business, mainly including Hong Kong offshore RMB deposits, remittances, foreign exchanges, and credit cards. Besides, the quota of RMB per person per day was 20,000 yuan. To meet the demand of RMB business in Hong Kong further, the Chinese government expanded the scope of personal RMB business in Hong Kong on November 1, 2005, and raised the upper ceiling of the personal cash exchange quota. Besides, the People's Bank of China announced *the Supplementary Provision to Expand the RMB Business in Hong Kong and the Mainland* on December 4, 2005. This provision has improved the upper ceiling of the RMB remittance from Hong Kong to the mainland, canceled the credit limit of personal RMB bank cards issued by Hong Kong banks, and permitted every personal account of Hong Kong residents to write checks within 8,000 RMB per day for consumption in Guangdong province.

Offshore RMB bond business was another important measure taken by the Chinese government to accelerate the development of offshore RMB business in Hong Kong after carrying out the Hong Kong offshore RMB deposit business.

The Chinese government has begun to allow domestic financial institutions to issue RMB-denominated bonds in Hong Kong since January 10, 2007. The People's Bank of China announced *The Interim Measures for the Administration of the Issuance of RMB Bonds in Hong Kong Special Administrative Region by Financial Institutions Within the Territory of China* to ensure it. In July 2007, the National Development Bank issued the first RMB bond in Hong Kong. In the embryonic stage (until the end of 2008), seven RMB-denominated bonds had been issued in Hong Kong, with a total amount of 22 billion yuan.

With the development of offshore RMB business, the construction of offshore RMB financial infrastructure was also carried out. The most important part among them was the Hong Kong RMB real-time gross settlement (RTGS) system. To support the development of offshore RMB business in Hong Kong, Hong Kong launched the RMB RTGS system in July 2007, which enabled the real-time settlement of RMB, the Hong Kong dollar, the U.S. dollar, and the euro. Since it was launched, the system has been operating smoothly.

At the embryonic stage, Hong Kong's offshore RMB market mainly focused on the offshore RMB personal business and domestic financial institutions' offshore RMB bond business. By the end of December 2008, the offshore RMB deposits in Hong Kong had reached 56.06 billion yuan, and the scale of offshore RMB bonds reached 22 billion yuan, though those bonds are all issued by domestic banking institutions. At this stage, the scale of offshore RMB business in Hong Kong was still limited and developed slowly. However, offshore RMB financial business in Hong Kong had made an important step. Its development provided a basic condition for the ultimate formation of an offshore RMB market in Hong Kong.

The formative stage

Hong Kong's offshore RMB market was mainly promoted by policies. Its formation significantly depended on the policy orientation of the government of the Chinese mainland. At this stage, in order to enlarge the size of Hong

Kong's offshore RMB stock, policies to promote the development of Hong Kong offshore RMB finance were introduced in succession.

First, on January 20, 2009, the People's Bank of China and the Hong Kong Monetary Authority signed a currency swap agreement to provide up to 200 billion yuan of liquidity support for Hong Kong, which provided an effective guarantee for Hong Kong's offshore RMB supply.

Second, on April 8, 2009, the State Council decided to make Shanghai, Guangzhou, Shenzhen, Zhuhai, and Dongguan (which is in Guangdong province) the initial pilots for RMB settlement in cross-border trade. The offshore areas were temporarily limited to Hong Kong, Macao, and the ASEAN countries. This policy made Hong Kong's offshore RMB deposits increase rapidly.

Third, in February, 2010, the Hong Kong Monetary Authority issued *The Illustration of Hong Kong RMB Business Regulatory Principles and Operating Arrangements*. Under these circumstances, as long as the RMB involved would not reflow into the mainland, Hong Kong banks were free to use the RMB funds they hold, which created an important condition for the free circulation of RMB in Hong Kong.

Fourth, on June 22, 2010, the People's Bank of China announced the expansion of the pilots for RMB settlement in cross-border trade to 20 provinces and cities and canceled the limit for offshore areas, which created an important condition for the initial formation of the Hong Kong offshore RMB market.

RMB settlement in cross-border trade was not only an important process of RMB internationalization strategy but also a significant measure for building the Hong Kong offshore RMB market. However, there are lots of restrictions on Hong Kong offshore RMB circulation: service types, holding scales, investment methods, and so on. Only by canceling part of the restrictions on Hong Kong offshore RMB business and establishing the ways for RMB reflowing into the mainland can the Hong Kong offshore RMB market be initially founded.

Therefore, on July 19, 2010, the People's Bank of China signed and revised *Clearing and Settlement Agreement of RMB business in Hong Kong Banks* with the Bank of China (Hong Kong). It also signed *Complementary Cooperative Memorandum of RMB Settlement in Cross-border Trade* with the Hong Kong monetary authority on the same day. Besides, the People's Bank of China issued *Notice on Issues Concerning the Pilot Program on Investment in the Interbank Bond Market with RMB Funds by Three Types of Institution Including Overseas RMB Clearing Banks* on August 16, 2010. Since then, the deposits in Hong Kong have been allowed to be used in inter-bank transfers, the upper ceiling of the RMB amount that enterprises could exchange had been cancelled, and the restrictions on Hong Kong banks opening RMB accounts for financial institutions and providing a wide range of services no longer exist. What is more, three types of institutions (including foreign central banks, Hong Kong and Macau RMB Clearing banks, and RMB cross-border trade settlements overseas participating banks) were allowed to invest in the mainland interbank bond market through special accounts within a certain limit. The establishment of the offshore RMB capital reflow mechanism was officially started then. The expansion of the sources of potential Hong

Kong offshore RMB holders, the increase of legal types of financial products, and the formal start of offshore RMB reflow mechanisms marked the primary formation of Hong Kong offshore RMB market from the perspective of policy.

Besides political promotion, actual business has also developed rapidly, which is mainly reflected by two aspects.

The first phenomenon is the continuous expansion of the offshore RMB deposit base. Liquidity is the basis of the formation of the Hong Kong offshore RMB market, which means that only when the amount of Hong Kong offshore RMB has reached a certain scale, can the Hong Kong offshore RMB market be established. Therefore, expanding the offshore RMB deposit base through exporting RMB to Hong Kong by RMB settlements in cross-border trade has become a necessary condition to establish the Hong Kong offshore RMB market.

The other aspect is that the offshore RMB product system is increasingly sound. During July and August in 2010, because of the revision of the settlement agreement and the construction of offshore RMB backflow mechanism, Hong Kong offshore RMB business and the innovation of offshore RMB products developed rapidly. Offshore RMB products such as certificates of RMB deposits, RMB structured deposits, RMB warranties, RMB investment funds, and RMB syndicated loans emerged in Hong Kong as the times required.

With a series of political promotions, the offshore RMB product market in Hong Kong has developed remarkably. On April 11, 2011, Hong Kong's first RMB IPO occurred. During that IPO, Hui Xian Real Estate Investment Trust (REIT) raised 10.48 to 11.16 billion yuan in total, with 5.24 to 5.58 yuan per unit. So far, Hong Kong RMB products have covered three aspects including fixed-income products, fund products, and IPO products. The framework of the Hong Kong offshore RMB product system has basically taken shape, which means the Hong Kong offshore RMB market has already formed in the aspect of actual business operation.

Box 5.1 Bank of Communications' RMB bond issuance and underwriting in Hong Kong

The rapid development of Hong Kong's offshore RMB center has contributed to the rapid development of the RMB bonds (dim sum bonds) market. The amount of RMB bond issuance in Hong Kong in 2013 was 3.76 times that of 2010.

From the view of term structure, more than 90 percent of the dim sum bonds are all short-term bonds with terms under 5 years. About 70 percent of them are 2-year or 3-year bonds. As the formation mechanisms of RMB exchange rate and interest rate are getting increasingly complete, the scale and proportion of long-term Hong Kong dim sum bonds will improve further in the future. From the view of the issuer's industry structure, financial institutions, especially Chinese funded financial institutions, are

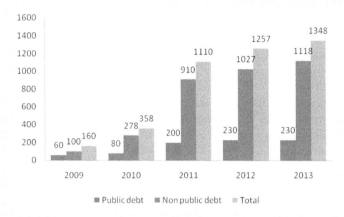

Figure 5.1 Offshore RMB bond issuance (0.1 billion yuan)

major issuers of dim sum bonds. The second type, the sovereign bonds (mainly Chinese government bonds), accounts for about 20 percent. The real estate enterprises (mainly Chinese-funded enterprises) have replaced manufacturing enterprises, becoming the third-largest type of issuers, accounting for about 15 percent of issuance (Figure 5.1).

The Bank of Communications Hong Kong Branch has taken full advantage of the development of RMB internationalization and the establishment of the Hong Kong offshore RMB center. With the support of its mainland branches, local (Hong Kong) experiences, and professional services, the Bank of Communications Hong Kong Branch had successfully helped issue many offshore RMB bonds such as public debt, political financial bonds, general financial bonds, and corporate bonds like as issuance and deposit agent, underwriter, financial arrangement, and some other status. Bank of communications has served as the lead bank, bookkeeping bank, and financial arrangement bank for many mainland enterprises such as Chenming Group, Port of Dalian, and Longyuan Power Group to issue RMB bonds in Hong Kong. During 2012, ten financial institutions within the territory of China had issued bonds in Hong Kong. The Bank of Communications participated in seven of them as the lead bank, with an issue amount up to 15.5 billion yuan.

The Bank of Communications Hong Kong Branch won "Excellent RMB Business Award" and "Outstanding Wholesale Banking Business Dim Sum Bonds (high grade) Category Award" presented by the Hong Kong offshore RMB center in 2012. It has a leading position and good reputation in bond rating and has made a great contribution to the establishment of Hong Kong offshore RMB center.

The overall construction stage

Strictly speaking, there is a huge distance between the initial formation and the completion of the Hong Kong offshore RMB market. Therefore, after the formative stage, the construction of the Hong Kong offshore RMB market entered the overall construction stage, where there will be more problems and greater challenges.

The national "twelfth five-year plan" announced clearly to support the development of Hong Kong as an offshore RMB business center and asset management center, which is the political base of the construction of the RMB offshore market in Hong Kong. On the "national twelfth five-year plan and economic, finance and trade cooperation development forum" held in Hong Kong on August 17, 2011, ex-Vice Premier Li Keqiang announced eight measures to actively develop the offshore RMB business in Hong Kong. This support from the central government for the development of Hong Kong offshore RMB business is regarded as the beginning of the overall construction of the Hong Kong Offshore RMB market.

Those eight political measures for the construction of the Hong Kong offshore RMB market, including the improvement of the offshore RMB backflow mechanism and the construction of offshore RMB bond market and product market, have played an important role in promoting the Hong Kong offshore RMB market into maturity.

On February 14, 2012, the first RMB-denominated exchange traded fund (ETF), "Hang Yuan gold ETF," was listed in Hong Kong Exchanges and Clearing Limited.

On September 17, 2012, the world's first currency settlement USD/CNH futures contracts launched in Hong Kong Exchanges and Clearing Limited officially.

In September, 2012, "the twelfth five-year plan of financial sector development and reform" was released. This plan had made it clear that the government would "support the development of Hong Kong as an offshore RMB business center and an international asset management center, consolidate and enhance the status of Hong Kong as an international financial center" on the political level.

On October 29, 2012, the world's first equity securities traded in RMB that listed overseas launched in Hong Kong.

On December 28, 2012, "Interim regulations of Qianhai RMB cross-border Loan" was formally approved by the People's Bank of China. Since then, mainland enterprises registered in Shenzhen Qianhai "special zone" can borrow RMB denominated loans from Hong Kong banks with lower interest rates. On January 28, 2013, the first batch of Qianhai cross-border RMB loan projects was signed in Shenzhen. In that batch of projects, fifteen Hong Kong banks lent around 2 billion yuan in total to fifteen enterprises registered in Qianhai. Those fifteen banks could be classified into three categories. The first category included the branches in Hong Kong of the five major state-owned banks and their holding banks, including the Bank of China (Hong Kong), Nanyang Commercial Bank, Industrial and Commercial Bank of China (Asia), and Hong Kong branches of Agricultural Bank of China, China Construction Bank and Bank of communications; the second category included Hong Kong branches of commercial banks and their holding banks, including China Development Bank Hong Kong Branch, China Citic Bank International, Hong Kong branches of China Merchants Bank and Wing Lung Bank; the third category includes four local banks of Hong Kong, including The Hong Kong and Shanghai Banking Corporation Limited, Standard Chartered Bank Hong Kong, Hang Seng Bank Limited, and Dah Sing Bank.

In 2012, the Hong Kong Monetary Authority implemented a number of measures to make Hong Kong the most open and convenient offshore RMB business platform. First, the operation time of the RMB interbank payment system (the RMB RTGS system) was prolonged to 15 hours per day to make the real-time RMB receipts and payments convenient for early operating customers that located in Europe and North America. Second, the Hong Kong Monetary Authority led the overseas roadshow to promote the Hong Kong RMB business platform actively. Besides, it also jointly held the cooperation forum with Her Majesty's Treasury, the Treasurer of Australia, and the Reserve Bank of Australia to promote the development of London and Sydney's offshore RMB business in Hong Kong.

On November 18, 2013, the Hong Kong Financial Services Development Council published six research reports, including recommendations for speeding up the construction of the Hong Kong offshore RMB center and consolidating Hong Kong's status as a main international financial center. Those reports put forward twenty-one suggestions from three aspects, hoping to reduce barriers and expand the construction path of the Hong Kong offshore RMB market on a political level, which included: suggesting Hong Kong SAR Government put forward suggestions to allow Shenzhen Qianhai to pilot QDII3 (Qianhai Qualified Domestic Institutional Investor Scheme) with a credit level of 50 billion yuan and $5 billion; permitting all the local financial institutions, including banks, securities, funds, and insurance companies, to invest overseas in order to improve the liquidity of RMB in Hong Kong; allowing institutions to provide RMB cross-border loans between branches of the same parent bank; suggesting the mainland allow foreign companies to issue RMB bonds and certificates of deposits in the interior of China and to choose to remit funds in terms of RMB currency under an approved amount; as for QDII3, the reports suggested encouraging capital to participate in RMB-denominated spot and futures trading in Hong Kong and extending the scope of RMB qualified foreign institutional investors (RQFII) to all the financial institutions registered in Hong Kong. Besides, for Hong Kong SAR Government and local financial industry, those reports suggested that they should strongly recommend the central government ease personal daily remittance restrictions and organize Hong Kong Financial Services Development Council, the Hong Kong Monetary Authority, and financial industry to promote Brazil, India, Russia, and other high-inflation- and high-interest-rate emerging markets to take advantage of third-party financing and other specific operations in the Hong Kong offshore RMB market.

The overall construction stage is an important step and process of the establishment of a mature offshore market after the initial formation of the Hong Kong offshore RMB market. At present, Hong Kong offshore RMB financial business has already had certain foundations but still has a big gap compared with a mature offshore market. Therefore, we must not stop strengthening the construction of the offshore RMB market.

The improvement of offshore RMB backflow channels and the development of the offshore RMB investment market are the centers of the construction of the Hong Kong offshore RMB market in this stage. Because the RMB capital account has not been completely opened, the Hong Kong offshore RMB market should be gradually constructed. Although the overall construction will make Hong Kong offshore RMB business develop rapidly, it is still difficult to establish a mature offshore RMB market in Hong Kong in the short term. The establishment of a mature offshore RMB market has numerous difficulties to overcome, so the overall construction of the Hong Kong offshore RMB market will be a long-term and arduous work.

The overall construction of the Hong Kong offshore RMB market needs not only political promotions but also the management of various impacts and risks brought by the development of offshore financial markets. To establish a mature Hong Kong offshore RMB market, we should start from its particularity and take enough consideration of more perspectives to improve the Hong Kong offshore RMB market continuously.

General evaluation

Hong Kong has become a major platform for RMB settlement in cross-border trade

With the active promotion from the authorities of the mainland and Hong Kong, the pilot area of RMB settlement in cross-border trade in Hong Kong keeps expanding. The entities' services covered keep increasing. The business scope of it is also getting more and more extensive.

New policies kept being introduced and demand kept increasing after the launch of *RMB Clearing and Settlement Agreement* signed by the People's Bank of China and the Hong Kong Monetary Authority, which made the RMB settlement of cross-border trade develop revolutionarily. Table 5.1 clearly reflects the trend of RMB settlement of cross-border business from 2010 to 2013.

While the Hong Kong cross-border RMB settlement business is gradually growing more mature, more and more enterprises choose RMB as the settlement currency in Hong Kong, making the RMB settlement amount increase continuously. With the arrival of the peak season of exports, the settlement would grow further as long as there is no drastic change in macro environment. After 4 years of development, with the continuous expansion of the scale of Hong Kong

Table 5.1 Amount of RMB settlement in cross-border trade (2010–2013; billion RMB)

	The amount of RMB settlement of cross-border trade in Hong Kong	Total amount of RMB settlement of cross-border trade	The proportion of RMB settlement of cross-border trade of Hong Kong
2010	369.2	506	72.9%
2011	1914.9	2080	92.1%
2012	2632.5	2940	89.5%
2013	3841.0	4630	83.0%

Source: The People's Bank of China

cross-border RMB settlement business and the continuous increasing of its proportion of RMB settlement of cross-border trade, Hong Kong has become the foremost RMB settlement platform of cross-border trade.

The basic framework of Hong Kong offshore RMB financial center has been initially formed

In July 2010, in order to create a better environment for the development of RMB business in Hong Kong, the mainland and Hong Kong signed a revision of *Clearing Agreement of Hong Kong Banks' RMB Business*, which made it more convenient for the Hong Kong financial institutions to operate their RMB business. Besides, the Twelfth Five-Year Plan's announcement to "support the development of Hong Kong as an offshore RMB business center" also indicates that Hong Kong will rise rapidly as an offshore RMB financial center. Along with the establishment of the RMB overseas backflow channel and the implementation of a series of work like RMB settlement of cross-border trade, the basic framework of Hong Kong offshore RMB financial center has been initially formed.

First, from the view of RMB deposit business, since the beginning of the pilot of the cross-border RMB settlement in July 2010, Hong Kong RMB deposits have increased rapidly and stably. The amount of RMB deposits of Hong Kong's banking system in 2009 was less than 56 billion yuan while, by the end of 2013, the RMB deposits in Hong Kong has already reached 860.5 billion yuan (not including the balance of CDs). About 10 percent of all the deposits in Hong Kong banks are RMB deposits. RMB has become the third important currency in the Hong Kong market after the U.S. dollar and the Hong Kong dollar. Meanwhile, because of the continuous expansion of the scale of RMB deposits, Hong Kong has become the largest offshore RMB funds pool outside the territory of China.

Second, the rapid growth of RMB deposits in Hong Kong has attracted many mainland enterprises and multi-national corporations with mainland business to finance in Hong Kong, which promoted the rapid development of Hong Kong offshore RMB financing business in return. Besides, the issuance of RMB bonds in Hong Kong market has opened up a new channel for enterprise to finance in offshore RMB markets. At the same time, as an important financing platform for mainland companies, the Hong Kong stock market launched the world's first RMB-denominated securities, which indicates that the aim that enterprises could raise RMB funds through the Hong Kong stock market directly has been achieved.

The degree of interaction between the mainland and the Hong Kong offshore RMB market keeps deepening

By looking at the market scale, you can see that the Hong Kong offshore RMB market is smaller than the mainland's. Therefore, the RMB price of the Hong Kong market should be made based on the RMB price in the mainland market.

What is more, because our country does not have the qualifications and conditions to open our capital market, the mainland market is still under strict control. Compared with Hong Kong's highly open financial market, the mainland market's sensitivity and response speed are relatively low. At present, affected by the international financial crisis, the international market fluctuates drastically. Under this condition, the Hong Kong offshore RMB financial market gets increasingly unstable, which will certainly shock the mainland market and deepen the interaction between the mainland and the Hong Kong offshore RMB market.

From the view of the market operation mechanism, when the international market fluctuates, capital tends to flow into strong currencies such as the U.S. dollar to avoid risks, making the whole market have a devaluation expectation for emerging market currencies. To avoid wealth loss caused by exchange rate changes, funds holders will reduce their demand for offshore RMB currency, which will lead to the devaluation of offshore RMB. However, due to the strict regulation, the impact of external shocks for the money market in Chinese mainland is much less than that of the Hong Kong offshore market, which will cause the difference between the exchange rates of the two markets. Along with the shrinking of RMB stock in offshore markets, interest rates of RMB will rise, and the cost of RMB will be elevated as a result, leading to a reduction of investment in offshore RMB bonds.

These changes will result in a downward trend in offshore RMB, making the reverse spread and the reduction in offshore RMB deposits larger. Conversely, when offshore RMB appreciates, monetary markets will form an expectation of appreciation. The entire process will be opposite. With the gradual cohesion of the settlement system between the mainland and Hong Kong, financial cooperation gets increasingly close. More and more business fields between the mainland and the Hong Kong offshore RMB markets interact. The degree of interaction between the mainland and the Hong Kong offshore RMB market keeps deepening, which will not only directly accelerate the financial reform in the mainland but also have an important influence on the development of the Hong Kong offshore RMB market.

Offshore RMB markets in other regions

London offshore RMB markets

There are two financial centers in London. The traditional financial center is located in the city, which is often called the City or Square Mile. There are Bank of England (BOE), the London Stock Exchange (LSE), the London Metal Exchange (LME), the Baltic Exchange, and more than 500 financial institutions and even more lawyers, accountants, and other professional firms in this small area. It is not only the economic heart of the United Kingdom and London but also the world's leading financial, commercial, and economic center. The new financial center is Canary Wharf, which is located in the east, mainly contains large multinational banks, such as Morgan Stanley, JP Morgan, Citigroup, Credit Suisse.

The London offshore RMB market is still young and is mainly concentrated in the city. In September 2011, during the fourth financial dialogue between China and the United Kingdom, former Vice Premier Wang Qishan clearly expressed support for London to become an offshore RMB trading center. In January 2012, during the British Finance Minister's visit to Hong Kong and Beijing, he signed a memorandum to support London to become the offshore RMB trading center. In April 2012, the CITY issued a formal plan of the construction of offshore RMB center. At the same time, HSBC issued the first offshore RMB bond in London, which also means the official beginning of the London offshore RMB market. In June 2012, the city of London began to publish relevant information of RMB markets.

Current situation of the London offshore RMB market

Markets referring to financial trading markets such as foreign exchange markets, bond trading markets, stock trading markets, and derivative product transaction markets are only in the narrow sense. Because the offshore RMB market has not formed yet, we need to expand the concept of market to overseas RMB deposits, loans, trade financing, and payment and settlement business in order to have a comprehensive consideration of the offshore RMB market's situation at the initial stage.

London's RMB deposit balance was about 14.5 billion yuan in 2013. Among them, interbank RMB deposit was 11.4 billion yuan, which had increased by 67 percent over last year, while RMB deposit balances of private banks and corporate accounts had decreased by 28 percent and 45 percent. Compared with that in the same period last year, at the end of 2013, Hong Kong's, Taiwan's, and Macao's total deposits reached 860.5 billion yuan, 182.6 billion yuan, and 85.8 billion yuan, respectively. The London market's RMB "pool" is still very small and unstable, with a decline in stable corporate and personal savings.

As to the use of funds, the RMB in London market is mainly used in short-term credit loans like trade financing. Long-term RMB loans are not much. In the first half of 2013, payments by RMB letters of credit in the London market

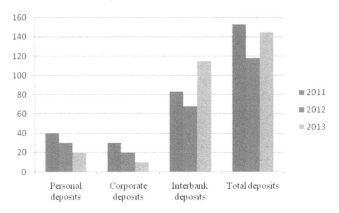

Figure 5.2 Deposit balance of London RMB market

Source: Information Report written by the CITY

had increased to 3.3 billion yuan, 240 percent higher than that in the last period; RMB settlement scale of import financing has increased to 20.3 billion yuan, 6 percent higher than that in the last period; RMB settlement scale of import financing decreased slightly by 3 percent, but the scale was still relatively stable, remaining at 4.3 billion yuan. However, long-term RMB loans are not much. In contrast, RMB loans in Hong Kong, Taiwan, and Luxembourg had reached 115.6 billion yuan, 12.7 billion yuan, and 67 billion yuan, respectively, by the end of 2013.

As to the foreign exchange market, the London RMB foreign exchange volume in the first half of 2013 increased by 32 percent over the volume in all of 2012. Among them, deliverable products increased by 101 percent, while non-deliverable products decreased by 26 percent, making the difference between them (deliverable products versus non-deliverable products) change from $14 billion in 2012 to $10 billion. As to the types of transactions, foreign exchange transactions mainly contained foreign exchange swaps and foreign exchange spots, with currency pairs focusing on USD/CNY, EUR/CNY, and GBP/CNY.

As to the issuance of RMB bonds in London, those bonds are all global now, which means they can be traded in the entire world (generally except the United States) and are listed and traded in several currencies. Usually bonds should use their issuance market's clearing system. For example, RMB bonds issued in the Hong Kong market are usually required to deliver and clear through the Hong Kong REGS system. The amounts of offshore RMB bonds and certificates of deposit issued in 2013 was 161.8 billion yuan and 248 billion yuan, respectively. Total balance of offshore RMB debt in the same year reached 593.7 billion yuan, with a year-on-year growth of 55.8 percent. Most of them were issued in Hong Kong, but they could be sold all over the world, including the London market. Actually, bonds issued in the London market do not occur often, mainly including the first offshore RMB bond issued by HSBC in 2011: 2 billion yuan

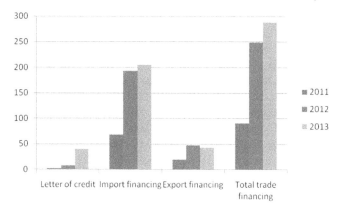

Figure 5.3 Total amount of trade financing in London RMB market

Source: Information Report written by the CITY

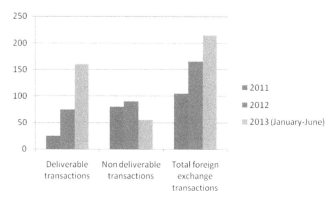

Figure 5.4 Foreign exchange transactions in London RMB market (daily: $100 million)

Source: Information Report written by the CITY

RMB bonds issued by ICBC in London on January 9, 2014, and 2.5 billion yuan RMB bonds issued by Bank of China in London, which refreshed the record of single RMB bond issuance in the London market. Up to now, there have been sixteen bonds traded in the London Stock Exchange in total, with an outstanding balance of about 15 billion yuan, which is very small compared with the entire balance of offshore RMB bonds.

Analysis of London offshore RMB market's prospects

The London offshore RMB market started to develop in 2011. From the view of stock, there are significant increases in deposits, trade financing, foreign exchange transactions, and many other fields but, as to RMB debt, RMB deposits account for only a small proportion of the local deposit market. According to the quarterly report of the Bank of England, the average share of RMB deposits is only 0.6 percent. Besides, the market growth in deposits is weak. Corporate and personal savings even decreased. What is more, the RMB funds "pool" of the London market is very small and mainly relies on interbank deposits. As to the application of assets, despite the great increase of trade financing in 2012, due to the limit of liability, its growth space will still be limited in the future and mainly relies on the mismatch support of interbank deposits. If affected by the reduction of leverage, the growth space will be compressed further. This also explains why the long-term RMB loans are difficult to increase.

Corresponding to traditional commercial banking business, foreign exchange and bond trading are two of the most special characteristics of the London market, because the London market is the world's largest foreign exchange market. The amount of RMB foreign exchange transactions increases rapidly, but its market share is still very low. According to the Bank of England's quarterly report published in December 2013 (see Table 5.2), the share of RMB bonds issuance and the share of daily foreign exchange trading volume are 0.83 percent and 0.59 percent, respectively.

Why does the amount of deposits in the London market increase slowly? The main reason is the mismatch of government promotion and market incentive, which means the governmental promotion has not stimulated the London market well. Meanwhile, the British government stimulates their economy by promoting more economics and trade rather than finance.

For example, in order to provide liquidity support, the Bank of England signed a 200 billion RMB/20 billion GBP bilateral currency swap agreement with the People's Bank of China in 2013. The Bank of England would not easily put this money into their currency system to create the RMB deposits. So now the growth of deposit "pool" in the London market mainly relies on traditional ways such as corporate trade and personal savings, which could explain why the growth is so weak.

Africa offshore RMB market

The scale of RMB settlement in cross-border trade keeps increasing

China has been the largest trade partner of Africa since 2009. The increasing trade volume between China and Africa accelerated the development of RMB settlement business in cross-border trade in Africa. The trade volume between China and Africa increased from around $10 billion in 2000 to nearly $200 billion in 2012 (Figure 5.6), 19 percent higher than the previous year.

The proportion of the trade volume of China and Africa increased from 3.8 percent in 2000 to 18.1 percent in 2012. Chinese investment in Africa amounted to more than $40 billion, among which the direct investment had reached $14.7 billion (Figure 5.7). There are more than 2,000 Chinese enterprises located in Africa involving various fields such as agriculture, telecommunications, energy,

Table 5.2 Financial activities denominated by foreign currencies in Britain and the proportion of RMB (2012; billion GBP, %)

	Total foreign exchange	*RMB*	*Proportion of RMB*
Bond issuance	149.5	1.2	0.83
Foreign exchange transactions per day	2536.8	15.1	0.59
Interbank deposits	1057.9	0.7	0.06
Non interbank deposits	1414.1	0.5	0.04

Source: Bank of England

and manufacturing. According to the Standard Chartered Bank's report, in 2012, RMB settlement of cross-border trade reached $5.7 billion. The number of African countries that use RMB as denominated currency in settlement of trade between China and Africa had increased from five in 2010 to eighteen in January 2013.

Box 5.2 "Bait problem" of London RMB market and its system

According to international experiences, the German mark, the U.S. dollar, the Japanese yen, and some other currencies' internationalizations are all closely related to their governmental promotion. Besides learning the international experiences, we also need to analyze the effect of Chinese governmental promotion in the past few years, which has an important meaning for further RMB internationalization. In order to facilitate understanding, a simple and clear analytical framework should be constructed and then applied to specific research on the development of the RMB market in London.

Basic concepts

Pool (capital pool): Using central bank's concept for reference, in the process of RMB internationalization, domestic RMB is the biggest pool. The People's Bank of China wants to export some RMB capital in this pool to construct an overseas RMB pool. Offshore RMB centers, namely offshore RMB pools, will be established in many places such as Hong Kong, Singapore, London, and Frankfurt. Theoretically, after the internationalization of the RMB, those small pools would be merged into a large offshore RMB pool. We will take Hong Kong and London for examples. These two offshore RMB funds pools are defined as Hong Kong pool and London pool.

Fish (market participants): Market participants can generally be divided into companies, individuals, and institutions. As to type of institutions, bank institutions can be subdivided into local banks, foreign banks, and Chinese banks. We set Chinese banks as a seperate category because they are more prominent in RMB business.

Bait (governmental promotion): Governmental promotion mainly contains clearing methods, economic and trade facilitation, capital opening policies, and some other supportive measures. At present, these measures are mainly produced by the People's Bank of China and put into effect after communication with foreign governments. To study the effect of the People's Bank of China's political promotion in RMB internationalization is to study the various effects of baits put into different pools.

The relationship among pools, fish, and baits

The Hong Kong RMB market was started in 2009. Because the Hong Kong pool is very small, RMB rapidly became an important currency in that pool. Besides, because most participants in the Hong Kong market are associated with the domestic market, RMB is familiar and popular to them. Therefore, fish in the Hong Kong pool adapt to the water well, making the Hong Kong RMB market grow rapidly. Of course, it also happens because the baits the central bank put in are very suitable. It located connections of the two pools mainly in Hong Kong, making Hong Kong smoothly become an offshore RMB deposit pool.

The London RMB market started later than Hong Kong's. Now there is no direct docking between London and the domestic RMB market, so only a portion of water in the Hong Kong RMB pool could flow to the London market. This part mainly refers to corporate and personal savings, while London interbank deposits are still in the accounts of London institutions in Hong Kong, which are in the Hong Kong RMB pool. Participants in the London market are more familiar with the dollar, the euro, the pound, and some other currencies rather than RMB. Therefore, only Chinese-funded institutions can adapt to and promote RMB capital pools. This also reflects that most RMB business such as RMB deposits and RMB trade financing in the London market are run by Chinese institutions. At present, baits put in the London market by the People's Bank of China (PBOC) is not much. Most of them are discussions, suggestions, and verbal support. The most practical, significant one was an 80 billion yuan RQFII quota given by the PBOC to the London market in 2013. However, because the participants there are not familiar with the RMB business, the number of institutions applying for the quota is much smaller than that of the Hong Kong market.

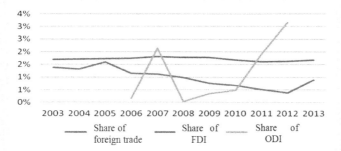

Figure 5.5 Share of Sino-British investment and trade (%)

Source: Counted basing on relevant data

Briefly, to breed fish you need water in the pool. If the pool does not have water, you can borrow other pools to breed fish. This is the relationship between pool and fish. Fish without bait, bait without fish, and fish not being adaptable to the bait are the problems that occur.

No water in the London RMB pool makes it difficult for the London RMB market to grow rapidly in the short term. In the last 10 years, the amount of Sino-British investment and trade accounted for only a small part of the entire Chinese foreign investment and trade (Figure 5.5). For example, its share of import, export, and FDI are all below 2 percent. ODI is also below 5 percent, though it has increased rapidly recently. Thus, so far, the London RMB market relies largely on the Hong Kong RMB market. It needs to borrow the pool to breed its fish and then progressively enlarge its capital pool.

From the analysis of the fish and bait, because the influence of Chinese-funded institutions (which is not the main force in the London market) is not that powerful, fish in the domestic and London market can be seen as two different groups. At present, the "bait" used by central bank to promote RMB internationalization mainly concentrated on real economy. For domestic enterprises, the internationalization of the RMB can reduce their exchange rate risks. However, for the London market participants, this will increase the burden of RMB exchange rate management. Based on the Sino-British balance of payments, the PBOC needs to promote and maintain good real economic links such as import, export, and direct investment between China and Britain. However, in the London market, what the market participants are really concerned about is the establishment of offshore RMB market and the opening process of domestic capital account.

Therefore, the London market will sink into an embarrassing situation called "no fish bait." With no fish interested in this kind of bait, it is no wonder that no financial institutions participate actively in offshore RMB markets. At present, relatively active banks, such as HSBC and Standard Chartered Bank, all rely on Hong Kong as their main capital pool to "borrow pools to breed fish." If the PBOC puts some suitable bait into the London market, it will negatively affect the domestic participants, which is not within the tolerance of the PBOC. It is this dilemma that caused the "fish without bait" problem. "Bait problem" is the biggest obstacle in the development of the London offshore RMB market.

Ricardo's "endowment theory" explained the necessity of international division of labor. In the international trade on the real economic level, various countries rely on their own advantages to complete commodity production in the international division of labor, but when it comes to currency internationalization, currencies can only replace one another. The internationalization of RMB is to replace other major currencies such as the U.S. dollar, the euro, and the pound to serve as the denominated currency in payment, trade, and deposit all over the world. As to the choice of transaction currency, it is not possible for the emerging international currencies and traditional international currency to exist together. Therefore, political measures introduced by one country's central bank to promote the internationalization process of its own currency will surely have bad effect on our countries' currencies, which is called the "bait problem."

The less relative the economic and trade relationship between the two markets, the more serious the "bait problem" would be. In other words, "endowment theory" corresponds to the "bait problem" in the monetary internationalization process. For the Hong Kong market, the internationalization of the RMB has made the relationship of economy and trade between Hong Kong and the mainland closer, which has supported the further growth of economy in Hong Kong.

Correspondingly, the impact of the Hong Kong (HK) dollar in the local market kept decreasing, while RMB has gradually become the denominated currency in Hong Kong. By contrast, in London, the economic and trade relationship of China and Britain is not very close, making the RMB internationalization there to stay only on a monetary level. It is impossible for the British government to strengthen the Sino-British economic and trade relationship through decreasing the impact of Great Britain pounds in the local market. According to the internationalization experiences of the U.S. dollar, Japanese yen, and other currencies, it is not difficult to find out that the usual method to solve the "bait problem" is to expand capital export. With the gradual opening of capital projects, we can use benefits/ wealth as a lever to raise the popularity of RMB in London market.

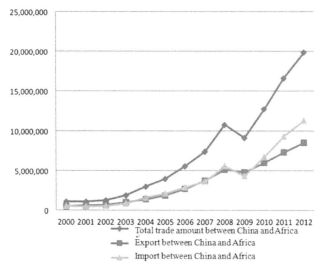

Figure 5.6 Amount of trade between China and Africa ($10,000)

Source: National Bureau of Statistics of the People's Republic of China

Until 2015, the amount of trade between China and Africa is expected to reach $100 billion; 40 percent of them will be settled by RMB. Besides, at least $10 billion of all the Chinese direct investment in Africa will denominate by RMB. Then RMB may replace the U.S. dollar to become the main currency in trade settlement between China and Africa.

Bank of China, Standard Bank of South Africa and Standard Chartered Bank have already put forward RMB trade settlement services in Africa.

The Bank of China successfully handled the first African area's RMB business of cross-border trade (RMB trade financing loan) in South Africa in January 2010, which is the first step of RMB internationalization in Africa. The Bank of China's RMB clearing business has covered more than twenty mainline banks of South Africa, Nigeria, Mauritius, Uganda, Kenya, Tanzania, Congo, Garner, Botswana, Namibia, Equatorial Guinea, Zimbabwe, Ethiopia, and other major African countries, becoming the main channel of RMB clearing in Africa; only in the first half of 2011, RMB settlement handled by the Standard Bank of South Africa exceeded 500 million yuan; Standard Chartered Bank has a history of more than 150 years in Africa with its branches located in more than forty African countries. These branches can open RMB accounts and receive and issue RMB letters of credit in forty African countries, which has removed financing difficulty of Chinese enterprises in Africa successfully through supplying chain financing.

For China's African trading partners, RMB settlement cannot only avoid the risks brought by fluctuation of exchange rate during transaction periods but can get the benefits of RMB appreciation. Meanwhile, for Chinese exporters, RMB settlement can avoid the risks brought by fluctuation of the U.S. dollar's

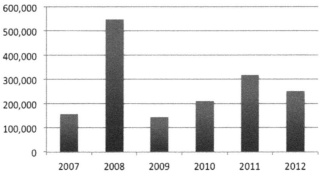

Chinese direct investment into Africa

Figure 5.7 Chinese direct investment into Africa ($10,000)

Source: National Bureau of Statistics of the People's Republic of China

exchange rate, reducing the loss caused by exchange. Besides, the enterprises using RMB to settle trade are free from verification. Their funds need not be inspected, which can help enterprises to improve their efficiency in the use of capital. RMB settlement also provides a more convenient and cost-saving channel for enterprises' cross-border investment and financing at the same time.

However, the range of RMB cross-border trade settlement in Africa is still limited. On the one hand, because most African countries face trade deficit in trading with China, African banks' inclination to use RMB is very slight. This can be reflected through the fact that 80 percent of African banks use the U.S. dollar in trade settlement. On the other hand, RMB is mainly used in trade between China and African countries. RMB is seldom used between African countries, which hindered the African countries' intention to use RMB in trade settlement.

The demand of RMB cash business increases day by day

Driven by the development of RMB settlement and clearing business, part of Chinese banks in Africa began to conduct RMB cash business. The Johannesburg branch of the Bank of China imported 5 million yuan RMB in cash to the National Bank of Mauritius in April 2013, making the Bank of China the first financial institutions that can provide RMB cash services in Mauritius. In August 2011, the Bank of China launched its RMB cash business in Zambia (capital, Lusaka), becoming the first commercial bank to launch cash business in Africa. Bank of China Johannesburg branch bought and sold more than 16 million yuan RMB in cash in Zambia. At present, the Bank of China Johannesburg branch has started to provide an RMB cash wholesale business for South African financial markets. Official and private demand for RMB in Africa grows rapidly.

RMB has become a new choice of African countries' foreign exchange reserves

Relying on the stable currency value and favorable prospects of the Chinese economy, the RMB has become a new choice for African countries to diversify their reserves and risks. In Africa, central banks of South Africa, Nigeria, Angola, Tanzania, Kenya, and some other countries have already absorbed RMB into their foreign exchange reserves.

Nigeria and Tanzania have absorbed RMB into their foreign exchange reserves since August 2012 and bought a batch of 3-year treasury bills with a total amount of $500 million through the National Development Bank, marking the rise of the RMB in African foreign reserve currencies. At present, Tanzania's foreign exchange reserves have reached $3.8 billion; Nigeria's foreign exchange reserves have reached $36.4 billion. They have become major Chinese government bond buyers. In March 2013, the South African Reserve Bank signed an agreement with the PBOC, deciding to invest 9 billion yuan in the Chinese interbank bond market. Central Bank of Nigeria (CBN) announced to increase its RMB reserves from 2 percent to 7 percent in February 2014, which meant CBN would raise its RMB holdings by about 13 billion yuan. There will be more African countries who want to diversify their foreign exchange reserves and absorb RMB into their foreign exchange reserve currencies in the future.

Development opportunities of offshore RMB markets

According to international experiences, there are some basic conditions needed in the construction of offshore RMB markets. The first conditions are political stability and growing economy in China. Only on these conditions can the value of RMB be stable. Second is the smooth flow mechanism of RMB, including RMB backflow mechanism and price formation mechanism. Nowadays, China has become the world's second-largest economy with political stability, which is the solid foundation of RMB internationalization. Promoting the internationalization of RMB needs not only a series of system arrangements to ensure RMB outflow and backflow but also a stable and acceptable exchange rate formation mechanism. For now, the development of the offshore RMB market is facing important opportunities.

Stable political situation and sustainable economic development

China with a stable political situation and the rapid development of the economy is attractive to foreign capital. China's domestic political situation has been very stable. The international status of China has also been improved greatly. In recent years, after the Western financial crisis, macro-economic fundamentals of China has remained healthy, and the inflation rate has also been successfully kept in an acceptable range. All these factors greatly enhanced global investors' confidence in RMB and have provided a solid foundation for the development of the offshore RMB financial center.

Under the background of global economic integration, the integration speed of China's economy and international economy keeps increasing and is entering a new stage of "bringing in" and "going out" to promote the opening up of China. As the result of economic globalization and financial liberalization, offshore business will surely play a more important role in this process. Since the opening up of China, the amount of foreign capital used by China has increased year by year. China's absorption of foreign capital has maintained positive growth for 11 consecutive months since February in 2013, which showed a steady development trend. The amount of foreign capital utilization reached $117.586 billion, with a year-on-year growth of 5.25 percent. Inferred from the current situation, capital is still scarce in China. Therefore, the absorption of foreign capital will still be an important policy for China for quite a long time in the future.

Along with the increasing influence of China's economy, the headquarters economy in China has also been developed considerably. More and more multi-national corporations moved their Chinese management headquarters and even Asia Pacific management headquarters (including financial centers, R&D centers, and investment centers) to China; currently most of the world's top 500 multi-national corporations have regional headquarters in China. Because regional headquarters of multi-national corporations usually manage their companies' domestic and overseas funds together—in the situation that there is exchange control in the territory of China—they need to manage their foreign exchange funds through offshore business.

With the deepening of financial management functions of multi-national corporations' regional headquarters, the corresponding cross-border group accounts, cash management, investment, financing, hedging, and other offshore financial demand will increase further. Offshore financial resources with the investment destination to invest in the China mainland are important international strategic resources that could and should be used by China. Permitting more domestic financial institutions to run cross-border financial business in the form of residents' running of nonresident business is essentially a method to use nonresidents' capital. Overseas capital attracted into China and domestic funds that spread overseas should be included in the scope of Chinese financial institutions' business in order to avoid wasting scarce resources. We should allow more domestic financial institutions, especially Chinese funded institutions, to run offshore business and encourage their offshore financial innovation in order to use these international financial resources to serve China's economic growth.

Meanwhile, the pace of China's overseas investment speeds up gradually. It is expected that China will become a large capital-exporting country in the coming decades. In recent years, the Chinese government acccelerated the implementation of the economic strategy called "going out" whose core is overseas investment by promoting Chinese enterprises to invest overseas. Under the trend of global economic integration, the demand of domestic enterprises to go out of China keeps increasing. From the view of directions where Chinese investments abroad flow, the number of foreign countries that have been invested in increased gradually. Enterprises that have been invested distribute in more than 150 countries and regions. The investment scope of industries also kept expanding and developing from the past with industries including manufacturing industry, transportation industry, commerce and service industry, mining industry, and so on. In addition, the methods of Chinese enterprises' foreign direct investment has also been expanded from setting up factories to cross-border mergers and acquisitions. These improvements provide an opportunity for the construction and development of an offshore RMB financial center.

On the other hand, the rapid development of the Chinese economy, further enforcement of international economic and trade cooperation, and the rapid construction of China's free trade area provides an important opportunity for the internationalization of RMB and the construction of the offshore RMB market. From none to some, from less to more, from neighboring countries to global multi-point distribution, currently China has built eighteen free trade areas with thirty-one countries and regions in five continents. Among them, twelve trade agreements involving twenty countries and regions have already been signed, including Closer Economic Partnership Arrangement (CEPA), Economic Cooperation Framework Agreement (ECFA), and many trade agreements signed with ASEAN, Singapore, Pakistan, Chile, New Zealand, Peru, Costa Rica, Iceland, and Switzerland.[1] Six free trade agreements involving twenty-two countries are still in the negotiating stage, including free trade negotiation between China and South Korea, Gulf Cooperation Council (GCC), Australia and Norway, as well as the China-Japan-Korea Free-Trade Area and the negotiation of Regional Comprehensive Economic Partnership Agreement (RCEP). The construction of free trade areas has not only provided new impetus to the internationalization of RMB from financial markets but also created new platforms and channels for offshore RMB markets.

Deep financial reform and innovation

China's financial reform provided a foundation and safeguard for the development of an offshore RMB market

Along with the deepening of financial globalization and the economic globalization of China, China becomes more and more important in global economy. Meanwhile, China's financial reform is facing a comprehensive situation including the global monetary excess, positive prospects of China's economy in the long term, active impact of hot money on China, and the increasingly serious difficulty in currency regulation. Under this condition, any important measures of financial reform must take internal and external influence into consideration, while speeding up the development of an offshore financial center can provide an important reference for many fundamental financial reforms in China.

The establishment of an offshore RMB financial center will promote the liberalization of domestic financial product pricing. The liberalization of interest rates is an inevitable direction of China's financial reform. Although China's market economic system has been initially formed, because of China's long-term interest rate control, an interest rate index based on the market is still absent. Besides, because China's financial system is relatively weak, in order to protect state-owned commercial banks and other financial institutions, it is still not the time to fully liberalize controls on interest rates. At the same time, as current official interest rates cannot accurately reflect the cost of capital, a reasonable interest rate reference for the development of national economy is still absent. Therefore, there is an urgent need for a reliable indicator of the RMB interest rate to provide a reference for the domestic capital market. The development of an offshore RMB financial center will form a fully market-oriented interest rate index, like London's LIBOR interest rate, which will offer an important reference for the liberalization of interest rates in China.

Diversification of offshore RMB market's products and channels

In the trend of deepening financial reform and financial innovation, an RMB backflow mechanism has been improved gradually. The establishment of each offshore market is smooth in general. Diversification of offshore RMB market's products and channels and the strengthening of the correlation between offshore markets have provided an important foundation for the further development of offshore RMB markets.

First, offshore RMB markets keep expanding to more countries and regions. The construction of the Hong Kong offshore RMB market is the initial attempt of the construction of an offshore RMB market. As the experience of Hong Kong market has accumulated gradually, China can construct more offshore RMB markets in more areas. The influence of RMB would increase through the competition among offshore RMB markets.

Second, offshore RMB products are more diversified. At present, the diversity and risk premium of offshore RMB products are still under strict control, making those products relatively simple and low risk. As the offshore market gradually matures, the offshore RMB products will be more diversified.

Third, the correlation between offshore market and onshore market will be strengthened further and finally be unified. Qianhai Shenzhen is piloting two-way cross-border loan business. China (Shanghai) Pilot Free Trade Zone is also trying to expand the degree of freedom in currency exchange under RMB capital accounts. These efforts will effectively strengthen the association between RMB offshore market and onshore market.

Chinese-funded financial institutions are increasingly competitive

In recent years, with the continuous economic growth in China, the overall strength of China's financial institutions has been enhanced continuously, which can be seen from the phenomenon that there are four Chinese commercial banks in the top ten biggest banks all over the world (ranked by market value). Here, we use four major state-owned commercial banks—Bank of China, Industrial and Commercial Bank of China, China Construction Bank, and Agricultural Bank of China—and four large commercial banks with full license of offshore RMB business—Bank of Communications, China Merchants Bank, Shanghai Pudong Development Bank, and Ping An Bank—as examples to analyze the international competitiveness of Chinese-funded financial institutions.

As to the basic situation, by the end of 2012, each of these eight commercial banks' market value had reached $80 billion yuan. As the largest commercial bank of these banks, the Bank of Communications' total market value has even reached 145.092 billion yuan and has stably maintained this value since 2009. It can be seen from Figure 5.8 that these banks' net operating incomes have shown a clear upward trend since 2009, especially that of the four state-owned joint-stock commercial banks including Industrial and Commercial Bank, Construction Bank, Agricultural Bank, and Bank of China. In addition, accompanied by an upward operating income, net profit of these commercial banks also kept growing. According to their annual reports, compared to 2011, the eight commercial banks' growth rates of net profit are all higher than 20 percent. The largest growth rate of net profit is Ping An Bank's, which reached 33.03 percent.

Meanwhile, these commercial banks never ignored the control of their own risk. It can be seen from Figure 5.9 that these commercial banks' capital adequacy ratio showed a stably rising and convergent trend since the beginning of 2009. As to the core capital adequacy ratio, it can be seen from the banks' 2012 annual reports, compared to 2011, that all these banks realized a growth in the core capital adequacy ratio except China Merchants Bank which declined slightly by 0.23 percent. The core capital adequacy ratio of Bank of Communications has increased by more than 21.25 percent with capital adequacy ratio and core capital adequacy ratio reaching 14.07 percent and 11.24 percent, respectively, which guaranteed the Bank of Communications at the leading level and laid an important foundation for the steady development of its offshore business.

As to overseas development, the scales of these banks' overseas institutions expand continuously; they set up branches, launching new businesses, and upgrading licenses in many big cities such as Hong Kong, Singapore, Frankfurt, Johannesburg, Tokyo, Seoul, New York, Sydney, and so on. The total assets of their foreign institutions have also grown continuously at high speed in recent years. Their operating ability, linkage ability between domestic and foreign, and competitiveness have been enhanced a lot. Take the Bank of China, which has the largest scale of overseas institutions, as an example. By the end of 2012, its overseas institutions had covered Hong Kong, Macao, Taiwan, and thirty-six countries all over the world. As to the development of overseas business, take the relatively mature business—cross-border RMB settlement business—as an example. In the first half of 2013, the cross-border RMB settlements of China Construction Bank, Agricultural Bank of China, Bank of Communications,

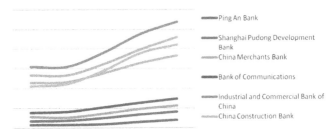

Figure 5.8 Net operating income of commercial banks

Source: Wind Database

Shanghai Pudong Development Bank, China Merchants Bank, and Ping An Bank were 395.122 billion yuan, 292.336 billion yuan, 354.632 billion yuan, 88.1 billion yuan, 124.803 billion yuan, and 55.6 billion yuan, respectively, with growth rates of 43 percent, 74 percent, 77 percent, 90 percent, 67 percent, and 330 percent, respectively, compared to the same period last year. The cross-border RMB settlements of Bank of China and Industrial and Commercial Bank of China were more than 1,000 billion yuan.

From the view of general environment faced by Chinese banks, on the macro-economic level, as the biggest exporter and second-largest economy in the world, China has been the largest trading partner of 124 countries and regions all over the world and maintained a sustainable economic growth. Nowadays, domestic enterprises want to go out, while foreign enterprises and capitals want to come in. This situation has provided a vast market for Chinese commercial banks' business, especially overseas business and offshore business; in addition, in the political aspect, China is steadily advancing the process of RMB internationalization and deepening the open degree of economy and finance, which also provides a valuable opportunity for Chinese financial institutions' overseas development.

In general, taking the basic situation of Chinese funded commercial banks, their overseas development situation, and China's economic policy environment

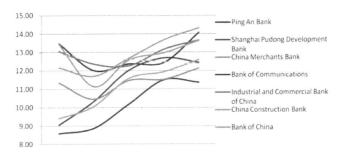

Figure 5.9 Capital adequacy ratio of commercial banks

Source: Wind Database

into consideration, the international competitiveness of Chinese financial institutions has shown a tendency of increasing, which largely promoted the development of offshore RMB business and RMB internationalization process.

Gradual formation of the RMB outflow and backflow mechanism

Currently, China has a managed floating exchange rate system based on market supply and demand with reference to a basket of currencies. The PBOC authorizes the China Foreign Exchange Trading System to publish the exchange rates' middle price of RMB against USD, EUR, JPY, HKD, AUD, CAD, SUR, and MYR in interbank foreign exchange markets on each trading day. Among them, the floating range of RMB against the USD has been expanded gradually, which means the exchange-rate regime is more and more market oriented.

Meanwhile, in order to promote the internationalization of RMB, China gradually accelerated the establishment and development of the offshore market. In August 2011, the Chinese central government demonstrated its positive attitude for the development of the Hong Kong offshore RMB business center. The mainland government would actively support the development of the Hong Kong RMB market, the expansion of the Hong Kong RMB circulation channel, and the innovation of Hong Kong offshore RMB financial products. Since then, Hong Kong has become the first offshore RMB market.

Besides Hong Kong, there are many areas attempting to become offshore RMB markets. As a global veteran offshore market, London is participating actively in the establishment of an offshore RMB market. On April 18, 2012, the HSBC Holdings PLC issued the first RMB-denominated bond in London with total volume expected to reach 1 billion yuan, targeting investors in Britain and Continental Europe, marking the first launch of offshore RMB-denominated bond issued overseas. Besides, the official launch of London as a center for RMB business also took place on that day. From January to April 2012, the British government set up two working groups with Hong Kong Monetary Authority and the City of London, respectively, in order to make London an important offshore financial center. At the same time, Frankfurt is also actively promoting becoming an offshore RMB financial center. In Asia, Singapore also shows a very positive attitude. The Singapore government said that Singapore would support the development of offshore RMB business; the PBOC has announced that Singapore would become the first regional financial center with RMB clearing bank outside China and authorize the Industrial and Commercial Bank of China, Singapore branch, to be the RMB clearing bank in Singapore. From the development process of RMB offshore markets, we can find out that a comprehensive RMB outflow and backflow mechanism has already been formed.

The inflow channels can be classified mainly into the following categories. The first is trading exit, which means using RMB to pay the imports in border trade. With the enhancement of China's economic strength, the acceptance of RMB is gradually increasing; however, using RMB in settlement when trade with developed countries still faces difficulties, it is feasible to promote RMB settlement when trading with East Asia and resource-based countries. The second is investment abroad, especially investment based on government projects or direct overseas investment of private enterprises. The third is currency swap. China has signed currency swap agreements with many countries such as South Korea, Malaysia, Belarus, Indonesia, Argentina, Singapore, New Zealand, Uzbekistan, Mongolia, Kazakhstan, Russia, Thailand, Brazil, United Arab Emirates, Turkey, Australia, Ukraine, and Brazil since 2008. The fourth is the purchase of special drawing rights. In 2009, China signed the agreement to purchase about $50 billion IMF bonds. Although the unit of measurement is the U.S. dollar, the payment was done through RMB.

The outflow channels can be classified mainly into the following categories. The first is trading entry, which means backflow through border trade payments. The second is banks' credit channels, including RMB deposits transferred to domestic banks from foreign banks. The third is foreign investment, which includes the amount that foreign residents use to buy assets, directly invest within the territory of China, and so on. On December 16, 2011, China Securities Regulatory Commission, the People's Bank of China and the State Administration of Foreign Exchange jointly issued "approaches on RMB qualified foreign institutional customers of fund management companies and securities companies investing in securities investment pilot," which officially allowed Hong Kong subsidiaries of securities companies and fund management companies who meet certain eligibility criteria to start RQFII as pilots. After that approach, certain amounts of RQFII were approved both in 2012 and 2013. RQFII is one of the important ways for offshore RMB to return to the territory of China.

Generally welcomed by the world's major financial centers

Along with the rapid growth of China's economy, the competition of the world's major countries and regions for the offshore RMB center is increasingly fierce. After Hong Kong's announcement of establishing the first offshore RMB center in September 2011, London's and Singapore's offshore RMB centers also have been established successively. Then many regions including Frankfurt, Paris, Tokyo, and Taiwan also expressed their willingness to become one of the offshore RMB centers.

When the RMB cross-border trade settlement pilot officially started in July 2009, Singapore had been actively participating in the development of the offshore RMB market, becoming the first batch of countries that finished RMB settlement of cross-border trade. Since January 2011, many Singapore banks such as HSBC (Singapore), United Overseas Bank, Oversea-Chinese Banking Company, and Development Bank of Singapore have started to accept RMB deposits and provide RMB financial products, which is the signal for the formal formation of an offshore RMB center in Singapore. RMB corporate business in Singapore mainly focuses on cross-border trade settlement, discounting letters of credit, and other fields related to cross-border trade.

RMB personal business in Singapore mainly focuses on RMB deposit and remittance. In May 2013, the RMB clearing business in the Singapore offshore market was officially launched, with Industrial and Commercial Bank of China becoming the first RMB clearing bank that was not selected by China. Besides, HSBC and Standard Chartered also took the lead in launching the first RMB-denominated bonds in Singapore. These measures have not only expanded the RMB international financing channels but also promoted the development of offshore RMB business. According to the Monetary Authority of Singapore, Singapore is the second largest RMB credit distribution channel besides Hong Kong, which has more than 20 percent of total global RMB trade credit. According to the RMB payment amount counted by the Society for Worldwide Interbank Financial Telecommunication, Singapore is one of the three largest offshore RMB centers.

The rapid development of offshore RMB business has brought infinite opportunities for the RMB market. Along with the continuous political promotion and the increasing economy of China, Luxembourg, Frankfurt, Tokyo, and Paris have also expressed their willingness to become an offshore RMB financial center. As the world's eighth-largest financial investment center, as the world's second and Europe's largest fund management center and as one of the most important financial centers in Europe, Luxembourg is discussing with China about allowing mutual recognition of investment funds in China and Luxembourg. Pierre Gramegna, Luxembourg's finance minister, said that he expected to lead a delegation to visit China in order to discuss the offshore RMB business. In addition Frankfurt, Germany, has already held a seminar on RMB internationalization and expressed the hope of becoming an offshore RMB center to strengthen economic communication and cooperation with China in July 2013. In November of the same year, in the press conference after the first Sino-French high-level economic and financial dialogue, Paris, which has the largest amount of RMB deposits in Europe, also expressed its achievements and willingness to develop offshore RMB business.

The study of how to choose offshore RMB financial center locations

According to historical experiences, there are two patterns of the emergence of an offshore financial market: the spontaneous market-choosing pattern and the top-down government-pushing pattern. Different from the earlier logical analysis, this section is based on the current situation. Here we attempt to study how to choose offshore RMB financial center locations all over the world through an analytic hierarchy process in China's perspective.

Box 5.3 Analytic hierarchy process

The analytic hierarchy process is a strategy used in operational research to select the optimal method among various alternatives. It divides the decision process into different hierarchies including goal, criteria, and plans. Decisions are made based on this foundation through qualitative and quantitative analysis. The specific steps are as follows:

Establish the hierarchical structure model

In order to use the analytic hierarchy process for the systematical analysis, first we need to divide the complicated problem into different elements. Then we classify these elements into several groups according to different attributes of them to form different hierarchies. Then the same level of elements as the criterion of certain elements on the next level play a dominant role at the same time that it is dominating a hierarchy of elements. Elements in the upper hierarchy dominate elements in a lower hierarchy as criteria. This up-down dominant relationship forms a hierarchical level. The top level usually has only one element. Generally, it is the predetermined target or ideal, commonly known as the *target layer*, which is followed by the criterion layer and the scheme layer. The number of layers is determined by the complexity of the problem. When there are too many layers, there can be a sub-criterion layer between the criterion layer and the scheme layer. Elements reflecting the detailed rules in a sub-criterion layer are denominated by the criterion layer and denominate the elements in the scheme layer (various alternative schemes). Various criteria are mainly used as reference to rank the schemes in the scheme layer. These criteria can be either qualitative or quantitative. All layers of a hierarchy model compose a decision tree. Figure 5.10 is an example of athree-layer model.

Determine the relative importance of different elements in the same layer

This is mainly done through constructing a decision matrix (paired comparison). Specifically, every element (digit) in the decision matrix represents the relative importance of two different criteria. A common method is to divide the relative importance of each two elements into nine levels as Table 5.3. Because the importance of Element *i* and Element *j* is symmetric, if X indicates the importance of Element *i* against Element *j*, 1/X indicates the importance of Element *j* against Element i. After getting the decision matrix, through a series of matrix calculations and consistency tests we can get the relative ranking of different schemes under the same criterion. This rank is reflected in the eigenvectors calculated by matrix

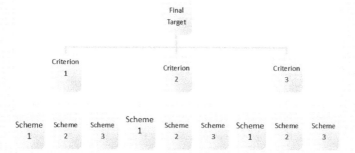

Figure 5.10 Decision tree of analytic hierarchy process

operations. The criterion or scheme that has larger numerical feature vectors is more important.

The weight score of each basic criterion (criterion in criteria layer under the target layer) is the product of all the digits in eigenvectors of all the criteria and schemes on the same branch of the decision tree.

The weight score of each scheme is the sum of all the weight score sunder its corresponding criterion. The higher the score is, the better the scheme.

Table 5.3 Scale of analytic hierarchy process' decision matrix

Digital scale	Definition
1	Element i is equally important as element j
3	Element i is slightly more important than element j
5	Element i is more important than element j
7	Element i is much more important than element j
9	Element i is definitely more important than element j
2, 4, 6, 8	Intermediate states of the states above

Model construction

Site selection criteria and metrics

Taking the political and economic characteristics of the international offshore financial center and practicability into consideration, we selected the following factors as the site selection criteria of an RMB offshore financial center: the overall business environment, information disclosure, the level of legal institutions, taxation environment, unemployment rate, and bilateral relationship with China. We have noticed that there is correlation between the measurement indices of these criteria, but this would not affect the feasibility of analytic hierarchy process.

Specifically, we use the ease of doing business (EODB) to measure the overall business environment. The EODB index is an indicator of the World Bank setting up evaluation of economic policy. The index based on the World Bank's survey results gives higher scores to regions with more concise government regulations and better protection of intellectual property. According to the latest statistics in 2013, Singapore, Hong Kong, New Zealand, the United States, and Denmark were the top five. The index took into account the ease of opening businesses, the ease of applying for a license, the ease of hiring and firing, the ease of registration of real estate, the ease of applying for loans, investor protection, tax strength, the ease of remote trading, enforcing contracts strength, and the ease of closing business. The EODB index covered a wide range. It considered the extent of government intervention in the country's economy and the degree of economic freedom and flexibility, making the index an important criterion for choosing the location of an offshore financial center.

The level of information disclosure is measured by a company information disclosure index and credit information depth index. These two indicators are also established by the World Bank and mainly used to evaluate a country's disclosure of financial information. The former pays more attention to corporate information, including financial data, transaction information, and so on; the latter cares more about bank credit information, including the amount of loans; the lender information and data are related to all kinds of credit. The establishment of offshore financial centers needs not only investors but also capital demanders, so how to ensure perfection and symmetry of information is also a key point to ensure the safety, stability, and effectiveness of offshore financial markets.

Legal level

A legal system is a necessary factor for offshore financial markets. A sound legal system is not only reflected in the complete legislation and effective law enforcement but also general respect and awareness of the law. These conditions, which are highly valued by investors, provide a good legal environment for the development of offshore financial markets. Laws are also an active factor of the construction and development of offshore financial centers, penetrating into the development of various other elements. Reform in the legal system clears the way for the development of economic and political reforms. The promotion of a legal system should be highly valued, especially by developing countries. When external conditions occur, if the internal financial market conditions of a country (region) can bind with them, the development of offshore financial markets would be promoted strongly. Whether capital will flow into offshore financial markets and whether financial institutions move into the center are decided by investors and financial institutions rather than offshore financial markets. When investors and financial institutions make these decisions, they would take into consideration every condition of the offshore financial market, especially the legal system. First, an offshore financial market usually is the most developed and modern area of a country (region). Competitors in the same level are often similar in the level of political stability, economic development, human resources, and infrastructures. Therefore, investors and financial institutions tend to focus on legal factors such as the ease of entry, whether their interests are guaranteed, and tax preferences. Second, a well-run legal system will set up the confidence of investors and financial institutions in their long-term development in the offshore financial market. The World Bank's index of legal power has provided a measurement for investors and financial institutions.

Tax environment

One of the main reasons that typical offshore financial centers of tax-haven models are able to attract numerous international commercial companies to register there is that companies can avoid double taxation there, and the tax burden there is slight. The tax burdens of all kinds of international business companies and offshore companies in Caribbean offshore financial centers is very slight, and almost all Caribbean offshore financial centers have signed treaties to avoid double taxation with major economic countries. For example, Antigua has set that international commercial companies are free of tax within 50 years since being founded; Bermuda is tax free for revenues, profits, and distributions within the island; the Cayman Islands do not impose income tax, capital gains tax, corporation tax, and inheritance tax. A superior tax environment can attract investors. We use the proportion of tax in profits as the metrics of tax environment.

Unemployment rate

We have to consider the stability of the host country when we choose the location for an offshore financial center. Large numbers of unemployed people mean not only a waste of human resources but also sufferings of individuals, families, and the society, which has negative effects on various aspects. Therefore, unemployment rate is an important factor that can affect social stability. In addition, a stable political and social environment, which can provide a good environment for living and working, is good for the establishment of offshore financial centers and the attraction of commercial companies and financial professionals. Moreover, the unemployment rate is a comprehensive economic and social indicator that can not only affect the stability of the society but also reflect the country's economic development level, labor market flexibility, and social security system.

Bilateral relations

Bilateral relations should all be taken into consideration when establishing an offshore RMB financial center. For example, because of cross-strait issues, some countries maintain so-called diplomatic relations with the Taiwan authority. With the absence of Chinese government to establish diplomatic relations with these countries, cooperation on trade will surely be difficult. Therefore, good diplomatic relations will promote the establishment of offshore financial markets. Here we considered the chronological order of the establishment of diplomatic relations with the host country and the proportion of their import and export trade with China in their GDP.

Alternative offshore financial centers

We chose alternative addresses for offshore financial centers by continent. Specific choices are as the following:

- Europe: Netherlands, Luxembourg, Malta, Switzerland, Cyprus
- American Continent: Panama, Dominica, Costa Rica, Uruguay
- Asia-Pacific: Hong Kong, Singapore, the Philippines, Japan, South Korea
- Middle East and Africa: Bahrain, Lebanon, Mauritius, Morocco.

Here we chose countries only as locations instead of specific to the level of city. The main reason is that macro-factors on the national level have a significant effect for the construction and function of offshore financial centers. Because in the negotiation process of the construction of offshore centers China lacks negotiating leverage and has little initiative, which is inconsistent with the basic premise of our "study of locations," we removed economic giants such as the United Kingdom, the United States, Germany, and France.

Model analysis and conclusions

In Europe, we selected the Netherlands, Luxembourg, Malta, Switzerland, and Cyprus to study. These five countries all have diplomatic relations with China. Switzerland was the first country that recognized the legal status among all the Western countries. It established diplomatic relations with China in 1950. Ranked in terms of bilateral trade, the Netherlands and Switzerland are the top two countries. The EODB of these two countries is also at the top of the world. On the whole, Switzerland scored 0.29, becoming the first of all Europe offshore RMB centers. The other four countries' ranking results are Malta, Cyprus, Holland, and Luxembourg. Malta's main advantage is its low unemployment rate, while Cyprus' mainly advantage is its high level of information disclosure and legal system.

In the Asia-Pacific region, we select Hong Kong, Singapore, the Philippines, Japan, and South Korea to study. Singapore and Hong Kong are the world's top two in terms of EODB. Besides, the information disclosure level of these two economies has also reached the world's leading level. Because the political and military confrontation attitude of Japan and the Philippines with China, these two regions are also greatly limited in economic and trade cooperation. According to the results of the analytic hierarchy, Hong Kong is the best place for offshore RMB center in this region. Other alternatives are ranked as the following order: Singapore, South Korea, Japan, and the Philippines.

In the American continent, we select Panama, Dominica, Costa Rica, and Uruguay to study. Because of the cross-strait issues, Panama and Costa Rica have not established diplomatic relations with China even now. What is more, these four countries' EODB are all ranked relatively low all over the world. Asset protection and the force of law in these four countries also need to be improved. After considering all these conditions, Costa Rica won narrowly as a candidate for the offshore RMB financial center in America.

In the Middle East and Africa, we select Bahrain, Lebanon, Mauritius, and Morocco to study. Mauritius becomes the candidate in the Middle East and Africa because of its relatively high EODB ranking and legal force.

Finally, we made a comprehensive comparison of Hong Kong from Asia, Switzerland from Europe, Costa Rica from America, and Mauritius from Africa. Hong Kong became the best location of offshore RMB financial center with a huge advantage eventually followed by Switzerland, Mauritius, and Costa Rica in ranking order. Hong Kong's advantages as an offshore RMB financial center are reflected in the following aspects.

The first aspect is the political and economic advantages of Hong Kong. Under the "one country, two systems" policy, Hong Kong has a very special political status. It belongs to China but is outside the territory of China; it is backed by the mainland and opened to the world. Under the background of "one country," Hong Kong is indivisible and closely linked with the mainland. Besides, it also has common national interests with the mainland. Therefore, Hong Kong has natural unparallel advantages in building offshore RMB markets. As to economic perspective, Hong Kong, which is separated from the mainland, is a relatively independent economy, with economic system, operation mechanism, financial system, and financial market different from those in the mainland. So the RMB financial market here belongs to offshore markets. Establishing an offshore RMB financial market here is not only beneficial to the internationalization of RMB but also effective for preventing the excessive impact on China's economy and financial markets caused by the inflow of numerous RMB capitals by forming a natural firewall to make some speculative RMB capital stay in Hong Kong.

The second aspect is the advantage of Hong Kong's financial system. Hong Kong has a sound market-oriented economic system and a sound, open, and transparent legal system. Besides, Hong Kong is a place that has a concise tax structure with low tax rates and no capital control, no interest rate control, and no currency exchange control. Therefore, as an international free port, Hong Kong has a strong attraction for international investors.

Specifically, compared with countries and regions all over the world, Hong Kong has a relatively low tax rate and provides tax preferences for offshore financial services. The degree of freedom of capital flow in Hong Kong is very high. Foreign investment accounts for a high proportion of the financial sector in Hong Kong. (For example, by the end of 2008, 181 or 90.5 percent of the 200 authorized institutions in Hong Kong had overseas capital injection.) Moreover, according to the survey of sixty-two financial centers all over the world done by the City of London and commissioned by the London government, Hong Kong ranked the fourth. Besides, Hong Kong also has a strong infrastructure advantage. Hong Kong has convenient traffic, a modern communication system, sound financial system, and an excellent payment and settlement system supported by the world's most advanced airports and seaports, the world's most advanced telecommunications system, which can communicate directly and conduct online financial transactions with more than fifty countries, a strong bank system, and numerous financial talent familiar with international financial operation mechanism. The number of foreign banks in Hong Kong ranked third in the world; almost all multinational banks have branches there. The Central Money Market Units established in 1990 is able to provide registration services for all countries' bond issuance and trading in Hong Kong. The RTGS system for HKD, USD, EUR, and RMB established in December 1996, August 2000, March 2003, and February 2007, respectively, can provide real-time delivery service for the exchange between major currencies and financial transactions denominated by major currencies.

The third aspect is Hong Kong's first-move advantage of RMB business. Since the beginning of the twenty-first century, Hong Kong offshore RMB business has entered a spontaneous, rapid, and comprehensive developing stage, which can provide a solid foundation for its further development. After the launch

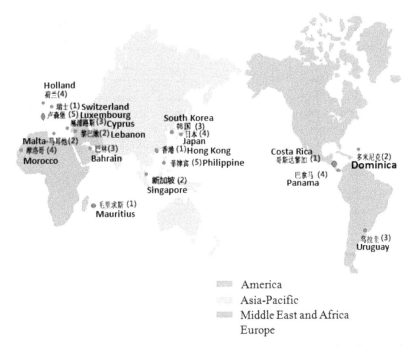

Figure 5.11 Global distribution of offshore RMB financial centers based on analytic hierarchy process

of RMB settlement and clearing arrangements on February 25, 2004, licensed banks authorized by the Hong Kong Monetary Authority began to provide personal RMB deposit, exchange, and remittance services. Since then, deposits have become the main form of RMB in Hong Kong instead of cash, with a rapid expansion of its scale. In addition, the RMB bond market has also been launched. June 8, 2007, the PBOC and the National Development and Reform Commission jointly issued the "management approach on domestic financial institutions' issuance of RMB bonds in Hong Kong Special Administrative Region" to promote the development of the Hong Kong RMB bond market. From July to September of the same year, China Development Bank, the Export-Import Bank of China, and Bank of China (Hong Kong) began to issue RMB bonds in Hong Kong successively, followed by Bank of Communications, China Construction Bank, HSBC, and the Bank of East Asia. The total sum of bonds issued by those banks is more than 30 billion RMB. Meanwhile, transactions of RMB derivatives also get increasingly active, mainly including the following three kinds of products. The first one is non-deliverable RMB forward contracts launched in Singapore in 1996. Because of geopolitical convenience and the needs of real transactions, a large number of NDF businesses were transferred into Hong Kong. The second one is non-deliverable RMB options. The third one is non-deliverable RMB swaps launched in August 2007. Numerous daily derivative transactions not only help RMB-related traders to avoid RMB exchange rate and interest rate risks but also act as an indication of the formation and adjustment of RMB spot rate and domestic interest rate. Besides, RMB structured notes and foreign currency deposits linked with the fluctuation of RMB exchange rate have also been launched in Hong Kong

Note

1 All agreements have come into effect except agreements signed with Iceland and Switzerland.

6 Challenges to building the offshore RMB market

There are two main challenges in general. First is how to establish an offshore RMB (CNH)market successfully. Based on the experience of Hong Kong and London, we must make efforts in products, institutions, technical support, and legal framework to achieve a faster development and thus promote the internalization of RMB actively. The other challenge is how to face the negative influences arising from the offshore CNH market objectively. According to the international experience, offshore markets might not only bring more risks to the private sector but also disturb the finance and taxation policies and currency circulation and even do harm to the entire economy. In summary, to establish offshore markets, we should forge ahead with determination and cautiousness as well.

Offshore CNH markets and financial institutes

Offshore CNH financial products

Ever since the 2008 financial crisis, interest rates overseas have decreased, and domestic monetary policy ranged from neutral to tighter. Under such circumstances, the exchange rate of RMB was still rising steadily, which made RMB bonds very popular. At present, 20 percent of offshore CNH bonds are issued by a third party (non-Chinese mainland or Hong Kong enterprises). Its buyers are from different parts of the world with various purposes, for example, the central banks of Australia, Nigeria, and Japan are prepared to treat it as foreign exchange reserve. German institutions have crossed boundaries and invested in CNH bonds in a prodigious amount. Taiwan also has issued its first "Treasury Bond." Besides, the offshore CNH bond with a total of ¥1 billion issued by China Construction Bank was so welcomed it sold out in an instant. All these phenomena show that CNH bonds are becoming more and more internalized. According to the Twelfth Five-Year Plan of Financial Development and Reform which was released in September 2012, China is in support of Hong Kong to develop into the center of offshore CNH businesses and international asset management and finally consolidate and increase its position of international financial center. It is predictable that Hong Kong will have a wider offshore

Table 6.1 A comparison of Dim Sum Bonds (DSB) and Synthetic Bonds

	Dim Sum Bonds (DSB)	*Synthetic Bonds*
Requirements for investors	Have a RMB account in Hong Kong, stricter requirements for investors	No need to have RMB funds, no special requirements for investors
Issuer	Domestic policy banks and commercial banks	Mostly domestic real estate companies and overseas-listed enterprises
Volume	¥1 to ¥1.5 billion	¥3.5 billion
Maturity	2 to 3 years	3 to 5 years
Rating	Yes	No
Liquidity	Less than ¥0.2 billion	¥0.5 to ¥1 billion
Issuer's RMB backflow	Yes, but under "one discussion for one case" approval system	Yes. Issuers can achieve the recycling of RMB by foreign exchange settlement and sales system because they get dollars instead of RMB
Influence of exchange rate	No influence because it uses RMB to price and settle	It focuses on the exchange rate of pricing date (or that on debt instructions) instead of the rate on settlement date. Investors will benefit when RMB appreciates

RMB market and more convenient financial transactions in the future, which will definitely promote the internalization process of RMB. Relying on the central clearing system of Hong Kong, the whole world will establish sub-centers across east and west continents: Taiwan-Singapore-London-America. Offshore CNH bonds will experience another explosive growth and potentially surpass Asian dollar bonds in several years. It will turn into one of the most important financing channels for enterprises

Besides, SFC of Hong Kong has also approved four RMB bond funds and gold-backed Exchange Trade Fund (ETF) priced and transacted by RMB. In December 2011, China implemented an RQFII program in Hong Kong stock market and began to arrange Hong Kong-listed firms to issue funds in the mainland stock market and are trying to release foreign exchange rate controls gradually and sequentially. RQFII stipulates that RMB capital raised by the Hong Kong branches of those mainland fund management companies and securities companies can be invested into mainland security markets. Because of this program, Hong Kong investors can step into mainland markets, and SFC of Hong Kong has approved nineteen RQFII funds amounting to ¥19 billion ever since.

In the aspect of the CNH monetary market of Hong Kong, volume was relatively small in early times compared to the CNH spot and forward market, whose liquidity situation has gradually improved. In fact, transactions in the monetary market experienced a temporary prosperity because of the news that overseas institutions were permitted to invest in the inter-bank foreign exchange market. CNH markets have two apparent levels, and banks that can deeply take part in cross-border trading settlement or have healthy accounts are very limited in number. Besides, CNK markets lack liquidity generally, nevertheless this situation is expected to improve as assets priced by CNH become higher. In the transaction aspect, CNH long positions can put their money in the clearing bank (within their inter-limitation boundary). The bid price of inter-bank monetary markets is calculated on the basis of clearing bank price. It is noted that this price is not the floor of CNH rates with extremely short maturity because banks taking part in RMB trade settlement businesses have limited ability to store CNH. CNH's scarcity maintains their lower price, however, the longer they mature, the higher the price will become. In a nutshell, the interest curve of offshore CNH is at least 50 base points lower than that of Shibor (CNO).

Recently, market pays more attention to a "new" currency—non-trade RMB. Actually, we have two CNH markets now. Standard Chartered Bank (Hong Kong) offers trade-related dollar/CNH price and also non-trade dollar/CNH price. Besides, trade-related CNH can replace CNO because Hong Kong Trade Settlement Banks have automatic access to the Clearing Bank while non-trade CNH cannot. Therefore, overseas branches of bank (for example, Standard Chartered Bank, United States) can buy CNH on commission through SCB

Table 6.2 CNH products

CNH products	Market	Comment
Spot	Yes	
Forward	Yes	RMB forward, NDFs and CNH forward curve.
FRA/CCS	Yes	
Money market	Yes	There are fewer institutes with CNH, so inter-bank transaction is relatively less.
CDs/structured notes	Yes	
FX options	Yes	Because CNH spot exchange rate has lack of transparency and pricing mechanism, the development of this option is restricted.
Structured products	Partial	
Bonds	Yes	CNH bond market of Hong Kong is under construction.
Mutual funds	Yes	The first offshore CNH Fund was introduced in August 2010.

Source: Global Research Department of SCB and updated by author

HK, but the kind of CNH, in a specific way, whether it is related to trade or is not, will decide how SCB HK closes the position and relatively clients' degree of satisfaction about long CNH and short dollars. Nowadays, clients are more satisfied with non-trade RMB, and foreign exchange counter sometimes buy non-trade RMB only when lacking liquidity.

Nowadays, there are CNH/HKD and dollar/CNH two kinds of products with a maturity from 2 years to the longest in the CNH forward market. However, its liquidity is still worse than the inland forward market and offshore RMB NDF market, so three different forward curves exist now. Therefore, 1-year dollar/CNH with the amount of $3 to $5 million is welcomed in the market and has better liquidity. While a trade settlement bank has limitations about its exposure in CNH markets, so sometimes the market is restricted in scale.

There are several problems in offshore RMB bond market. The market has less liquidity but more volatility. On one hand, dim sum bond (DSB) in Hong Kong could accommodate only 17.7 percent of offshore RMB by the end of 2012, and people lack RMB investment channels. Therefore, DSB supply is not enough to satisfy the demand, and DSB holders prefer to continue to hold it rather than trade in secondary market. (Offshore RMB in Hong Kong can be invested in only deposit and DSB, and the latter are more profitable.) In fact, DSB's fluidity is far weaker than Eurobonds and dollar bonds, even less than other Asian bonds. On the other hand, DSB's popularity relies on people's expectation of RMB appreciation. Once this trend cannot continue or exchange rate begins to fluctuate both ways, investors would sell bonds in large numbers, resulting in a big undulation in the market.

The market lacks an efficient credit-rating system and relative credit-rating institution. It is bad for investors and the market.

The RMB reflow mechanism is not perfect now; synthetic bonds like DSB may be used to reflow hot money to the mainland, which would influence macro-economic stability and obstacle macro-control over it.

The lack of long-time financing tools means long-time investment projects have to rely on bank loans instead of issuing bonds. This obstacle has long caused the mismatch of long-time projects and short-time bank loans. In order to solve this problem and adapt to the demand of urbanization in the future, China should pay more attention to developing the bond market. It is estimated that investment demand in infrastructure will be ¥20 trillion to ¥30 trillion in the next 10 years, and the Twelve Five-Year Plan requests the percentage of direct financing increase to 15 percent. Therefore, the scales of municipal bonds and corporate bonds are likely to double during the next 5 years. However, there are still big challenges to develop offshore bond markets and improve the efficiency of markets. For example, how to consolidate fragmented onshore and offshore bond markets? How to supervise the issuing process and establish a perfect market system? Besides, it is important to involve more international financial institutions to deepen and broaden mainland bond markets. And the development of bond markets will in turn stimulate banks to pay more attention to financing demands of small and medium-sized enterprises and consumers.

Offshore CNH financial institutions

Offshore banks are also called *offshore units*: banks or other financial organizations located in offshore financial centers. They can do business only with other offshore banks or foreign institutions other than in the domestic market. The appearance of offshore banks leads to the emergence of offshore markets. In a traditional international market, transactions are between resident and nonresident. In a financial market, institutions like banks offer loans to foreign organizations or underwrite negotiable securities, and investors purchase nonresident negotiable securities in secondary market. While offshore financial markets offer intermediary services to nonresident investors and borrowers, institutions generally accept foreign currency deposits from nonresidents and provide foreign currency loans to nonresidents. Usually, this kind of business has nothing to do with residents and national economic activities, so it is called *transitional* or *offshore business*.

Offshore bank business in China has experienced a tortuous process. People's Bank of China and State Administration of Foreign Exchange approved China Merchants Bank of China (CMBC) to take the lead of offshore bank business in Shenzhen in June 1989. Afterward, they approved Shenzhen Development Bank (SDB), Guangdong Development Bank (GDB), and its Shenzhen branch, Industrial and Commercial Bank of China (ICBC), Agricultural Bank of China (ABC), and their Shenzhen branches to run offshore bank businesses. However, affected by the Asian Financial Crisis in 1997, People's Bank of China stopped offshore services of these five banks at the beginning of 1999. Offshore businesses of Chinese-funded banks entered its cleanup-and-rectify stage. In June 2002, People's Bank of China approved CMBC and SDB to rerun their offshore businesses and Bank of Communications and Pudong Development Bank to develop their offshore businesses. At present, offshore services of banks listed above are well developed. It is roughly estimated that the assets of offshore bank business had been over $2 billion by the end of June 2006. Their gross offshore savings were around $2 billion, gross international settlements nearly $20 billions and gross profits stood at over $20 million.

Generally, Chinese-funded bank businesses can be categorized into several groups: foreign exchange proceeds deposit, foreign exchange loan, foreign exchange inter-bank lending, international settlements, issuing negotiable big amount certificate of deposit, foreign exchange guarantee, advisory service, and other businesses approved by State Administration of Foreign Exchange. Investors can open HKD savings accounts, foreign currency savings accounts, HKD current accounts, USD checking accounts, HK financial accounts, foreign currency financial accounts, online accounts, and import and export L/C. In November 2003, People's Bank of China offered clearing arrangement to banks that have personal RMB business in Hong Kong. In February 2004, banks in Hong Kong began to run personal RMB businesses, and by the end of that year, Hong Kong RMB current deposit and fixed-term deposit had reached ¥12.127 billion. In 2005, RMB deposit in Hong Kong increased significantly because the trade activities settled by RMB were increasing, and the upper bound of

RMB flowing from Hong Kong to inland banks had updated to ¥8,000, and HK residents could sign a check within this boundary per account per day for consumption in Guangdong Province. By November 2012, institutions ran RMB businesses, which were permitted by Hong Kong economic and financial administration, and had reached 138 with nearly 3 million RMB current and savings accounts and 750,000 RMB fixed-term deposit accounts. Compared to RMB deposit business, RMB loan business began later, which was officially opened to the public in 2011. However, RMB outstanding loans show a strong growth momentum, which increased from ¥2 billion in 2010 to ¥30.8 billion in 2011. Furthermore, by the end of November 2012, a total of ¥2.6 trillion had been exchanged to HKD and other currencies by institutions that are permitted to do RMB businesses by Hong Kong. Meanwhile, HKD and other currencies that were the equivalent of ¥2.6 trillion had been exchanged to RMB. In the aspect of remittance, there were 28,434 remittances from Hong Kong to the mainland with the amount of ¥160.35 billion.

The characteristics of offshore bank business in China

All kinds of businesses develop at a rapid speed but still on a small scale. Since the overall recovery of the offshore bank industry in 2002, the Chinese-funded commercial banks in China experienced a steady increase of their offshore businesses. It is roughly estimated that its total assets, its total outstanding deposit, and its total international settlement reached $1.6 billion, $1.2 billion, and $6 billion, respectively, in 2004. These three numbers reached $1.7 billion, $1.55 billion, and $15 billion, respectively, in 2005. All three indicants increased at a rapid speed, particularly the international settlement business. However, the offshore bank businesses in China are still small in scale. By the end of June 2006, the total offshore business assets of the four Chinese-funded banks had been $2 billion, even including foreign banks' offshore business assets in China. In fact, the total number of offshore business assets and debt was no more than $20 billion, which is far less than those of international offshore financial centers, like London, Hong Kong, and Singapore. It has not been developed into a perfect and mature offshore financial market yet.

It has only a few service varieties and a narrow business scope. In general, offshore businesses of Chinese-funded banks in China stay in the traditional businesses, like deposits, loans, and international settlements, focusing on developing international settlement and risk-free trade financing. Their services concentrate on Chinese domestic institutions and foreign enterprises in Hong Kong, Macao, and Taiwan regions only. Clients from Europe, America, and Japan are rare.

Single capital resource and irrational asset-liability structure are limited by service targets and products; offshore business volumes of Chinese domestic commercial banks are clearly small and show a shortage of capital with a single capital resource. Meanwhile, their asset-liability structures are irrational: Sshort-term liability accounts for more while long-term assets play a more important role. This short-save and long-loan structure will cause liquidity problems.

Profits increase at a faster speed, but its profitability is normal, and external competitiveness is weak. The amount of profit realized by Chinese domestic commercial banks through offshore businesses was $5 million, $11 million, and $22 million, respectively, by the end of June 2004, 2005, and 2006. Its year-on-year growth rate was more than 100 percent, which was a greater number. However, because of the small volume of liability business, scale and scope of the asset business are limited. Besides, considering the volume of liability and term structure, banks have to hold a lot of positions to maintain their liquidity. Therefore, offshore business has a lower return rate and a lower profit rate. Actually, the profit rate of Chinese domestic bank offshore business was only 1 percent in June 2006.

What is more important is that we will face more challenges to establish an RMB offshore center in sovereign states.

First, like London, there are just a few entity economic agencies to support the establishment of an RMB offshore center, and this problem is limited to several people at the policy level. Because London is the biggest exchange rate transaction center in the world, its RMB storage is so small that it has limited actual profit. However, the plan to build an offshore RMB European center is mainly pushed by the British Cabinet and Treasury and constantly stressed by British mainstream media and politicians. It is mainly because Britain will be the first nation to benefit once RMB becomes convertible on capital account, but it still encounters difficulties.

Second, an offshore domestic commercial bank in London should pay more attention to solving the peer regulation problem. After the financial crisis in 2008, the British authorities adopted prudential supervision and denied the supervision of China Banking Regulatory Commission (CBRC) over Chinese domestic banks in London. They required that an overseas offshore Chinese commercial bank should be a legal entity wholly owned by an onshore domestic bank (a requirement applicable not only to China). That is to say, an offshore subsidiary company and parent company should have independent accounts. We prefer another form to build offshore banks. Specifically, supposing that the British authorities and the CBRC have peer regulation system and criterion and share common supervision results, then Chinese banks can freely build branches in London instead of wholly owned subsidiaries. And because branches share a common account with a parent company, it can satisfy only one capital adequacy rate requirement and run a larger scale and scope of businesses than subsidiaries. However, because of the financial crisis, especially the bankruptcy of Lehman, the British authorities realized that they could not forbid capital reflow from London to New York parent companies and thus did harm to normal British depositors once the financial crisis happened. Thus, after the crisis, British authorities adopted the prudential supervision and reset the standard, and require that offshore subsidiaries should accept the overall supervision of British authorities to protect British normal depositors, but the requirement has disadvantages, that is, it will limit the business scale of multinational banks in London. Chinese domestic banks have constrained the business scale in London nowadays. In the next half of 2013, British Treasury

Secretaries said they might scrap the limit of this aspect and permit Chinese banks to build branches conditionally to push London to become one offshore RMB overseas center, but it is still an oral plan rather than a policy.

Finally, state-owned commercial banks have their own problems. In one aspect, state-owned Chinese enterprises adopt a quasi-public servants system, and its salary system is based on an administrative level and technical title. These characteristics are applicable to the Chinese system but have lots of problems in developed countries. Take a subsidiary company in London as an example; it can recruit only those Chinese employees with a low level of education and financial qualities. The top financial graduates will not apply to these companies mainly because of their personnel policy and salary system. These systems lack incentives and have no competitiveness over other foreign capital offshore banks. In another aspect, Chinese banks have limited profitability. They are used to the inland big interest gap between deposits and loans and make monopoly profits. They are actually far away from financial reservoirs and have become monopolist in the mainland of China. However, to have a better development in developed countries needs a high level of competitiveness and creativity. For those subsidiaries of state-owned banks that do not have any intermediary business innovation or market business innovation, they do not have other profit resource, and their growth will be constrained.

Interaction between onshore and offshore financial markets

A traditional international market is also called *onshore* market, which is in charge of a country's international debit and credit of its currency and is regulated by its policies and regulations. Its main traits are: the market is regulated by its country's laws and rules; the debit and credit costs are high; transactions are between its residents and nonresidents; institutions usually run the country's credit business, which is actually a kind of capital export. Comparatively, a new international market is called *offshore* market or *foreign* market, which is a place for nonresident to borrow or lend currency overseas. Main traits include: its services target nonresident, and transactions are between foreign borrowers and lenders; people trade with worldwide-convertible currencies instead of domestic currency; capital financing business has nothing to do with domestic policies and rules. We can observe that private capital plays a more important role on the international stage as the financial market's globalization becomes faster; developing countries have a larger proportion of investment; the number of large-scale mergers and acquisitions grows; the multinational bank has realized business integration and Web-based goals. And the international market will become more and more important.

The international market can stimulate the international trade and investment to develop, adjust the balance of international payments, and push the development of production and capital internationalization, while it will also detach the international financial part from the real economy, extend financial risks because of the financial integration and huge capital flow between countries.

Based on the actual situation and market characteristics, China should take steps to establish offshore financial markets gradually. Nowadays, the non-convertibility of RMB is inconsistent with the free flow of offshore center capital; therefore, in order to build offshore markets, we should adopt an outside-inside separation mode to segregate onshore and offshore business. When the Chinese financial market completely opens its capital accounts and the exchange market is free enough, then the offshore center operation mode can be adjusted, and inland residents can trade with offshore accounts.

In the short term, we should still hold the separation mode. The reasons are as follows:

1   RMB is not freely convertible for the exchange regulation, financial institutions operate as monopolies, and interest rate liberalization is still under way, so it is important for the government to intervene and macro-control the market and maintain the independent of its monetary policy to stablize and develop the Chinese financial market; and the separation mode is more suitable for the Chinese experience.
2   The separation mode will isolate two markets and protect onshore markets from offshore market's violation and shocks and maintain its stability and safety; and the offshore market can act as a demonstration, helping to stimulate the transfer of Chinese financial markets and take full use of worldwide surplus liquidity.
3   At the beginning of the development stage, separation between the two markets can significantly avoid backward effects which could enlarge the gap between regional economies.

In the long run, China should transfer its mode to a partial infiltration kind to attract foreign investment and develop its economy. The separation model will set up walls for financial risks and prevent outside economy variability from harming the domestic economy, but it will also prevent communication between the domestic side and foreign side, and thus foreign capital cannot influence the Chinese economy in a good way. It is meaningless to develop offshore markets in this aspect. So when the Chinese economy has developed to a suitable level, a financial supervision system becomes more and more perfect, and the offshore market is well operated with rich experience, it is important to transfer the development mode and build a usual flow channel between onshore and offshore accounts. Specifically, only offshore capital infiltrating inland markets was permitted in the early days, and inland capital infiltrating offshore market was forbidden. And the infiltrates can choose loans only in the initial stage. Financing tools like bonds and securities will gradually be permitted. This is called *conditional two-side* infiltrate. We should consider every aspect from policy designs to operations and manage this business efficiently, in time, and in good control. We should also set a lower infiltrate proportion no matter the volume to avoid big-scale capital from entering onshore markets.

Settlement and clearing system of offshore RMB markets

At present, RMB offshore businesses are paid and settled through agency banks. Inland commercial banks open RMB inter-bank current accounts for foreign financial institutions, set fundamental funds and provide fundamental funds services, and sell and buy RMB within the legal boundary at the request of foreign organizations. Commercial banks act as an RMB payment and settlement system, provide RMB liquidity to offshore markets, and realize the reflow of the RMB. Specifically, there are four categories:

1   Agency banks are the interface of foreign banks to an RMB high-value payment system (HVPS). Inland agency banks (on behalf of foreign banks involved in trades and its clients) do RMB cross-boundary settlement business with inland settlement banks (on behalf of inland clients involved in trades) through RMB HVPS.
2   Agency banks provide liquidity for RMB trade settlement to a certain extent. Because of the non-convertible capital account, companies that take part in international trade settlement may not get RMB in exchange markets. To solve this problem, People's Bank of China allows agency banks to buy and sell RMB within a certain boundary to enrich its fluidity.
3   Agency banks are members of inland inter-bank markets and can borrow or lend RMB in inter-bank markets, which is a guarantee of extra fluidity to offshore markets.

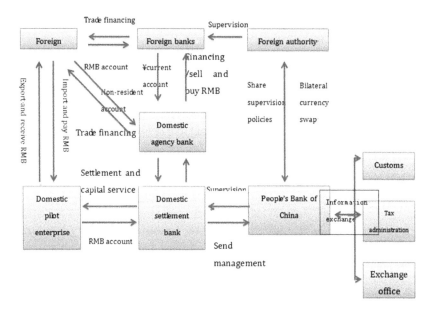

Figure 6.1 Settlement and clearing system of agency banks

As the internationalization of RMB and the development of offshore RMB markets grow, other supporting measures should be taken to transfer the settlement risk because of the birth defect of the agency bank model. Specifically, branches of non-central commercial bank, acting as agency bank, have troubles in maintaining financial stability:

1 The safety of payment information relies only on foreign agency banks.
2 Branches of non-central commercial banks have no ability to ensure this sudden block trading (and even have position limitations in some countries). Once the agency bank is caught in a bad situation for some reason, the risk will at once be transferred to the payment and settlement part and becomes a settlement risk.
3 Offshore payment and settlement platforms should be systemically important institutions, while the foreign commercial bank agency system was not. So there are big weaknesses in the supervision level.

Therefore, an offshore RMB market requires an efficient offshore settlement system. Take the example of the Clearing House Interbank Payments System (CHIPS): most of the cross-boundary settlements have lower efficiency requirements, and it is not asked to accomplish within seconds. So if CHIPS costs less, though it costs more time, more clients will go for it. And the future RMB offshore market can refer to the CHIPS system to build its own settlement system (Table 6.3).

Domestic monetary policy and financial regulation will be under greater pressure

Development of offshore markets may interfere with domestic monetary policy

Since the 1990s, the development of offshore financial markets has gradually added some discordant factors to the stability of the world economy including the interference with the effects of domestic monetary policy. Currently, challenges to monetary policy when building the offshore market include the following three aspects.

First, when the cost in the offshore market is less than the cost of the currency in the onshore market due to the absence of reserve requirements in the former, the result is the formation of domestic monetary tightening pressure. In the process of the development of the offshore financial market in Singapore, the domestic deposits were subjected to the reserve requirement, which was 26 percent in the early 1980s. The requirement included 6 percent cash balance and 20 percent double cash flow ratio. Its domestic depository institutions used offshore institutions to evade the deposit reserve requirements, thus reducing costs in order to provide customers with more attractive interest rates. Of course, doing so would lead to the expansion of the domestic deposit base and reduction of money supply, thereby forcing domestic interest rates to rise. Later, the Singapore regulatory authorities strengthened supervision, and only

Table 6.3 CHIPS and offshore RMB settlement system

	CHIPS	*Offshore RMB settlement system (plan)*
Settlement	Netting settlement	Netting settlement
Shareholders and organization form	CHIPS is a system operated by commercial institution CHPC, whose shareholders consist of the Clearing House Association LLC(organization member), 18 A-class members(international banks) and 4 AA-class members (international banks).	It plans to be operated in the model of business. Its shareholders consist of inland big banks and several international banks with a number limitation of 10. It will also absorb 50–100 domestic banks and international banks as members.
Operation model	CHIPS require all participating banks to have deposit branches in the USA and enough financing channels to satisfy the capital demand at the beginning and ending of each day. Transactions within member banks are accomplished by the inner system and those inter banks are realized through CHIPS. Any non-member bank can become a member bank to deal with its cross-border payments.	Cross-border RMB payment system can be used directly here. Other financial institutions can commit IPSR member bank to deal with its own cross-border RMB payments. Actually, all agency banks participating in the domestic system should be absorbed as IPSR members

then was the situation curbed. What is more, when the host government uses monetary easing to stimulate economic growth, a large sum of money will flow to offshore financial markets pursuing higher returns. At this time, the government will have to take a series of measures, including raising interest rates to curb capital outflows. As a result, the expansionary policy would be difficult to implement.

Second, offshore financial markets may bring imported inflation. Because the offshore market intermediation activities make one country's idle money become another country's money supply, this adds a new means of credit expansion that makes the country's inflationary pressures increase. When commercial banks raise money from the offshore markets to provide domestic enterprises with a large number of foreign currency loans and the enterprises exchange the foreign currencies for domestic currencies, the domestic money supply will be under expansion pressure. Meanwhile, when the government of an offshore market tightens the money supply to curb inflation, domestic banks and businesses can borrow from offshore financial markets at lower interest rates, thereby weakening or even completely offsetting the monetary policy effect of their government. As for the situation in Thailand, large amounts of foreign debt borrowed through the offshore market known as the Bangkok

International Banking Facilities and foreign capital inflows at the times of good market expectations are generally exchanged into baht to use. As a result, the domestic capital position becomes loose, and with the rapid expansion of domestic credit, there is an increasing expansion pressure on the domestic money supply, which impacts on the operation of its own monetary policy.

In addition, the development of offshore financial markets makes the determination mechanism of interest rates and currency exchange rates more complicated for the currency issuers. The situation that offshore interest rates and domestic interest rates coexist while offshore and domestic exchange rates coexist will severely test the government's domestic economic and financial policy formulation and effective implementation.

Specific to challenges of the development of RMB offshore market to domestic monetary policy, there are mainly two key issues.

FIGHTING FOR THE PRICING POWER OF EXCHANGE RATES AND INTEREST RATES DURING THE CONSTRUCTION OF THE OFFSHORE MARKET

Developing offshore financial markets under the background that interest rates and exchange rates in China have not yet been fully market-oriented will inevitably lead to offshore financial markets' impact on the economy. Especially when the offshore market develops to a certain size, it will have some effects on the domestic market and may bring some risks to the country.

First, we can consider the issue from the perspective of the impact on the pricing power of the exchange rate. In general, offshore markets are quite sensitive to exchange rate movements of overseas markets because of factors like the higher degree of financial liberalization. A slight change in the international market will make a highly liberalized and less bureaucratically run offshore market quickly react to the change, with an appreciation or depreciation trend occurring prior to the onshore market. Thus, RMB exchange rates of the offshore market play the leading role in the price discovery in the onshore market spot rate. However, at the early stage of the development of the offshore market, domestic market size is much larger than the offshore RMB exchange market, so the influence of RMB exchange rate of the offshore market is quite limited, and the pricing power of exchange rate is still within the grasp of domestic markets but, in the long term, with the expansion of the offshore market, its influence will finally grow and take over the pricing power of exchange rate from the domestic market.

Second, we can consider the issue from the perspective of the impact on the pricing power of interest rates. At present, interest rates of China's mainland market have not been fully market-oriented and are still under control. Because the offshore market does not have reserve requirements, its deposit insurance fees and taxes are lower, and its RMB interest rates are much different from those of the domestic market. However, due to the presence of the control of the capital account, low interest rates of the offshore market cannot lead to large-scale capital flows, so the domestic interest rates will not be directly and significantly impacted but, in the long run, the control of the capital account will be gradually relaxed. With massive arbitrage prompting a large amount of RMB capital to pour into the mainland market, the domestic money supply will increase. In order to suppress excessive growth of the money supply, the People's Bank of China generally adopts a tight monetary policy such as raising the deposit reserve requirements and deposit and lending interest rates. Through this transmission mechanism, the offshore market can influence interest rates of the domestic market greatly.

PROMOTING THE TRANSITION OF MONETARY POLICY FROM AGGREGATE PATTERN TO
PRICE-BASED PATTERN

Since reserve requirements of offshore markets are lower, the money multiplier is larger, and therefore the scale of funds is larger. Vast capital inflows will result in monetary authorities having difficulties in monitoring domestic monetary aggregates, so continuing to use quantitative tools will reduce the effectiveness of monetary policy. With the constant improvement of the offshore market, the marketization of interest rates will continue to deepen, and the effectiveness of the use of price instruments will also increase. In this context, the shift of the monetary policy from aggregate pattern to price-based pattern will help with the effective price transmission between inside and outside markets and help to promote cross-border capital flow freely. It can also avoid capital movements on a large scale, ensure the realization of the monetary policy target, and maintain the independence of monetary policy.

The development of offshore financial markets may also undermine the effectiveness of domestic monetary policy. For example, if the central bank tightens the money supply when confronted with domestic inflation, it may lead to higher interest rates. If domestic interest rates are higher than those of RMB offshore markets, it may lead to a net capital inflow, which may offset the effect of the central bank's monetary policy. When the domestic economy experiences persistent surplus, RMB will be under the pressure of appreciation. To maintain stable exchange rates, the central bank will have to sell a certain amount of local currency. However, if the exchange rates of offshore financial markets are higher than domestic ones, arbitrage activities may make a part of RMB capital within the country flow to the offshore financial market, which may partially offset the central bank's efforts for stable exchange rates.

In short, arbitrage opportunities will inevitably arise between offshore financial markets and the domestic market before the marketization of interest rates in China is completed. The inflow and outflow of speculative capital may have a certain impact on domestic financial markets. In the meantime, the transmission mechanism from offshore financial markets to onshore markets and the influence of offshore financial markets on domestic expectation are both uncertain. These factors will definitely increase the difficulty of practicing domestic monetary policy and the uncertainty of the effects of the policy.

Box 6.1 Experience of Japan's Offshore Financial Market (JOM)

In December 1986, the Japanese Offshore Financial Market (JOM) was formally established. Offshore financial transactions are usually exempt from interest withholding tax, deposit reserve, and deposit insurance, and there are no interest rate cap provisions. Unlike financial markets of London and the United States, transactions in the JOM are required to pay state and local government revenues, which limit the attractiveness of JOM to some extent.

Restrictions on market participants and business activities

1 *Operation restrictions:* To ensure the externalities offshore accounts, transfers between offshore accounts and onshore accounts are strictly limited. The inflows and outflows between offshore accounts and general accounts in Japan and daily net inflows from offshore accounts are controlled to be less than 10 percent of the previous month's average balance of nonresident assets, while total monthly inflows cannot exceed total monthly outflows of monthly outflows. Banks and institutions engaged in the offshore business are responsible for reviewing the funds in offshore transactions and must ensure that "the counterparties use these funds outside the country."

2 *Restrictions of trading partners:* JOM's trading partners are limited to foreign legal persons, foreign governments, international agencies, and overseas branches of foreign exchange banks (banks approved by a government to operate offshore accounts). Overseas branches of Japanese companies and individuals, even though they are nonresidents, cannot become trading partners. Foreign exchange banks in the offshore business are obliged to carry out a review of the nature of trading partners.

3 *Restrictions on fund-raising and usage:* In the JOM trading business, only non-settlement deposits and loans from nonresidents, other offshore accounts, and parent banks are allowed. Certificates of deposit are not allowed to be issued. Deposits gathered from the nonresidents and other offshore accounts are required to meet the following three conditions. First, for the deposits with agreed periods, the terms for foreign non-financial institutions should be at least 2 days and at least overnight for foreign governments and international organizations; second, for the deposits without agreed periods, they can be gathered only from financial institutions, foreign governments, and international institutions and should be paid the day after the termination notice; and third, loans borrowed from foreign non-financial institutions should not be less than 100 million yen or

equivalent foreign exchange. Funds in offshore accounts cannot be used for foreign exchange transactions, bills trading, securities trading, and swaps trading (i.e., banks operating offshore business are limited to do general deposit and lending business with foreign residents; other transactions can be done only in the general accounts of the banks).

JOM offshore business is carried out through the "special international financial transactions account" approved by the Ministry of Finance. Financial transactions conducted between "special international financial accounts" are exempt from the deposit reserve. However, due to the characteristic that the inside and outside of JOM are separated, funds in "special international financial accounts" have to go through the "fund transfer related accounts" established by the Bank of Japan and pay the deposit reserve when transferred to domestic market. The "fund transfer related account" is the link between the Japanese onshore market and offshore market: On one hand, the regulatory authorities can learn about transactions between the offshore market and onshore market by monitoring "fund transfer related account"; on the other hand, the Bank of Japan can adjust the deposit reserve ratio of "fund transfer related account" to control the amount of capital flowing from the offshore market to the onshore market. In December 1986, when JOM was just set up, the deposit reserve ratio was 25 percent. In October 1991, the ratio was down to 15 percent. The adjustment of deposit reserve ratio of the "fund transfer related account" provides the Bank of Japan with a special tool in the regulation of mutual penetrations between the offshore market and the onshore market. In exceptional circumstances, if there is excess liquidity in Japan so the authorities do not want the offshore funds to penetrate to onshore market, they can impose a 100 percent reserve on the "fund transfer related accounts" to achieve their goal.

Problems in JOM's operation

Regulatory authorities originally intended to separate inside from outside when JOM was established, but penetration of offshore funds to onshore market occurred in the actual operation. Development of a country's offshore market is inevitably accompanied by reform and opening up of domestic financial markets. In June 1984, the Japanese government abolished foreign exchange restrictions, which meant foreign exchange could be freely converted into yen and used as domestic funds in principle. With foreign exchange restrictions abolished, banks could exchange an unlimited amount of foreign exchange into yen or absorb the euro-yen and use it in a domestic market.

Because transferring offshore funds to domestic accounts through a "special international financial transactions account" needed to pay the reserve, Japanese commercial banks operating offshore business lent a lot of offshore-raised foreign exchange funds to their overseas branches in Hong Kong and Singapore in the motive of profit. Their overseas branches then lent these funds to domestic financial institutions and enterprises. These offshore foreign exchange funds were converted freely into yen in the form of external liabilities and came into the Japanese domestic market, bypassing regulatory channels set by the government for offshore funds into the onshore market.

The practice of Japanese commercial banks mentioned above complied with the framework of the Foreign Exchange Management Act, and the separation between the offshore market and the onshore market was bypassed, resulting in lots of foreign exchange inflows into the onshore market in Japan through these paths. In the operation of JOM, there was actually no separation between outside and inside. A "refinancing game" dominated by the banking industry was played out between the onshore market and offshore market. In other words, these funds in fact only circulated among Japanese. Japanese banks played the game's leading role, and offshore centers such as London and Hong Kong became the main channel for the capital to move in and out. During 1984 to 1990, external assets of Japanese banks soared from $105 billion to $725 billion. Over the same period, external liabilities of the banking sector in Japan soared from $130 billion to $904 billion while the net inflow of funds increased from $25 billion to $180 billion. This refinancing game became an important reason for Japan's long recession. After the bubble crisis in 1990 and the Asian financial crisis in 1997, the development of Tokyo offshore market and the international process of yen fell backward simultaneously.

Development of offshore market demands a higher level of financial regulation

One of the reasons why offshore financial markets appear is to avoid domestic regulations, so the development of offshore financial markets will inevitably demand higher levels of financial regulations.

First, in offshore financial markets, capital can flow freely, which will result in higher costs of hot money controls and increasing difficulties to monitor cross-border capital flows. If we cannot set a reasonable firewall, the speed and depth of the spread of an international financial crisis will exceed market expectations and be out of control. Therefore, we must determine the "degree" of financial openness prudently to avoid potential risks caused by excessive financial openness.

Second, the full convertibility of RMB, marketization of exchange rates and interest rates and other reforms will be realized before the offshore financial centers. Once these reforms are carried out, China's current regulatory policy of capital account, exchange rate policy, interest rate policy, and bank industry regulatory measures will be faced with great challenges. This requires China to establish a new set of macro-prudential financial regulation mode. At present, China is overall at the initial stage of the construction of macro-prudential supervision system, so it is undoubtedly a major challenge to the regulatory authorities to develop a new prudential regulatory system suitable for domestic offshore markets. We have to enhance the current situation that various departments only carry out their duties but cannot coordinate effectively as soon as possible, otherwise it cannot adapt to the huge impact from the full opening-up of international offshore markets and thus lead to a systemic financial crisis.

Finally, in the three channels of existing cross-border trade in RMB payment, through our own channels for an RMB cross-border payment system, which brings great security risks to the cross-border flow of RMB funds. Each capital change is vulnerable to real-time monitoring of some countries with ulterior motives, which severely restricts China's economic and financial cooperation with countries in the Middle East, Africa, and other politically sensitive areas. The daily trading volume of RMB has reached $120 billion, which means RMB becomes the world's ninth largest foreign exchange market trading currency. It is quite imminent to build an independent cross-border payment system for RMB.

Market risk prevention and regulatory issues are the most concerning parts in the financial sector, so is the case with the RMB offshore market. Whether the offshore business can develop well is largely dependent on the level of regulation and regulatory capabilities. In order to ensure the smooth conduct of offshore business, it is necessary to take into account both regulatory effectiveness and possible hindering effect of excessive regulation to offshore banking business in the implementing of regulation, so it is important to determine the "degree" of regulation. We must learn lessons from predecessors and carefully analyze the risk prevention and regulatory mechanism for the building of the offshore RMB market so that the smooth and healthy development of the RMB offshore market can be assured.

REGULATION OF CURRENCY-ISSUING COUNTRY

In general, foreign reserve assets selected by foreign central banks, whether they are in the form of bonds or deposits, are realized by a large amount of capital provided by the government and the banking system of the currency-issuing country. The huge flows gradually change into loanable funds through circulation of the banking system and expenditure mechanism of the government, thus creating revenue. With the constant standardization and strengthening of market access management and streamlining the approval process of RMB business, any bank conducting offshore business should get approval from the Chinese and the foreign relevant authorities rest with where the offshore financial institutions stand. In the approval process, the different types of licenses should also be issued based on the applicant's own situation at the same time; the scope of business of the applicant should also be clearly classified so it can be managed more effectively.

HOME COUNTRIES' REGULATION OF OFFSHORE FINANCIAL INSTITUTIONS

Offshore financial institutions act as "bridges" throughout the market. For example, some commercial banks and investment banks could not only guide the direction of funds to providers but also provide valuable information to those who need funds. The importance of this reconciliation cannot be underestimated. Therefore, in order to ensure the effectiveness of this reconciliation, the home country must take responsibility to ensure that any offshore banking institution is absolutely under adequate supervisions. According to the relevant regulations issued by the Basel Committee and accepted by the international community, there are three aspects that we need to pay attention to. First, we should implement the regulatory way that the home country regulators directly in charge of banks and businesses of banks throughout the world are subject to this regulation. Second, the establishment of cross-border branches of banks should be approved by the home country supervisory authorities. Regulators should have the ability to prohibit or hinder the establishment of legal persons under consolidated supervision, or regulators should have the ability to stop the banks to establish branches in suspected countries. Finally, the home country supervisory authorities should have inside and outside information of cross-border banking institutions to monitor various business indicators.

LEGISLATION OF A REGULATORY SYSTEM FOR RMB OFFSHORE FINANCIAL CENTERS

First, we need to improve the financial legislation for RMB offshore markets. In this process, the legislation should not be too restrictive while helping to lower the transaction costs. Second, we need to establish industry regulatory standards. We should not only adjust liquidity ratio appropriately but also introduce tax deduction and exemption policies related to offshore financial markets. Third, enhancing market access regulation is essential. We should start from the standardization of the approval process and ask offshore banks to make a clear classification management of the holdings of different licenses and make the head office bear the business risk as the final insolvent person. Finally, we need to introduce other necessary regulatory regimes. In addition to requiring financial institutions involved in offshore business to hold a rigorous and comprehensive internal control system, we demand their keeping in touch with the State Administration of Foreign Exchange in any situation. In addition, we should separate inside and outside offshore financial markets so that the independence of the offshore financial markets are continuously monitored.

7   Conclusions and suggestions

The *Internationalization of RMB: Annual Report*, annually issued by Renmin University of China, faithfully records the whole process of RMB internationalization and takes a deep look into the major theories and policies of different stages. The report uses a new index—RMB Internationalization Index (RII)—to reflect the actual international usage of RMB in an objective way so that people from all walks of life both at home and abroad can easily and timely catch up with RMB's international status as well as its process. Through the horizontal and vertical comparative analyses of RII, enterprises and financial institutions can estimate the market development and benefit from potential opportunities; researchers can explore topics with academic values that require further study; and administrative authorities can verify their policies and see whether the system functions are as planned to determine the focus of the next step. In the foreseeable future, RII could also be referred to or used by foreign companies, financial institutions, governments, and international organizations.

Main research conclusions

RII ushers in a single-digit era

RMB internationalization steadily increased in 2013 and zoomed from 0.56 in the beginning of 2012 to 1.69 in the fourth quarter of 2013, reaching another historical peak. RII remains strong, which is mainly fueled by four aspects. First, China's economy continued growing steadily, and the increasing rate of GDP remains the highest increase in the world. In 2013, the GDP of China increased by 7.7 percent, reaching 56.89 yuan. Despite the slowdown of the GDP growth rate, China's economic growth remained at the top of the world. Therefore, there is no doubt that the bright economic prospect laid a solid economic foundation for the internationalization of RMB. Second, as the real economy grows, the increasingly expanding RMB demand is the main driving force for RII growth. In 2013, with annual total volume of imports and exports exceeding $4 trillion for the first time, China became the world's largest trading nation. The great growth potential of its domestic market and broad involvement in the international market increased the percentage RMB took in pricing and settlement in trade. Third, the comprehensive and in-depth reform has tremendously boosted the market's confidence in cross-border use of RMB. China has introduced a series of reform measures to accelerate interest rate liberalization, making RMB convertible under capital accounts, improving the market-oriented RMB exchange rate mechanism, and raising the opening up of standards with China (Shanghai) free trade area as a pilot project. Thanks to these measures and the institutional dividends brought by them, the obstacles and doubts about RMB internationalization have been gradually removed. As people from both domestic and foreign markets become more confident in RMB, the actual demand to use RMB internationally has increased. Fourth, the rapid development of offshore financial markets has further enhanced RMB's international appeal. The amount of offshore RMB deposits has increased substantially in Hong Kong, Taiwan, Singapore, London, Luxembourg, and Frankfurt, and there are constant innovations in financial products priced by RMB as well. Offshore trading cannot only offer liquidity but also create a new channel to preserve and increase the value of RMB assets, which makes it much more convenient for and appealing to cross-border RMB users and holders and thus accelerates RMB internationalization.

Cross-border trade settlement and direct investment remain the top two driving forces for RMB internationalization. According to the banks, in 2013, cross-border RMB trade settlement amounted to 4.63 trillion yuan, with a 57.5 percent increase compared with last year. RMB foreign direct investment added up to 533.7 billion yuan, 1.9 times that of the year before. RMB trade financing and cross-border M&A are in great demand. The three pilot districts—Qianhai of Shenzhen, China (Shanghai) free trade area, and Kunshan of Jiangsu—take the lead in cross-border RMB lending and facilitating foreign direct investment to help bring about a great increase in RMB cross-border financial transactions. By the end of 2013, People's Bank of China had signed currency swap agreements with twenty-three countries and regions with the total amount of 2.57 trillion yuan. The international acceptance of RMB as a reserve currency continued to expand.

In terms of the major currencies' internationalization indexes, the international status of the U.S. dollar remained level, that of the euro and GBP increased slightly, and that of the Japanese yen declined. Generally speaking, in 2013, the American economy had done better than expected. Exiting from QE sped up the global capital recycling to America, causing the appreciation of the USD, so the dollar investment demand of the market rose sharply. However, the USD's percentage in global foreign exchange reserve declined. By the fourth quarter, the USD internationalization index reached 52.96, leveling off with the previous year. During the second half of 2013, the Eurozone economic recovery was speeding up and the gap between regional economies narrowing, and the trade and direct investment scales surging. All those factors contributed to the improvement of the real economy base of international usage of the euro, making the euro's percentage in global foreign exchange reserve rise remarkably. In the fourth quarter of 2013, the euro internationalization index was 30.53, increasing by 3.85 percent. As the U.K. economy recovered, GBP's role as a safe-haven currency has been enhanced, reflected by the share edged up in the international credit market. However, the potential danger of the U.K. economic dependence can hardly be ignored. With weak export and under-investment of corporations, output and orders of the manufacturing sector remain less than the pre-crisis level, causing a slight drop of GBP in 2013 Q4 international foreign exchange reserve. The 2013 Q4 GBP internationalization index was 4.30, with year-on-year growth of 2.87 percent. Affected by Abenomics stimulus, the depreciation of JPY has played a positive role for a stronger Japanese stock market, expanded export, and consumption spending. Nevertheless, its domestic economy has already shown signs of falling back from the peak. Moreover, political and diplomatic frictions with its neighbors also depressed international confidence over JPY, compromised the yen's hedging function, and causing a significant fall of the yen's share in global foreign reserve. The 2013 Q4 internationalization index of JPY was 4.27, 7.25 percent down from the year before.

Public opinion paid extensive attention to RMB and held a positive attitude toward its prospect

In 2013, public opinion had paid extensive attention to RMB internationalization

The majority held a positive attitude toward the prospect of RMB internationalization, and most officials and scholars of European continent countries like Germany and France seemed to like that prospect. Many scholars believe that in order to realize RMB internationalization, the goal of the next stage is to achieve regionalization and focus on Southeast Asia. With respect to the potential risks and problems facing RMB internationalization, a more consistent view is that they might involve not only the economic and financial sectors but also other fields like politics and international relations. Many analyses point out that the Chinese government has played a significant role in economic operation. Only when the government and market join their forces to reform and push forward continuously can RMB internationalization be delivered successfully.

According to the public opinion analysis of RMB internationalization, the international community has paid much more attention to RMB since 2010, and the relevant reports have multiplied. Europe always remains highly concerned about RMB issues, with Britain being the keenest spectator. In all the European reports related to the yuan, British news has always accounted for more than 80 percent, which has some bearing on the status of London as an international financial center. And some people always believe that it might be an important way for London to enhance its future competitiveness if it develops offshore RMB business. Asia's concentration on RMB is right after Europe. India accounts for the majority of RMB cross-border trading, demonstrating its value on the financial cooperation mechanism of BRICS countries.

Though public opinion focuses mainly on economy and trade as well as finance, when it comes to RMB, the focus varies distinctly

European concerns tend to be more general. In their RMB-related reports, the commonly used words would be *economic growth*, *monetary crisis*, the *Chinese government*, *internationalization*, and so on, while the United States pays more attention to high-tech products, for example, iPhone's export to China. Since 2012, America has become highly focused on RMB internationalization and its impact on the dollar. Yet, South American media concerns focus on trade and agriculture. Asia's concerns about the yuan differ greatly from place to place. For instance, East Asia and Southeast Asia media focus on growth, direct investment, finance, and yuan's replacing the dollar, while West Asia values oil exports and trade.

Offshore market construction promotes currency internationalization

The offshore market is the corollary for developing international trade and financial market

The offshore market has several main characteristics including loose regulation and low cost in money transaction. It is wider, deeper, and more open, and it mainly deals with nonresidential transactions. Multi-national banks are an important powerhouse for offshore finance development. The offshore market cannot function only as a platform to deliver safe monetary payment and convenient liquidation and settlement with high efficiency and low cost but also as a key national platform to manage risks and carry out the third-party transactions. The historical experience suggests that the offshore market makes a big difference in strengthening a currency's international status. However, since the offshore market has paralleled with its homeland's monetary system and has not been under its own government's regulation, the development of the offshore market would inevitably pose new challenges to the macro-economic management of international currencies' issuing countries.

RMB internationalization cannot be realized without building and developing the offshore market

Speaking from the real situation of the yuan's internationalization at the present stage, the cross-border usage of yuan would not be sustainable if relying solely on RMB pricing and settlement in trade. However, now is not the perfect timing at all to completely let go of the capital account, which at least is not ready to be reformed through radical approaches. Hence, if the RMB offshore market can be cultivated actively, the risk of capital flow could be firmly controlled within the offshore market, and the disguised capital account relaxation could help to boost yuan's internationalization. Such transitional financial arrangements are, in fact, the best choice under today's limited situation. Efforts should be made to build and develop the RMB offshore market as well as improve RMB financial products and services, which could make RMB more accepted and used in this region to form a global currency network and also improve the safety of yuan transactions to encourage possession of RMB assets by both local and foreign residents.

Major international currencies consolidate their statuses via the offshore market transactions of international financial centers

International currencies are a kind of assets with strong network externality. The low trade and information costs of the offshore markets play a decisive role in forming the external network of the international currency and expanding its geographic distribution. The research on offshore market development shows that the global distribution of a certain international currency would be affected by many factors, such as the scale of trade or financial transactions, its homeland's economic scale, the financial development degree, the law system, the language, and culture. Geographical distance does not exert significant influence on the distribution of the international currency offshore markets. Whether the major international financial centers trade RMB assets and the trade's scope and degree are completely up to the market, the initiative belongs to the local market and the various trade participants within. Therefore, in the long run, the yuan's offshore financial transaction scale and trade proportion in the major international financial centers will be a touchstone to see whether RMB has already become one of the major international currencies.

The international layout of RMB offshore markets

The international RMB offshore financial market grows rapidly

The basic framework of the Hong Kong RMB offshore financial center has taken shape, which is a main platform for cross-border yuan trade settlement. As the offshore RMB investment channels have become increasingly diversified, Hong Kong and the mainland yuan markets have been more interrelated. The building of London's RMB offshore market recently relies mainly on the Hong Kong RMB market, by breeding fish in borrowed ponds to gradually expand the capital pool. After the signing of currency swap arrangement between the ECB and People's Bank of China, the RMB deposits and bonds have increased remarkably in places like Frankfurt, Paris, and Luxembourg. In Africa, nations like South Africa, Nigeria, and Kenya that are closely related with China in economy and trade are taking active parts in discussing the feasibility of developing offshore yuan markets.

The development of the offshore yuan market is faced with a rare opportunity

There are three main reasons. First, the internationalization of China's real economy is accelerating, the political situation is stable, and the economic growth enjoys a sustainable high speed. Second, China has carried out a comprehensive and deep financial reform and innovation. The yuan's outflow approach and backflow mechanism are gradually taking shape, and the competitiveness of the main Chinese-funded financial institutions has been improved. Third, the RMB offshore market products and channels have been diversified, and the RMB has been generally welcomed in the main world financial centers.

The international offshore financial centers are undergoing a deep change

The competition has intensified, so it is urgent to find a new driver of growth, which offers a strategic path to build and develop RMB offshore markets. The initiative to launch RMB business in global offshore financial centers like New York and London is held by the market, and it is going to take a long period of time because success will not come unless conditions are ripe. If China wants to actively boost offshore markets, it has to carefully select the target market. China should not only strive for the acceptance of the major global financial centers of Europe and the United States as early as possible but also take an active part in developing the trading potential of the RMB business in the emerging international financial centers. After a comprehensive study of trade, the real economy, capital, investments, geographical factors, politics, cultures, and system construction, through the analytic hierarchy process, the global location research of an RMB offshore financial center finds that the first choices for China to actively build offshore markets are Hong Kong in Asia, Switzerland in Europe, Costa Rica in the Americas, and Mauritius in Africa, among which Hong Kong's advantage is the most distinct.

The main challenges facing RMB offshore market construction

Hong Kong's RMB offshore market develops rapidly, but it faces big challenges

RMB financial products lack diversity and financial institutions are suffering from insufficient capability of innovating and offering technical support. There is a big gap between CNH and CNY, so the motive to speculate and straddle in the market is rather intense. The liquidity of the RMB bond market is poor, and the market volatility is excessive. There is no efficient credit-rating mechanism or credit-rating agency, which is bad for the institutional investors to allocate their assets. The backflow mechanism is unsound. The Chinese-funded financial institutions are now the main force of the offshore yuan markets, but peer regulation and the different salary system limit the development of Chinese institutions' offshore business.

The payment and settlement of the offshore RMB business is mainly fulfilled in the proxy pattern, which has a big defect

The safety of payment information depends fully on the overseas agent bank. Once the bank is caught up in bad management because of some other reasons, the risk would pass on to the areas of payment and settlement, causing settlement risks. The sound development of offshore RMB markets asks for building a highly efficient offshore clearing system like Clearinghouse Interbank Payments System (CHIPS) as soon as possible.

RMB offshore finance is still in the initial stage

The formulation of a unified "offshore financial law" is premature. Therefore, the practice of current major offshore financial centers in the rest of the world is needed to provide the legal regulation details. Different from offshore financial centers' indirect and guiding regulation, China conducts a direct and injunctive one. It is necessary for offshore RMB markets to complete the top-level design of legal regulation from the general perspective and especially focus on the reform of offshore financial regulation. In addition, since a confidentiality clause, which is widely adopted by offshore financial centers, is so different from the confidential system of the Chinese financial institutions, the related law can be effectively prompted and improved only through comprehensive international cooperation and coordination.

Offshore financial centers tend to breed money laundering

It is easy to operate because of the strict financial security measures, preferential tax treatment, and the loose regulatory climate of offshore international financial centers as well as the transfer of electronic funds. The financial institutions in the United States, Britain, and other advanced countries have had anti-money-laundering and strict information-sharing systems, which presents new challenges to the Chinese enterprises to conduct RMB offshore business and maintain good market reputation. It is inevitable to face international conflicts of law during the building of offshore RMB markets. Thus, the imperative dispute settlement mechanism must be taken into account when a top legal system is designed.

The development of offshore financial markets could weaken the effects of China's domestic monetary policy to some extent

It may lead to deflationary monetary pressure in China or transmitted inflation. Moreover, offshore market transactions could make interest rate and exchange rate mechanisms of the international currency more complicated. For example, CNH plays a greater leading role than CNY, which may take the pricing right of RMB foreign exchange rate away from the mainland market as the offshore markets expand. With the control of capital accounts' relaxing gradually, massive arbitrage will drive large RMB capital into mainland markets, forcing PBC to adopt a tight-money policy and having great impact on domestic interest rate. It can be concluded that the further development of offshore RMB markets will inevitably drive the control target of China's monetary policy.

Tax-haven offshore markets

The main part of the offshore financial market, tax-haven offshore markets bring many impacts while effectively dispatching and allocating global capital. The impacts include more severe risk and information asymmetry, a less functional tax system, financial revenue and expenditure, wider gap between revenue distributions, poorer resource-allocation efficiency in developing countries, and more overall risks in the international financial market. Most of the foreign capital attracted and used by China is from offshore financial centers, tax havens that include Hong Kong, Singapore, British Virgin Islands, Barbados, and Cayman Islands. In turn, those mentioned markets are places where our foreign direct investments concentrate. The challenges brought by offshore RMB markets include much less revenue and safer methods for corrupt officials to transfer assets overseas. In addition, some companies or individuals can use offshore enterprises to conduct illegal activities, which definitely harm national interests.

Policy proposal

Internationalizing real economy and cementing the foundation of RMB internationalization

RMB is steadily pushed to the center of the international monetary arena by China's trade scale and share of yuan trade settlement. Therefore, the fundamental guarantees for RII's augment include promoting and supporting China's enterprises to "go out," raising the internationalization level of enterprises and real economy, and making more enterprises the influential transnational corporations and decision makers of international division of labor. In the short term, through guiding RMB appreciation expectation, monetary speculation aimed at arbitrage is likely to bring a financial transaction that is a dozen times larger than a trade settlement and make RMB internationalization reach the next stage rapidly. However, the RMB internationalization promoted by monetary speculative transactions is volatile. As the financial transaction scale will plummet when RMB expectation reverses, monetary speculation is undesirable. From a long-term perspective, it is critical to lay solid fundament of RMB internationalization by promoting the development of transnational companies headquartering in China, speeding up the internationalization of real economy, and turning the RMB speculative transaction of some enterprises into investment activities.

Properly dealing with the concerns of different countries and regions and creating good environment for public opinion

In the past 2 years, the world has paid much more attention to RMB, demonstrating the increasingly close economic exchanges and interest ties between China and the rest of world. Different countries and regions have distinct concerns about the economic activities related to RMB. Those opinions show not only the sentiment of local people but also foresight and guidance, which has a substantial effect on RMB internationalization. China should figure out the other's actual demands and major concerns and specifically lead the outside public opinion on foreign trade and investment so as to create a good public sentiment. The obstacles rooted in ideology for RMB internationalization should be cleared through generating a lot of positive coverage in the international community.

Solving the problem of RMB internationalization through interaction between China and the rest of the world

After rapid advancement in recent years, the path RMB internationalization followed is increasingly clear. Meanwhile, some deep-seated problems become visible. Given the current limited open capital account, one of the main challenges faced by RMB in elevating its international status is to guarantee and continuously expand the liquidity of offshore RMB markets while making RMB more attractive to foreign holders. The interaction between offshore RMB markets and domestic RMB business can help solve the above-mentioned problems. The strategic thinking about "interaction between China and the rest of world" needs two conditions to work. First, a pattern should be adopted in which offshore financial centers at home and abroad are independent from one another. Second, the Chinese-funds banks extend the advantage of local currency business at home to overseas through internationalization.

In the long term, it is necessary for RMB to be fully convertible before it becomes an important international financial transaction currency or an international reserve currency. Efforts should be made to create conditions for deeper and broader use of RMB in the international market through the reform of capital accounts. However, before the time is ripe to open capital accounts, adjusting and controlling the scale and structure of the offshore RMB market as well as increasing the channels between offshore and onshore markets in a timely and orderly way will ensure that open capital accounts and RMB internationalization promote one another. From this perspective, the development of offshore RMB markets has created a valuable time window to deepen capital account reform in an orderly manner and achieve the strategic goals of RMB internationalization ultimately.

Seizing the favorable time window, accelerating the construction of offshore markets, and improving the layout of offshore markets

We should seize the favorable time window and fully use the historic opportunities of structural transformation of the domestic market economy, adjustment of the international offshore financial centers, and seeking haven currencies on international market, so as to promote the RMB internationalization by building offshore RMB markets. In terms of specific measures, what should be done is to establish offshore RMB markets in major international financial centers. The significant role of offshore markets in global resources allocation have to be valued; the objective law of offshore financial centers' development should be respected; the top-level design on the basis of mutual benefit should be accomplished; offshore RMB markets on all continents should be properly located in line with the development of our trade and investment, so as to enable RMB internationalization to serve real economy. As Hong Kong is the best choice for current offshore RMB markets development, efforts should be made to gradually break down the institutional barriers that restrict the development of the offshore market in Hong Kong, and make Hong Kong an international offshore RMB market.

The development pattern, path, and schedule of offshore RMB financial markets must be in accordance with China's reality and needs, and we must keep the balance between financial reform and stability. First, with more sophisticated offshore RMB markets and larger amounts of offshore RMB, RMB should generally play a bigger international role. Second, work should be done to solve the problem of investment channels of RMB being too few, and the recycling mechanism does not work well through accelerating financial instrument innovation, enriching and developing overseas financial products of RMB, and creating various and high-quality bonds issued in RMB. Offshore RMB products should develop more core competence to enter essential investment markets. Third, efforts should be made to steadily reform the domestic financial system, RMB interest rate and exchange rate; open capital account in an orderlyway; improve China's financial supervision system; and coordinate more with the home countries of offshore markets in investor confidentiality, anti-money-laundering, tax evasion, and regulation. The risks of offshore RMB markets should be controlled as well as the impacts of offshore financial markets on domestic economy in order to secure domestic economy and finance. Finally, the offshore RMB capital pool should be brought into currency regulation for overall consideration. Innovations of monetary-policy tools and transmission mechanism as well as keeping initiative prudential are necessary for PBC to have the pricing power of RMB interest rate and exchange rate iunder control and maintain the effect of monetary policy.

Creating an efficient offshore RMB clearing system

As the offshore RMB markets become larger and more widespread, it is much more urgent to create an independent and efficient offshore RMB clearing system. Without an efficient offshore RMB clearing system, the proportion of offshore RMB trade in the international financial centers will be inevitably limited. An offshore RMB clearing system is required to build up as soon as possible based on American CHIPS, in order to realize an effective link between offshore and onshore RMB markets and efficient currency conversion between RMB and other major foreign currencies in trade and nontrade. The system should be an RTGS system with coincident performance period. The credit exposure should be controlled by market access and law of surplus account; liquidity risk should be controlled by synchronous payment and multilateral netting; and operational risk should be reduced by improving the management of operation and service.

Improving the legal institutions and frameworks of offshore markets

The development of legal regulations is a specific challenge that cannot be avoided during the building and development of offshore RMB financial centers. Especially, the institutional arrangements and designs of financial regulation, tax preference, judicial system, and dispute settlement play a significant role in offshore RMB financial markets' development, including its attraction to foreign investment, coordination with major international financial centers, and in China's macro-control for financial order. In this regard, offshore RMB financial centers must set up an independent financial regulator and sound regulatory system; establish a comprehensive, targeted, and powerful basic legal system as well as facilitate a friendly and efficient offshore carrier legal system; and improve independent and efficient judicial administration systems, lawsuit system, judge behavior system, and lawyer management system as well as a pragmatic system for dispute settlement.

In addition, it is especially significant to perfect confidentiality rules (articles) and a strict law system of anti-money-laundering and contain the illegal transfer and flow of foreign capital. In order to promote the development of offshore RMB markets, the Australian experience—giving tax preference to certain offshore agencies or actors—should be referred to. Efforts also should be made to increase the international revenue at home, strengthen the cooperation mechanism of bilateral and multilateral international revenue, crack down on tax evasion, guard against tax avoidance, and maintain China's tax order, which is in line with related law.

Actively promoting the international language and cultural exchanges, and increasing the international acknowledgement and influence of the Chinese culture

Currency internationalization seems to be that the international community acknowledges and adopts certain sovereign currencies on economic and financial levels. However, from a deep level, it is that the non-citizens approve or even follow the culture, arts, innovation capacity of science and technology, social and political system, military force, and other factors of the issue country that matter. The "familiarity effect" caused by common language in the international exchanges makes traders more likely to approve one another so as to make the deal easier and dramatically increase the economic and financial exchanges between the two parts, which is very helpful for the currency internationalization. Offshore RMB trades mainly occurred in Hong Kong and Singapore. It is obvious that RMB is more popular in local markets than in London or any place else, which is bound up with similar language and culture. Therefore, with further promoting Confucius Colleges, China shall increase its cultural influence abroad, and more foreigners will approve China's value, so as to improve the level of RMB internationalization.

As for the future, the economic zone of the Silk Road is regarded as the longest economic corridor with the most development potential in the world.

Since ancient China left many valued legacies on the way of the Silk Road, including commercial prosperity, national fusion, and peaceful development, the Chinese culture enjoys greater acknowledgement and attractiveness in the region. The construction of the Silk Road economic zone builds a new platform for China to expand regional trade and foreign direct investment. RMB internationalization is expected to make a breakthrough in valuation of commodities, such as oil, infrastructure investment, and credit, so as to create a new chapter for RMB widely used in other regions in Asia besides East Asia.

Postscript

RMB internationalization is one of the most important national strategies. The *Internationalization of RMB: Annual Report* has been published annually since 2012, recording the actual course of RMB internationalization and studying in depth the key theories and policies of every stage.

The report of 2014 is about "the establishment and development of RMB offshore markets". The research group has studied the internal logic of the promotion effect offshore markets have on RMB internationalization, and focused on the implications and effects that the establishment and development of RMB offshore markets have on RMB internationalization. Combining this with the current situation of offshore markets, the research group has discussed the realistic path for RMB internationalization to follow given the circumstances that capital accounts are not fully open.

First, the report of 2014 focuses on three points. First, the RII keeps rising steadily, reaching a rate in single digits, and it is more obvious that trade together with financial services expands cross-boarder RMB use. Second, the confidence given by RMB to the international community is mainly on an economic level, while advanced offshore financial markets are necessary for RMB to maintain its attraction on a global stage. Moreover, the rapidly growing RMB offshore markets have more realistic implications on RMB internationalization, which keeps the potential risks of cross-border capital flows within the scope of certain offshore markets, and raises the share of RMB in finance by relaxing the control over capital in a distinct way, to further improve the capital account in an orderly manner and create the valued time window. Third, most major financial centers in the world welcome the establishment of RMB offshore financial centers, and emerging international financial centers are competing especially fiercely for RMB offshore business. The layout of RMB offshore markets should not only respect traditional implementation patterns but also should not easily prevent the possibility of cultivating markets. In addition, Hong Kong's experience and its generalizability are both worth deeper study for the balance between offshore market and real economy.

The *Internationalization of RMB: Annual Report* is the result of a joint study conducted by Renmin University of China and the Bank of Communications, written by IMI and supported by an international finance teaching team of

Financial and Monetary Institute. It is also supported by the School of Statistics, the School of International Relations, and the Business School as well as the the international business department of Bank of Communications. A dozen graduate students of the university participated in the groundwork, including data collection and information processing. The Bank of Communications has demonstrated practical experience and achievements in cross-border RMB business. Our special thanks to Cao Yuanzheng, chief economist of the Bank of China, Lian Ping, chief economist of the Bank of Communications, Hu Yifan, chief economist of Haitong International, Huang Zhiling, chief economist of the China Construction Bank, Zeng Songhua, former deputy director general of the IMF's Asia–Pacific department, Xiang Songzuo, chief economist of the Agricultural Bank of China, and Zhan Xiangyang, financial chief research officer of the Industrial and Commercial Bank of China for their contributions to the report of 2014. Our thanks also go to the People's Bank of China, the State Administration of Foreign Exchange, Commerce Department, National Development and Reform Commission, China (Shanghai) the Pilot Free Trade Zone Management Committee, the Authority of Hong Kong-Shenzhen Modern Service Industry Cooperation Zone in Qianhai, Shenzhen, the Global Economic and Financial Research Institute of Chinese University of Hong Kong, Hong Kong Monetary Authority, China Development Bank, Hua Xia Bank, China Merchants Bank, JP Morgan School of Economics and Finance, Goethe University, the Bank of England, Commerzbank, the branch of ICBC in Frankfurt, Bank of China Hong Kong, Hong Kong and Shanghai Banking Corporation and other institutes for their support in data acquisition, market surveys, and verification of policies. Experts from many areas, including Sun Lunjun, Wang Yi, Wang Zuogang, Zhang Yixiong, Huang Jinlao, and Wu Zhifeng, have attended panel discussions and proposed amendments and suggestions which have contributed to the improvement of the report. We wish to extend our heartfelt thanks for all their efforts.

The division of work for the report is as follows:

- Introduction: Chen Yulu
- Chapter 1: TuYonghong, Zhao Xueqing, He Zhiyun, Wu Chaomin, Kang Meiwen, Sun Lu, Liu Nanxi, Li Yingxie
- Chapter 2: TuYonghong, Yao Yulin, Wang Jiaqing, Rong Chen, Xiao Xiao, Li Yafeng, Deng Weihua, Zhou Hang, GaoRenfei, Ma Junhui
- Chapter 3: TuYonghong, Dai Wensheng, Cao Yuanzheng, Lian Ping, Hu Yifan, Huang Zhiling, Zeng Songhua, ZiangSongzuo, Zhan Xiangyang, Xiao Xiao, Zhao Xueqing, Rong Chen, Wang He
- Chapter 4: Wang Fang, Liu Yang, He Qing, QianZhongxin, RenQian, Yang Shuyun, GuoJunjie
- Chapter 5: Hu Bo, Wang Fang, Fu Zhilin, Wu Cong, Huang Jinlao, QianZongxin, GuoXingyi, Wang Aoran, Zhang Ying
- Chapter 6: Wang Fang, Zhang Chengsi, Gang Jianhua, Zhang Wenchun, Zhang He, Hu Tianlong

- Chapter 7: TuYonghong, Wang Fang
- Appendix 1: Zhang Wenchun, Zhang He
- Appendix 2: Wang Fang, HuaJingjing, Pan Yahuizi

IMI of Renmin University of China
June, 2014

Appendix I

Taxation comparison of offshore financial centers

The offshore financial center, as an important means in international financial markets all over the world, not only brings huge international capital flows but also promotes the development of financial, service industry, and employment, which plays a significant role for economic development of a country.

Offshore companies are very different from general limited companies. In addition to its lax financial regulation, convenient financial operation, and confidential information, another important factor is its tax policy, which takes low-tax as main characteristics.

"Direct tax exemption" model

The so-called mode of income tax exemption, also known as *pure tax haven* or *traditional tax haven* mode, refers to countries or regions concerned with simple tax law and less taxes levying only a small amount of indirect taxes excluding the income taxes and property taxes such as personal income tax, corporate income tax, capital gains tax, inheritance tax, property gift tax, and so on, which means any business or individual income is not subject to local government tax revenue. Countries and regions that take such mode are Bahamas, Zi Lu, Bermuda, Greenland, Costa Rica, Vanuatu, British Cayman Islands, the Virgin Islands, New Hebrides, New Caledonia, Faroe Islands, Somalia, Saint Pierre Island, Micronesia, Turks and Caicos, and so on, among which Baja Maharashtra and Bermuda are mostly typical.

The Bahamas is located in the Bahamas in the northernmost of America's West Indies, and its revenue mainly comes from tourism, international financial services targeting the exchange rate, and the oil re-export industry. With a simple tax system and fewer taxes, Bahamas's basic taxes are mainly on stamp duty, service fee, departure tax, gambling, tax and other indirect taxes, which do not take up much proportion in fiscal revenue. On the other hand, it does not levy income tax, estate duty, inheritance tax, estate tax, dividends, interest, withholding tax, or disclosure fee, even the sales tax, tonnage tax into and out of the territory, and the like. Any manufacturing company established in its territory can enjoy tax exemption for 15 years. All companies and enterprises that obtain a license in Grand Bahama Island Freeport Zone (no tax area) can be guaranteed excise duty, stamp duty, and most tariffs exemption before the year of 2054. The legal system of company in the Bahamas is very flexible. It does not need to submit audited accounts for companies (except bank and safe company) registration. Any company can issue bearer shares and redeemable shares. Directors of the company can be of any nationality and can hold board meetings anywhere in the world. Companies that mainly engage in business activities overseas can obtain the status of nonresident company, not subject to foreign exchange restriction of the Bahamas. To the 1990s, the number of a variety of companies in the Bahamas has reached more than 16,000, which contributes to around $4,000 annual contribution to the local economy and provides more than 3,000 jobs. However, most companies are of typical non-substantive business organizations such as shell company, mailbox company, or paper company with the purpose avoiding tax. For example, Bank of America has established more than 100 financial branches here mostly to get rid of direct capital export restrictions of the U.S. government.

Bermuda is located in the western North Atlantic. It implements low taxation with exempting direct tax but only levying tariffs, stamp duty, payroll tax, social security tax, land tax, passenger tax, foreign currency purchase tax, and other small taxes, of which the tariff constitutes the main revenue sources. Currently, Bermuda is brewing a low rate of income tax but has guaranteed not to impose it on foreign companies before 2006. A company established in the territory can merge through registration without submitting financial statements to the government according to corporation law. Besides, the government keeps aloof from the nationality of shareholders or managers in the company, and it is legal for companies established in the territory to engage in business activities abroad. Currently there are more than 7,000 kinds of companies, mostly established by overseas personage, with the purpose of using low tax legal environment activities to evade taxes.

"Overseas income tax exemption" model

The so-called overseas income tax exemption model refers to the countries and regions concerned abandoning resident tax jurisdiction and implementing source tax jurisdiction instead, which means levying income tax derived only from the territory instead of abroad or overseas. Such countries and regions mainly are Ethiopia, Liberia, Panama, Venezuela, Argentina, Costa Rica, Brazil, Bolivia, Guatemala, Nicaragua, Ecuador, Dominica, Paraguay, Jersey, Malaysia, Brunei, Singapore, Hong Kong, Macau, and so on, which can be represented by Singapore and Hong Kong.

Singapore is a famous free port with statutory taxes as income tax, inheritance tax, property tax, stamp duties and tariffs, and the like, levied based only on income derived from the territory. Its tax system is characterized by fewer types, simple structure, and low tax rate. Singapore implemented tax reform in 2002, which stipulated the income tax rates for both companies in the territory and individuals changed from current 24.5 percent and 26 percent to 20 percent within 3 years. A subordinate company in Group can offset the gain or loss, uses single tax system, handles income tax of foreign business flexibly, exempts intellectual property development expenditure tax, write-downs for obtaining intellectual property subsidy, establishes deferred tax system, exempts personal interest income, foreign personal income remittances, employee fees and personal pension overseas, and other personal income tax.

Hong Kong adheres to source of jurisdiction only on income obtained in the territory for the long term. The beneficiary who does not set up offices in Hong Kong is still subject to profits tax. In contrast, it is unnecessary to pay tax on income obtained outside Hong Kong unless they are deemed to come from Hong Kong, whether there is remittance to Hong Kong. In addition, Hong Kong is famous for a low tax rate, simple taxation, and generous offers all over the world.

"Certain income tax exemption" model

This model refers to the countries and regions involved with abandoning personal income tax and levying corporate income tax instead. Such countries and regions are mainly Grenada in the American West Indies, islands economies located in the western Caribbean, Kuwait, Saudi Arabia, Jordan, Iran, Syria, Oman in the Middle East, and so on. One of the more typical is Kuwait.

Kuwait is a famous petroleum export country, also known as a simple tax regime and low tax burden; 95 percent of its revenue comes from public revenues and royalty revenue from oil, and business tax accounts for only about 3 percent. It levies only a few taxes as tariffs, corporate income tax. Companies bear a small rate of taxation burden, and 90 percent of corporate income tax is paid by the Department of Petroleum. Kuwait implemented tax reform to increase the proportion of non-oil revenues for revenue increase in 2002. The main contents include levying sales tax on imported products from January 1, increasing import tax on cigarettes and tobacco from 70 percent to 100 percent, and tax on domestic non-essential consumer goods by up to 10 percent. Meanwhile, it also reforms income tax to impose 5 percent of net profit for private companies, reducing the tax burden on foreign companies up to 25 percent.

"Low tax rates applicable to overseas income" model

The low tax rates applicable to overseas income model means that although countries and regions involved levy personal and corporate income tax, corporation net property tax, and personal property tax when executing resident tax jurisdiction, they implement preferential tax rates significantly lower than the rate applicable to the territory on residential income obtained overseas to attract foreign investment. Such countries are mainly the Channel Islands, the Cook Islands, Belize, the Netherlands Antilles, Barbados, and Montserrat and Antigua, and so on, which take the Netherlands Antilles and Barbados as examples.

Netherlands Antilles is one of the most important international tax havens. The islands include the collection of a variety of taxes, like the personal income tax, corporate income tax, property tax, real estate tax, inheritance tax, gift tax, and turnover tax and, at the same time, the practice of domiciliary jurisdiction and territorial jurisdiction. However, for offshore companies whose business activities are overseas, the islands provide tax-free preferential terms and implement the following tax incentives for foreign investors: ff the nonresident shareholders hold more than 25 percent of corporate stock, the tax of the dividend and capital gains tax will not be collected; if the company is established in accordance with the relevant provisions of the tax law, the tax of the nonresident shareholders can be avoided; nonresident taxpayers are exempt from inheritance tax and gift tax; withholding income tax of the dividends and interest paid by the resident company for the nonresidents can be avoided; the customs in company free zone of Curacao and Aruba can be avoided; and only 2 percent profit tax will be paid for the income of the company exporting.

Barbados implements a low tax or tax-free system for an offshore company, and there is no capital gains tax or foreign exchange control in this area. Marginal tax rate of current companies is up to 40 percent, but for the international business companies and offshore financial companies, only 0 percent to 2.5 percent income tax is needed. For foreign sales companies and tax exemption insurance companies, the income tax, withholding tax, and property transfer tax are exempted, and no tax returns and financial disclosure are needed. By the end of 2000, there were more than 8,000 international businesses, marketing, insurance companies, and offshore banks registered in Barbados. In the offshore financial business, nearly $70 million fiscal revenue will be gained annually.

"Low tax rate applied to income tax and general property" model

The so-called low tax rate applied to income tax and general property model means that although the income tax and general property tax are collected, the relevant tax rate is lower, and the tax burden is lighter. The countries and regions belonging to this type are mainly distributed in Alberta Alderney, Andorra, Ann Guerra, Bahrain, the British Isle of Man, Kampen, Cyprus, Gibraltar, Guernsey, Israel, Jamaica, Jersey, Lebanon, Liberia, Ethiopia, Liechtenstein, St. Helena, St. Vincent, Sark, Switzerland (except for some states and municipalities), Tonga, Argentina, Costa Rica, Venezuela, Haiti, Panama, Malaysia, and so on, among which Liechtenstein and Cyprus are typical.

Liechtenstein is a miniature hill country situated between Austria and Switzerland where the tax system is simple and the tax rate is low. All residents and nonresidents are obliged to pay personal income tax and corporate tax, but the object of corporate income tax is the net income of the company with the implementation of a progressive tax rate of 7.5 percent to 15 percent; 4 percent withholding tax is levied on the stock dividend. Inheritance tax is levied based on the real value of the heritage, and if the decedent's heirs are relatives, up to 5 percent progressive rate is applied. If not, the maximum tax rate will be as high as 27 percent.

Indirect tax as the main body is implemented as a simple tax structure in Cyprus. Corporate income tax is levied based on the net income of the resident company and the local branch of the foreign companies, and the related tax rate is 20 percent to 25 percent. The tax of the companies established in Cyprus is levied according to their income. The tax of the franchise fees gained by nonresidents of Cyprus is levied at 10 percent; interest is levied according to the company tax rate and, under certain circumstances, the tax may be exempted. The bonus income of the shareholders is levied individually, and this tax can be offset only against tax in advance. Nonresidents may apply for a refund of its entire pre-tax. Shareholder dividends of overseas companies are exempted from taxes: 0 percent to 30 percent of excess progressive tax rate is implemented at a personal income tax rate. For the handling of real estate or company stock with real estate by companies or individuals, a 20 percent capital gains tax will be imposed. The tax liability of real estate transactions will be calculated at a tax rate of 5.%–8% of its selling price or market price.

"Tax preference for specific industry or business pattern" model

The so-called tax preference for specific industry or business pattern model is a new model formed gradually in recent years. The system originally was strongly opposed to some developed countries implementing a tax-free system. Out of the consideration for attracting foreign investment, a number of flexible tax measures were developed and, for certain industries or specific operations, special tax incentives are provided, such as specific tax incentives provided by Luxembourg for holding companies, the Netherlands for a real estate investment company, Britain for the international financial sector, Greece for maritime industry and manufacturing, and Wyoming and Delaware for limited liability companies, which not only enable the foreign enterprises and individuals coming to invest directly because of low tax burden, but also help to reach the goal of evading the tax burden of certain countries. So such an area is regarded by related countries, especially the developing countries, as an international tax haven. Luxembourg and the United Kingdom are examples.

Luxembourg is the world's seventh-largest financial center as well as one of the most important European fund-raising markets and capital returning financing markets with a sound tax system where the perfection of rate varieties and the height of the tax rate is better than that of the other Western European countries. Low-tax or tax-free systems are implemented by Luxembourg for other holding companies of different varieties. Besides, there is no central bank or deposit reserve system here, and strict bank secrecy system is implemented. All of the factors mentioned above make it a famous tax haven for holding companies and there are at least 7,000 holding companies active currently in Luxembourg.

Britain has become an important international tax haven due to a series of tax incentives it provides for the International Finance Corporation. The tax law sets that any foreigner owning an account provided by U.K. financial institutions and involving the trade activities with British companies can enjoy the exemption of capital gains tax. The corporate income tax rate applicable in Britain is relatively low among all the countries in the EU and if the annual revenue of IFC is below 30 million pounds, the rate applied is only 23 percent. For nonresident International Finance Corporation, tax is levied only on income from abroad. Meanwhile, a company registered in the United Kingdom can also use bilateral tax treaty signed between the United Kingdom and other countries to conduct tax avoidance activities. A company that chooses a country that has a bilateral tax treaty with the United Kingdom as its management and operation base can enjoy tax exemption policy legally. United Kingdom implemented preferential tax laws to new Companies IFC Headquarters Company in 1994, which set that companies of which the headquarters is in United Kingdom and 80 percent of revenue has come from abroad can enjoy tax exemption on profits back to the United Kingdom from abroad. And the company did not need to pay taxes even if this part of the fund was reallocated after the withdrawal. The measure became an effective tool for the British government to promote the return of capital gains to foreign shareholders, and a large number of billionaires living in London currently are the beneficiary of the measure (Table A1.1)

Table A1.1 Characteristics of partial offshore financial centers

Area	Population (2010)	The main features
Cayman	56,000	The world's top hedge fund domicile, residence of many large banks
Mauritius	1,299,000	Neighboring India. Less pressure compared with offshore financial centers in Europe
Jersey	93,000	Close to London. Paradise of offshore trusts. No income tax and capital gains tax
Luxembourg	507,000	Firmly resist the EU transparency requirements. The world's second largest mutual fund market after U.S.
Switzerland	7,664,000	Tax evasion is legal in Switzerland. The world's third-largest private wealth management center
Singapore	5,086,000	Regional centers. Connecting link to western offshore financial centers

Source: Based on data compilation by a British economist

Table A1.2 Tax policy comparison of different offshore financial centers

	All-in-one inside and outside	Separated inside and outside	Penetrating inside and outside	Tax havens		
	London	Hong Kong	New York	Singapore	Cayman Islands	British Virgin Islands
Corporate income tax	Small low-profit enterprise: 20% General enterprises: 23% Petroleum enterprises 19%/30%	Individual: 15% Companies and other legal persons/groups: 16.5%	Small low-profit enterprises: 8% General enterprises: 23%	17%	NA	15%
Personal income tax	Exemption amount: 9,440 GBP Progressive tax rate: 20%–45%	Standard rate: 15% Progressive tax rate: 2%–17%	Progressive tax rate: 10%–39.6%	Exemption amount: 20,000 USD Progressive tax rate: 2%–20%	NA	Exemption amount: 10,000 USD Ordinary enterprises: 14% Encouraged investment areas: 0%
Business tax	NA	NA	3.5%–9%	NA	NA	NA
VAT	Zero tax rate Preferential tax rate: 5% Standard rate: 20%	NA	NA	NA	NA	NA
Consumption tax	Tobacco, alcohol, lottery, petroleum products	NA	New York: 4% Local tax: up to 8.75%	7% Export goods and services: 0%	NA	NA
Stamp Duty	Stocks, real estate transactions Commercial property: 1%–4% Residential property: 1%–15%	Quota: 3–100 HKD Fixed rate: 0.1%–3.75%	NA	Real estate transfer and lease, acquisition, real estate mortgage and stock	Real estate transactions: 7.5%–9% Guarantee: 1%–1.5%	Exemption for international offshore companies
Tariff	Up to 30%	NA	Companies which set up factories in the free trade area may not need to pay any import and export duties	NA	20%	5%–20%
Registration fee	NA	NA	NA	NA	NA	350–1,100 USD

Appendix II

Chronicle of events of RMB internationalization

Date	Events	Details
January 25, 2013	The launch of an agreement on RMB clearing business between the PBC and the Taipei Branch of Bank of China	On January 25, the PBC and the Taipei Branch of Bank of China signed an agreement on RMB clearing business. According to the clearing agreement, financial institutions on both sides of the Taiwan Straits could settle cross-border RMB transactions for their clients via an agent bank or the RMB clearing bank.
February 6, 2013	The launch of the cross-strait currency settlement mechanism.	The cross-strait currency settlement mechanism got under way. Forty-six banks in Taiwan began offering RMB-denominated deposits, loans, remittances, and wealth management business. With such great demand for RMB funds, offshore RMB business in Taiwan was growing faster than in Hong Kong.
February 8, 2013	The PBC authorized ICBC Singapore Branch as the clearing bank for RMB business in Singapore.	On February 8, in accordance with the arrangements for strengthening bilateral cooperation in financial services between the PBC and the Monetary Authority of Singapore, after a comprehensive review, the PBC authorized the Industrial and Commercial Bank of China (ICBC) Singapore Branch to act as the clearing bank for RMB business in Singapore.
March 7, 2013	The PBC renewed the bilateral local currency swap agreement with the Monetary Authority of Singapore and increased the size of the swap.	On March 7, the PBC renewed the bilateral local currency swap agreement with the Monetary Authority of Singapore. The size of the swap facility was doubled from 150 billion yuan, or SGD 30 billion, to 300 billion yuan, or SGD 60 billion. The agreement will remain in effect for 3 years and can be extended by mutual consent.

Date	Events	Details
March 13, 2013	The PBC allowed QFIIs for access to the interbank bond market.	On March 13, the PBC issued the *Notice on Issues Related to Investments in the Interbank Bond Market by Qualified Foreign Institutional Investors* (PBC Document [2013] No. 69), allowing QFIIs to apply to the PBC for access to the interbank bond market.
March, 2013	Bolivia's central bank announced an increase in the number of RMB purchases.	Bolivia's central bank announced an increase in the number of RMB purchases, having achieved the goals of international reserves diversification and hedging against inflation.
March 26, 2013	The launch of a bilateral local currency swap agreement between the PBC and the BCB.	On March 26, the PBC signed a bilateral local currency swap agreement with the Banco Central Do Brasil (BCB). The size of the swap facility is 190 billion yuan, or 60 billion real. The agreement would be valid for 3 years and could be extended by mutual consent.
March 26, 2013	The PBC and South African Reserve Bank signed an agreement for latter's investing.	On March 26, the PBC and South African Reserve Bank signed an agreement for the latter to invest in China's interbank bond market via the PBC.
March, 2013	QFII and RQFII were permitted to enter domestic interbank bond market transactions.	QFII and RQFII were permitted to enter domestic interbank bond market transactions.
April 9, 2013	The improvement of trading mode between RMB and the Australian dollar.	On April 9, 2013, with the authorization of the PBC, the China Foreign Exchange Trade System (CFETS) announced it would improve the trading mode between RMB and the Australian dollar ($A) and launched direct trading between the two currencies on the interbank foreign exchange market. This was an important step in strengthening bilateral economic and trade connections between China and Australia. Development of direct trading between RMB and $A would contribute to the formation of direct exchange rate between the two currencies. This would help to

Date	Events	Details
		lower currency conversion cost for economic entities, facilitate the use of RMB and Australian dollars in bilateral trade and investment, and promote the financial cooperation and enhance economic and financial ties between the two countries.
April 24, 2013	Australia to shift 5 percent of foreign reserves to China.	The Reserve Bank of Australia revealed that they would hold around 5 percent of Australia's foreign currency assets in China, bringing RMB into their foreign reserves.
April 25, 2013	The PBC issued the *Notice on Issues Concerning Pilot Securities Investment Program.*	On April 25, the PBC issued the *Notice on Issues Concerning Pilot Securities Investment Program by RMB Qualified Foreign Institutional Investors on the Domestic Market* (PBC Document [2013] No.105), specifying details on the opening of deposit accounts for RQFII.
May 5, 2013	The SAFE issued a document to strengthen the administration of Foreign Capital Inflows.	On May 5, to support compliant enterprises to carry out normal business activities and to prevent BOP risks, the SAFE issued the *Notice of the State Administration of Foreign Exchange on Strengthening Administration of Foreign Capital Inflows* (SAFE Document [2013] No.20) in order to strengthen administration of the comprehensive position of banking institutions in terms of the purchase and surrender of foreign exchange, category management of foreign exchange receipts and payments of import and export firms and foreign exchange inspections.
May, 2013	RMB deposits in Hong Kong rose to 698.5 billion yuan.	RMB deposits in Hong Kong rose to 698.5 billion yuan ($113.60 billion) in May, 3.1 percent up from the month before. Cross-border trade settled in RMB increased to 318.1 billion yuan.
May, 2013	Standard Chartered Global index broke the 1,000 yuan mark.	Standard Chartered Bank announced the latest Standard Chartered Yuan World Index, 5 parts of the index rose to a new peak at 1002, breaking the 1000.

Date	Events	Details
		Rapid growth of international payments in HKD and RMB-related foreign exchange transactions in London was the main driving force behind the rise.
June 22, 2013	The PBC signed a bilateral local currency swap agreement with the Bank of England.	On June 22, the PBC signed a bilateral local currency swap agreement with the Bank of England. The size of the swap facility was 200 billion yuan, or 20 billion pounds. The agreement would remain effective for 3 years and could be extended with mutual consent. The establishment of a bilateral local currency swap arrangement between the PBC and the Bank of England would provide liquidity support for the development of the London RMB market, promote the use of RMB in overseas markets, and facilitate bilateral trade and investment. The signing of the bilateral local currency swap agreement marked the new progress in the monetary and financial cooperation between the PBC and the Bank of England.
June 29, 2013	ICBC's RMB clearing bank in Singapore liquidation amounted to over 60 billion yuan.	ICBC's RMB clearing bank in Singapore liquidation amounted to over 60 billion yuan.
June 2013	SAFE approved three institutional investors.	China's SAFE approved three institutional investors in June: ICBC (Asia) Investment Management Limited; Hang Seng Investment Management Limited; and Pacific Asset Management (Hong Kong) Limited. RQFII Institutions showed that the Commission had approved eight qualified institutions during the first half of 2013.
June 5, 2013	Deutsche Bank completes 1st RMB bond issuance.	Deutsche Bank had completed its first renminbi (RMB) bond issuance in Taiwan in a deal worth 1.1 billion yuan. The bond was listed on the Gre Tai exchange in Taiwan, which meant that Taiwanese retail investors were able to directly invest in it.

Date	Events	Details
June 2013	Luxembourg became the second largest offshore RMB market.	The number of RMB bonds issued in Luxembourg during first half of 2013 surpassed that in Hong Kong and London, becoming the second largest offshore RMB market after London.
July 1, 2013	BOC Taipei Branch had made total payments of 240 billion yuan.	By late June 2013, BOC Taipei Branch had opened RMB clearing accounts for sixty-four participating banks; had handled 36,000 RMB settlement and clearing transactions, with total receipts and payments of 240 billion yuan; and had handled over 1,000 RMB purchase and sales transactions, with a total amount of more than 10 billion yuan.
July 8, 2013	Shanghai FTA became a testing ground for the internationalization of RMB.	Shanghai Free Trade Area launched opening policies on five areas including finance, trade, and shipping, especially innovations on management, tax, regulation, and other aspects. People were expecting innovations and the ability to participate in internationalization through breakthroughs in investment system, adding TPP and TTIP into our tax system.
July 9, 2013	Deregulation of RMB cross-border use.	On July 9, the PBC issued the *Notice on Simplifying the Procedures for Cross-border RMB Business and Improving Relevant Policies* (PBC Document [2013] No.168), which simplified cross-border RMB business procedures under the current account, relaxed regulations on the maturity and quota of account financing, and standardized overseas RMB loan and guaranteed businesses by domestic non-financial institutions, and so forth.
July 10, 2013	Banks in Singapore would be able to obtain RMB directly from China's domestic RMB market.	Singapore Deputy Prime Minister and Finance Minister Tharman Shanmugaratnam recently revealed that all participating banks and commercial banks in Singapore would be able to obtain RMB directly from China's domestic RMB market since July 9.

Date	Events	Details
July 10, 2013	Dongxing test area was approved to conduct personal cross-border trade RMB settlements.	Central Branch of People's Bank of China in Nanning issued *managements on personal cross-border trade RMB settlements in Guangxi*, which was limited to the implementation of Dongxing test area, making Dongxing test area the second pilot area after Yiwu conducting personal cross-border trade RMB settlements.
July 11, 2013	Standard Chartered Hong Kong signed cross-border bilateral RMB loan agreement with Shenzhen International.	Shenzhen International Holdings Ltd and Standard Chartered Bank (Hong Kong) Ltd ("Standard Chartered Hong Kong") jointly announced the signing of a 1-year RMB100 million Qianhai cross-border bilateral renminbi loan agreement, showing that cross-border loans would continue to increase.
July 12, 2013	Bank of China White Paper: the internationalization of RMB-denominated function needed to be strengthened.	Bank of China issued the 2013 annual cross-border RMB business white papers, summarizing cross-border RMB businesses during the last 4 years, providing insights and understandings of internationalization of RMB and showing two functions need to be strengthened: RMB as an international measurement of value and the use of offshore renminbi circulation.
July 12, 2013	CSRC claimed that RQFII pilot program would be expanded to London and Singapore.	The spokesman for the China Securities Regulatory Commission (CSRC) told reporters that the Renminbi Qualified Foreign Institutional Investor (RQFII) pilot program would be expanded to London, Singapore, and other unnamed locations. Taiwan-invested financial institutions were permitted to invest in mainland's capital markets via RQFIIs. Regarding financial institutions from the Taiwan region, Singapore and London participating in RQFII pilot, relevant existing rules and regulations on Hong Kong-based financial institutions participating in RQFII pilot would be adopted.

Date	Events	Details
July 25, 2013	HKMA introduced new measures to enhance the RMB liquidity.	To enhance the liquidity of RMB business in Hong Kong, the Hong Kong Monetary Authority ("HKMA") introduced two optimization measures RMB current funding arrangements:
		1 HKMA announced that the central bank would use the signed currency swap agreement to provide next day settlement (T +1) of a day's liquidity. 2 HKMA claimed that it would provide same-day settlement (T +0) overnight funds to provide RMB funds to assist the bank to meet liquidity needs that day. Due to intra-day settlement funds overnight using the HKMA's own offshore Renminbi funds is expected to provide same-day settlement funds to total no more than 100 billion yuan. 3 The new measures can enhance participation in RMB business in Hong Kong–authorized institutions liquidity management, which would contribute to Hong Kong as an offshore RMB business center for further development.
August 1, 2013	Belarus announced to hold renminbi-denominated assets in their foreign exchange reserve portfolios.	Belarus announced to hold renminbi-denominated assets in their foreign exchange reserve portfolios.
August 9, 2013	Citi China became the first international bank to launch a paperless processing solution for RMB cross-border settlement.	Citibank (China) Co., Ltd. ("Citi China") announced that it would be the first international bank to launch a paperless processing solution for RMB cross-border settlement. Citi's solution followed a series of measures aiming to simplify the cross-border RMB settlement process announced by the PBOC on July 10, 2013. By connecting Citi's electronic banking solution to the Balance of Payment Declaration (BOP) system operated by the State Administration of Foreign Exchange (SAFE), transactions could be completed entirely electronically, resulting in a reduction of manual

Date	Events	Details
		error, processing cost, and risk. Clients benefited from significant efficiency gains as documents associated with a cross-border RMB transaction.
August, 2013	Shanghai unveiled its first RQFLP domestic investment business.	Shanghai unveiled its first RQFLP (RMB Qualified Foreign Limited Partner) domestic investment business. RQFLP provided a new channel for offshore RMB and will greatly broaden oversea funds, especially those investing in mainland China.
September 3, 2013	Coca-Cola completed cross-border lending in yuan.	Coca-Cola Beverages (Shanghai) Ltd. had completed a 250 million yuan ($40.85 million) inter-company loan to London-based Atlantic Industries, a Coca-Cola subsidiary, with the help of Citibank China.
September 4, 2013	RMB exchange rate against the Indonesian rupiah cash services started.	The start of the RMB exchange rate against the Indonesian rupiah cash services conducive to promoting economic and trade cooperation between China and ASEAN countries to further deepen, and it helped to enhance the renminbi in Asia, especially the influence of the ASEAN region, and promoted the process of internationalization of the RMB.
September 6, 2013	RMB became one of the top 10 traded currencies.	The survey by the Bank for International Settlements showed the share of renminbi rising to No. 9 from No. 17 on the list, which was the first time in history for renminbi to become a member of the world's most important currencies.
September 6, 2013	HSBC became the first mainland Chinese to carry out cross-border RMB business of foreign banks bidirectional loans.	HSBC China announced that it had assisted a Taiwan-funded enterprise located in Kunshan City, Jiangsu Province, to carry out two-way cross-border renminbi loans business, becoming the first mainland Chinese to carry out this business with foreign banks.

Date	Events	Details
September 9, 2013	The PBC signed a bilateral local currency swap agreement with Hungarian National Bank.	On September 9, the PBC signed a bilateral local currency swap agreement with the Magyar Nemzeti Bank (Hungarian National Bank). The size of the swap facility was 10 billion yuan or 375 billion ISK. The agreement would be valid for 3 years and could be extended upon mutual consent.
September 11, 2013	The PBC and the Central Bank of Iceland renewed their local currency swap agreement.	On September 11, the PBC and the Central Bank of Iceland renewed their local currency swap agreement. The size of the new swap facility was 3.5 billion yuan or 66 billion ISK. The agreement would be valid for 3 years and could be extended upon mutual consent.
September 12, 2013	The PBC signed a bilateral local currency agreement with the Bank of Albania.	On September 12, the PBC signed a bilateral local currency agreement with the Bank of Albania. The size of the swap facility was 2 billion yuan or 35.8 billion lek. The agreement would be valid for 3 years and could be extended upon mutual consent.
September 17, 2013	Yiwu financial reform will highlight cross-border RMB settlement, foreign exchange management.	Zhejiang Yiwu international trade comprehensive reform of the financial special programs on the seventeenth officially announced that Yiwu special finance reform was officially launched. Yiwu financial reform highlighted cross-border RMB settlement, foreign exchange management, and trade finance innovation. Yiwu was expected to become a prior test area for the internationalization of RMB.
September 22, 2013	The world's first CRI released by BOC	On September 22, BOC released Cross-border RMB Index (CRI) to the world, which followed the rate of use of the RMB in the complete capital cycle from cross-border outflow, overseas flow to cross-border backflow, reflecting the activity level of RMB use in cross-border and overseas trade. Consisting of outflow, flow, and backflow, the index followed up capital flow via current accounts, flow via capital accounts, overseas flow, and so on.

Date	Events	Details
September 23, 2013	The PBC issued the *Notice on Issues Concerning the RMB Settlement Business of Investments in Domestic Financial Institutions by Overseas Investors.*	On September 23, the PBC issued the *Notice on Issues Concerning the RMB Settlement Business of Investments in Domestic Financial Institutions by Overseas Investors* (PBC Document [2013] No.225) to standardize the use of the RMB settlement business by overseas investors for their investments in the establishment, merger and acquisition, and holding of equity in financial institutions in China.
September 27, 2013	The State Council has approved and promulgated the *Framework Plan for the China (Shanghai) Pilot Free Trade Zone (the Framework Plan).*	The State Council approved and promulgated the *Framework Plan for the China (Shanghai) Pilot Free Trade Zone (the Framework Plan),* which not only specified a list of financial sectors in banking, insurance, finance leases, and other departments but also provided a clear direction for financial reform from aspects of openness and innovation. The objectives of setting up FTZ include liberalization of the RMB capital accounts, implementation of a taxation policy which promoted investment, and development of offshore financial business. One of the highlights of *the Framework Plan* was the reform of a foreign exchange management system, to explore and establish an international foreign exchange management system that would be suitable for the free trade zone, which facilitated trading and investment and helped to promote the openness of RMB capital account.
October 1, 2013	The PBC and Bank Indonesia renewed their local currency swap agreement.	On October 1, the PBC and Bank Indonesia renewed their local currency swap agreement. The size of the swap facility was 100 billion yuan or IDR175 trillion. The agreement would remain in effect for 3 years and could be extended upon mutual consent.
October, 2013	The monetary authorities of Taiwan held renminbi-denominated assets in their foreign exchange reserve portfolios for the first time.	The monetary authorities of Taiwan held renminbi-denominated assets in their foreign exchange reserve portfolios for the first time.

Date	Events	Details
October 8, 2013	The PBC and the ECB signed a bilateral local currency swap agreement.	On October 8, the PBC and the ECB signed a bilateral local currency swap agreement. The swap line had a maximum size of 350 billion yuan or 45 billion euro. The joined hands between RMB and the world's second-largest international currency, euro, not only marked another big step in RMB internationalization but also showed that the position of RMB in the international financial sector was rapidly increasing.
October 11, 2013	FTA will build crude oil futures platform, possible for RMB-denomination.	The world's first futures in road-paving material (bitumen) generated strong investor interest after launching on the Shanghai Futures Exchange on October 9. With the accelerated launch of domestic crude oil futures, the Shanghai Free Trade Zone provided a good opportunity for it.
October 15, 2013	UK got an initial quota of 80 billion yuan RQFII.	During a visit to China, UK chancellor George Osborne secured an agreement to extend Hong Kong's renminbi-qualified foreign institutional investor (RQFII) scheme to the UK, with an initial quota of 80 billion yuan.
October 24, 2013	RMB becomes the second real-time clearing currency in the Philippine market foreign currency.	Chinese Economic and Commercial Counselor Embassy in the Philippines at the twenty-third news release, RMB fund transfer system (RMB Transfer Service, referred to as RTS) marked the start of the renminbi as the Philippine market following the U.S. dollar after the second real-time settlement of foreign currency, would finance the Philippine institutions, traders, and investors to provide high efficiency and low cost of RMB settlement meaning while effectively avoiding exchange rate risk and foreign exchange financing for higher returns. Bank of China's next phase would further develop Philippine domestic RMB market, the introduction of more RMB investment products; the future would also provide cross-border RMB clearing services, to

Date	Events	Details
		further reduce costs and improve the efficiency of cross-border RMB trade payments.
October 27, 2013	The "383 Plan": to realize the internationalization of RMB within a decade	The government-affiliated think tank released the "383 Plan," claiming that it would take less than a decade to make renminbi a major international settlement, investment denomination currency, and international reserve currency in some markets, thus forcing reforms in foreign exchange market, cross-border investments, bond markets, comprehensive managements of domestic and foreign currency in financial institutions, and some other fields.
November 3, 2013	Iranian oil trades with China can be settled in renminbi.	Iranian parliamentary Speaker Ali Larijani announced that their oil trades with China could be settled in renminbi.
November 5, 2013	The Province of British Columbia, Canada, became the first foreign government to issue bonds into CNH market.	The Province of British Columbia, Canada, became the first foreign government to issue bonds into the Chinese renminbi (CNH) market, making RMB one of the Canadian government's financing vehicles.
November 12, 2013	South Africa's Reserve Bank announced to invest $1.5 billion in purchasing Chinese bonds.	South Africa's Reserve Bank announced that it was investing $1.5 billion to purchase Chinese bonds, bringing its reserve assets held in RMB up to 3 percent of the total to reduce systemic risk.
November 12, 2013	SEC authorized four unlisted Renminbi Qualified Foreign Institutional Investor (RQFII) funds.	SEC authorized four unlisted RQFII funds—JF Asset Management Limited; Mirae Asset Global Investments (Hong Kong) Limited; Shanghai International Asset Management (HK) Co. Ltd.; and China Everbright Assets Management Limited— allowing the RMB funds raised overseas to invest in domestic capital market. There were thirty-nine authorized RQFII unlisted funds until the end of December.

Date	Events	Details
November 18, 2013	The openness of capital promoting reforms, Shanghai Free-Trade Zone Capital Open Promoting reform, free trade zone to leading the charge.	The *Decision of the CCCPC on Some Major Issues Concerning Comprehensively Deepening the Reform* issued on the 15th claimed to build a new open economic system, including relaxing control over investment access, speeding up the construction of free trade zones, and further opening up inland and border areas. Financial reforms would be an important pioneer in foreign investments in China and RMB overseas investments.
November 21, 2013	Shanghai Futures Exchange prepared to launch crude oil futures that year, which might be denominated in RMB.	Shanghai Futures Exchange prepared to launch crude oil futures that year, and the underlying assets of such "Chinese version" of crude oil futures was sour crude oil, which might be denominated in RMB. The basic idea of crude oil futures was to provide an international platform, net trading, and bonded delivery for international investors to freely enter the platform for transactions; the relevant ministries considered some policies related to foreign exchanges, and crude oil futures could be listed after getting approvals.
November 22, 2013	LME planned to launch renminbi-denominated contracts,	LME planned to launch in Asia for iron ore and thermal coal contracts. Futures based on RMB-denominated non-ferrous metals exchanged contracts as the inevitable result, not only to promote renminbi-denominated financial derivatives development but (even more important to the central government) how to value the process of RMB internationalization services gaining significance.
November, 2013	Singapore launched the first RMB denominated bonds .	British banks HSBC and Standard Chartered in May had separate sales placing a total 1.5 billion yuan ($245 million) of bonds. Later in November, ICBC Singapore Branch issued a 2-year 2 billion yuan Lion City debt.

Date	Events	Details
December 2, 2013	ABC and StanChart jointly offer RMB Clearing Business in the UK.	Agricultural Bank of China (ABC) and Standard Chartered Bank offered renminbi (RMB) clearing services in the United Kingdom (UK). Moreover, both parties continued to expand their cooperation in terms of the SME business and the support to overseas expansion of Chinese enterprises.
December 3, 2013	Renminbi outperforms euro, becomes second-most popular trade finance currency	Renminbi replaces the euro to become the second most widely used currency in global trade after that of the United States in 2013, according to the SWIFT network responsible for international financial transactions. The currency has the largest share of letters of credit and collections. China, Hong Kong, Singapore, Germany, and Australia were the top users of renminbi in trade finance.
December 3, 2013	China clarifies issues regarding RMB Cross-Border Direct Investment.	The Ministry of Commerce released the *Announcement on Issues Regarding the RMB Cross-Border Direct Investment* (Announcement [2013] No.87, hereinafter referred to as *Announcement*), which facilitated cross-border RMB direct investments and improved relevant regulations. The *Announcement* stated that foreign investors applying to exchange the foreign currency for capital contribution into RMB do not have to go through the approval procedures for modification of contracts and articles of associates with relevant authorities.
December 5, 2013	Bank of China (Hong Kong) partners with UnionPay International to pioneer the RMB Settlement Service of Union Pay Card for Hong Kong Merchants.	Bank of China (Hong Kong; "BOCHK") and UnionPay International jointly announced to pioneer the RMB settlement service of UnionPay Card for merchants in Hong Kong, which was previously settled with HKD.

Date	Events	Details
December 5, 2013	China (Shanghai) FTA first cross-border renminbi business two-way cash pool Whispering BOC	On December 5, the Bank of China successfully benefit Kerry (Shanghai) International Trade Co. Syria to do two-way cross-border renminbi business cash pool, which is China's (Shanghai) Free Trade Zone first cross-border RMB test. Two-way cash pool operations but also China (Shanghai) FTA financial reform policies were introduced after the first single banking.
December 9, 2013	NCD in interbank market set up the wholesale market of RMB international financing activities.	PBOC published guidelines to allow banks to issue negotiable certificate of deposits (NCD) in interbank market, setting up the wholesale market of RMB international financing activities.
December 17, 2013	IFC's Act to Boost RMB-denominated Trade Finance in Emerging Markets.	IFC, a member of the World Bank Group, and Standard Chartered Bank have signed a landmark risk-sharing facility, which will increase the amount of RMB-denominated trade finance available to Chinese banks as well as corporates and businesses in China and across Asia and other emerging markets involved in imports and exports to China. This marks IFC's first venture into RMB-denominated cross-border trade finance, building on the success of IFC's award-winning global trade programs.

Index

383 Plan 226

Abe, S. 14, 28, 61, 195
Africa 4, 58, 93, 126, 150–1, 155–7, 197
agency banks 183–4, 198–9
Agricultural Bank of China (ABC) 24, 82, 143, 161, 178, 228
Albania 223
allocated reserves 47, 50
Americas 4, 170–1
analytic hierarchy process 166–8, 171
Angola 157
Annual Report on Exchange Arrangements and Exchange Restrictions (AREAER) 66
Antigua 169, 210
ANZ Bank 30, 60
Apple 92
appreciation 15, 46, 61–2, 64, 73, 75–6, 101
arbitrage 15, 101, 115–16, 119–20, 187, 199
Argentina 92, 209
Aruba 211
Asia 15, 88, 92, 195–6
Asia-Pacific 4, 16, 170
Asian financial crisis 72, 80, 178, 190
Asian Tigers 115
asphalt futures 43
Asset Management 73, 142
asset-liability structures 179
Association of Southeast Asian Nations (ASEAN) 17, 24, 139
asymmetric information 9, 126
Australia 2, 4, 133, 203; chronology 216–17; current situation 51, 53–5, 57, 60–1; future of offshore market 143, 159; internationalization index 15–16, 26; public opinion 86, 93

backflow mechanism 96–9, 140; challenges 177, 198; future 142, 157, 160, 163–4
Bahamas 208–9
Bahrain 171
baht 186
bait problem 151–4
Baja Maharashtra 208
balance of payments 9, 32–4, 71, 77, 116
Baltic Exchange 147
Bangkok International Banking Facilities 185–6
Bank of China (BOC) 17, 21, 58, 60, 149; Africa 155–6; chronology 215, 219–20, 229; competitiveness 161–2; HK offshore market 137, 139, 143, 173; public opinion 72, 96, 100–1
Bank of Communications (BOCOM) 21, 48–50, 73–5, 161, 205–6; Hong Kong 140–1, 143, 173
Bank of East Asia 173
Bank of England (BOE) 30, 51, 111, 147, 150, 218
Bank for International Settlements (BIS) 9, 11, 14, 39, 79, 128
Bank of Japan 56–7, 189
Bank of Shanghai Cooperation Organization Initiative 72
banks 5, 49–50, 139, 142–3, 172; African 155–6; clearing and settlement 183–4; competitiveness 160–3; economists' views 81, 83; internationalization index 17–18, 20, 30; offshore 72–3, 109–11, 178–81, 192; public opinion 90, 92–3
Barbados 210–11
Basel Committee on Banking Supervision 81, 192
Beijing 49

Belarus 2, 26, 221
Belize 210
Bermuda 169, 208–9
bilateral cooperation 16, *see also* currency swaps
bilateral relations 169–70
Bolivia 2, 24, 50, 209, 216
Bombay Sensitive Index 38
bonds 2, 117, 173–5, 177; African forex reserves 157; comparison of major currencies 27–8; current situation 35–7, 49–50, 67; economists' views 76, 78; futures 43–4; internationalization index 9–10, 20, 23–6; London 30, 148–9; offshore 73, 138–41, 146; public opinion 97, 100, 102–3
Bosera Asset Management 96
Brazil 51, 83, 92, 119, 143, 209, 216, *see also* BRICs
Brazil Bank 30
Brent crude futures 43
Bretton Woods 77
BRICs 18, 38, 80
Britain *see* UK
British Columbia 37, 226
Brunei 209
bubbles 76, 119–20

CAC40 38
Canada 2, 37, 51, 53–4, 86, 88, 226
Canary Wharf 147
Cao Yuanzheng 71–2
capital, cost of 97, 102, 112–13
capital absorption 158
capital account 3, 9, 13–14, 182, 196–7, 201; convertibility/liberalization distinction 71; current situation 34, 66–70; economists' views 73, 75–7, 80, 82; historical implications 117–21, 134; public opinion 103–4, 107
capital adequacy ratio 161
capital export 154
capital flows 124–5
capital markets 45, 71
capitalism 81
Caribbean 121, 169
cash 156
Cayman Islands 111, 169, 208, 213
CCB 59, 78
Central Asia 16–18
central banks 50–3, 56–7, 79, 157; bait problem 151–4, *see also* reserve currencies
Central Money Market Units 172

Channel Islands 210
Chenming Group 141
Chicago Board of Trade (CBOT) 78
Chicago Mercantile Exchange 25
China 120 Index 41
China Banking Regulatory Commission (CBRC) 180
China Citic Bank International 143
China Construction Bank 30, 96, 143, 161–2, 173–4
China Development Bank 21, 96, 143, 173
China Financial Futures Exchange 25, 43
China Foreign Exchange Trading System (CFETS) 59, 163, 216
China International Trust and Investment Company 96
China Merchants Bank 96, 143, 161–2, 178
China Securities Regulatory Commission (CSRC) 45–6, 164, 220
China Southern Fund 96
Chinese University of Hong Kong 100
Citigroup 147, 221
clearing 15–16, 19–23, 100, 183–4, 202–3; economists' views 73, 83; historical implications 114, 132, 134
clearing banks 5, 58, 137, 176
Clearing House Interbank Payments System (CHIPS) 184–5, 199, 202
Clearing and Settlement Agreement of RMB business in Hong Kong Banks 139
Clearstream 59
Closer Economic Partnership Arrangement (CEPA) 47, 137, 159
CNH 174–7, 198–9; financial institutions 178–84
Coca-Cola 222
collective investment securities 68
commercial banks 161–2, 183–4, 190
commercial credit 69
commercial paper 105
commodity-pricing 78
comparability 8
competitiveness 75–6, 160–3, 181
Complementary Cooperative Memorandum of RMB Settlement in Cross-border Trade 139
conditional two-side infiltrate 182
confidentiality 110, 122, 199, 203
Confucius Institute 135, 203
consumption 76–7
convertibility 3, 73, 78, 118–19, 190; vs. liberalization 71–2

Cook Islands 210
corporations, multinational 110, 158
cost of capital 97, 102, 112–13
Costa Rica 4, 171, 208–9
country risk 114
CPC Central Committee 13, 82, 227
credit 69; creation 107; international
    19–21
credit information depth index 168
credit markets 46–7
credit ratings 102, 177
Credit Suisse 147
cross-border business 93, 96–9, 139,
    144–5, 158, *see also* offshore
Cross-border RMB Index (CRI) 223
crude oil futures 43, 45, 225, 227
CSI-300 43–4
cultural factors 106, 127, 133, 136, 203–4
Curacao 211
currency: conditions for
    internationalization 6; functions
    8; major currencies 27–8; of price
    77–8, *see also* appreciation; reserve
    currencies; RMB Internationalization
    Index (RII)
*Currency Composition of Official Foreign
    Exchange Reserves* (COFER) 51, 53
currency risk 114, 122–3
currency swaps 50–3, 77, 139, 150, 164;
    chronology 215–16, 218, 223–4;
    internationalization index 26–7, 30
currency wars 57
customer-centered mechanism 48
Cyprus 170, 212

Dah Sing Bank 143
data 11, 128
DAX index 38
Decision on Major Issues Concerning
    Comprehensively Deepening Reforms
    13, 81–2
decision process 166–7
deficits 75–6, 109, 116, 124
deflation 4, 199
Delaware 212
Delphi method 84
demand 12–13
deposits 73, 114, 145, 173; Japanese
    offshore market 188–9; London 147,
    149–50; rates 112
deregulation 111, 219
derivatives 39, 41–3, 45, 68, 117, 173;
    foreign exchange 55; offshore

73; promotion of exchange rate
    liberalization 60–1
Deutsche Bank 24, 218
devaluation 57, 146
development 157
Development Bank of Singapore 164
dim sum bonds (DSB) 100, 102, 140–1,
    175, 177
diplomatic relations 169–70
direct investment 34–5, 69, *see also* foreign
    direct investment (FDI); overseas
    direct investment (ODI)
disclosure index 168
diversification 160
dollar (Australian) 51, 53–5, 60–1, 129,
    216
dollar (Canadian) 51, 53–4, 61; derivatives
    39
dollar (Hong Kong) 14, 61, 154
dollar (US) 3, 14–15, 27, 155–6, 194;
    current situation 36–7, 51; derivatives
    39, 41–2; economists' views 75, 77–9;
    exchange rate 59, 61–2, 64; hegemony
    80; historical implications 122–6;
    offshore 109–10, 114–15, 127–9;
    overseas loans in domestic financial
    institutions 46; public opinion 92–3,
    105
dollarization 81
Dominica 171, 209
Dongguan 139
Dongxin City 18
Dongxing 31, 220
double drive model 1
double surpluses 77
Dow Jones 38
Draghi, M. 51
dual-currency bonds 103
Dubai 43, 83

e-commerce 75
ease of doing business (EODB) 168,
    170–1
East Africa 16
East Asia 72, 88, 92, 196
ECB 51, 57, 197, 225
Economic Cooperation Framework
    Agreement (ECFA) 159
economic growth 12–13, 23, 115, 122–3,
    193
economic reforms *see* reforms
economists' views 77–82, 103; on banks'
    offshore business 72–3; on reserve

currency 73, 75–7; on Shanghai zone
71–2; on strategic thinking 82–3
economy, real vs. virtual 7, 80–1
Ecuador 209
effective exchange rate 62–5
Eighteenth CPC Central Committee 13,
31, 80, 82, 107
empirical research 128–33
endowment theory 154
England 129, 134, *see also* UK
English Media Directory 84
enterprises 48–9
entry and exit 96
Ethiopia 209
euro (EUR) 14, 27–8, 79, 194;
current situation 36–7, 51, 56,
61–2; derivatives 39, 41; historical
implications 122–3, 127–30; overseas
loans in domestic financial institutions
46
Eurobonds 177
Eurodollar 105, 109, 127
Europe 4, 15, 24, 78, 195; current
situation 51, 58; debt crisis 14, 29, 61,
86; future of offshore market 165, 170;
historical implications 111–12, 115,
123–4; public opinion 86–7, 92; stock
markets 38
European Central Bank (ECB) 51, 57,
197, 225
European Union (EU) 27, 29
exchange rate 56–7, 59–65, 134, 146,
153; marketization 60–1, 64, 72, 163;
pricing power 186–7; public sentiment
89, *see also* appreciation
exchange rate channel 73, 76
exchange traded funds (ETFs) 142, 175
experts 103, 105–7
Export-Import Bank of China 173
exports 32, 57, 62; of RMB 116–17;
settled in RMB 15, *see also* trade

familiar effect 133, 203
Faroe Islands 208
FATF 122
Federal Reserve 1, 27, 56, 80–1, 101, 105,
119
finance 9; public sentiment 90, 92–3, *see
also* virtual economy
financial capitalism 81
financial centers 81, 110, 125, 132–6,
164–5, 197–8; location choice model
165–73; taxation comparison 208–14,
see also Hong Kong; London

financial cooperation 17–18, 146; UK
29–30
financial crises 80, *see also* Asian financial
crisis; global financial crisis
financial institutions 83, 96, 99, 139–41,
143, 147, 192; competitiveness 160–3
financial markets 78; development 125–6;
domestic vs. international 25
financial products 101–3, 134
financial reform *see* reform
financial services 48–50, 74
financial settlement and clearing 19–23
first-move advantage 172–3
fiscal policy 76, 105
fish without bait 154
Fitch 100
Five Year Plan, Twelfth 142, 145, 174, 177
fixed-income 78
flexibility 8
flow indicator 9–10
foreign direct investment (FDI) 2, 20,
22–3, 34–5, 71, 194
Foreign Exchange Management Act 190
foreign exchange market 14, 55–7, 79,
128–9; derivatives 39, 41; London 148,
150
foreign exchange reserves *see* reserve
currencies
Forex Sale and Purchase 60
forward curves 177
forward market 55–6, 173; non-
deliverable (NDF) 62, 64–5, 173
franc (Swiss) 39, 51, 133
France 38, 86–7, 165
Frankfurt 2, 4, 15, 58, 163–5
free trade agreements 16, 158–9
free trade zones 5, 13, 19, 21, 104, 160,
194; chronology 219, 227; current
situation 31, 34–5, 43, 45, 47;
economists' views 71–2, 75, 83
FSF 122
FTSE100 38
FTZ 48, 75
fund transfer related accounts 189
futures 25, 41–5, 123, 142, 225, 227

GBP *see* pound sterling
GDP 12, 77, 129, 193
geography 126, 133
Georgia 57
Germany 15–16, 38, 53, 58, 81, 86–7, 165
Germany Institutes 174
global financial crisis 7, 54, 59, 80, 121–2,
180; public sentiment 89–90

Global National Bank 72
globalization 110–11, 121, 158–9
goods trade 32–3
governmental promotion 151–4
Gramegna, P. 165
gravity model 129
Great Britain *see* UK
Greece 212
Greenland 208
Grenada 210
growth *see* economic growth
Guangdong 48, 138–9, 179
Guangdong Development Bank (GDB)
    178
Guangxi 18, 31
Guangzhou 139
guarantee 69
Guatemala 209
Gulf Cooperation Council (GCC) 159
Guosen Securities 96

Haitong International 77
Hang Seng Bank 21, 143
headquarters 158
hedge funds 123
hedging demand 122–3
hegemony 80
hierarchy model 166–7
high-value payment system (HVPS) 183
HKD *see* dollar (Hong Kong)
HKEx 41
Hong Kong 2, 4, 197–8, 202, 209–10; bait
    problem 151–4; challenges 174–9;
    current situation 37, 43, 45, 47–9, 58;
    economists' views 75, 81–3; future
    of offshore market 137–46, 160–1,
    163–4, 170–3; historical implications
    120, 133–4; internationalization index
    14–16, 24; Japanese offshore market
    190; London comparison 147–8;
    public opinion 96–104, 106
Hong Kong Exchanges and Clearing
    Limited 142
Hong Kong Financial Services
    Development Council 143
Hong Kong Monetary Authority
    (HKMA) 100, 117, 137, 139, 143–4,
    173, 221
Hong Kong and Shanghai Banking
    Corporation (HSBC) 24, 30, 100, 143,
    147–8, 154, 163–5, 173, 222
Horgos Cooperation Center 74
hot money 76, 116, 119–20, 190
Huang Zhiling 77–8

Hubei 48
Hui Xian Real Estate Investment Trust
    (REIT) 140
Huiduitong 48
Hungary 51, 223
Huoerguosi 17

Iceland 223
imports 15, 78, 148, *see also* trade
index *see* RMB Internationalization Index
    (RII)
index futures 43–4
India 57, 86, 88, 93, 119, 143, 195, *see also*
    BRICs
Indonesia 17, 222, 224
Industrial and Commercial Bank of
    China (ICBC) 24, 30, 58, 81, 83, 143,
    149, 161, 163, 165, 178, 215, 218
industrial policy 76
inequalities 76–7
infiltration 182
inflation 5, 78, 116, 185, 199
inflation target 56
information asymmetry 9, 126
information cost 135
information disclosure 168
infrastructure 172
insurance 69
integration 115, 158
interbank market 20, 24, 26, 44, 55, 139,
    176
interest rate 57, 104, 112–13, 120, 134,
    146; derivatives 39; futures 25; market
    deepening 72; offshore interference
    with domestic 184–7; parity 115;
    reform 41, 60, 160; spreads 23, 102,
    112–13; swaps 42
international credit 19–21
international currency regions 123
international finance *see* finance
International Finance Corporation (IFC)
    24, 212–13, 229
International Monetary Fund (IMF) 7,
    11, 47, 51, 53, 66, 71, 79–80, 93, 164
International Monetary Institute (IMI) 7,
    96, 100, 205–7
International Petroleum Exchange 43
international trade *see* trade
internationalization of the RMB
    196–7, 201–4; chronicle of events
    215–29; defined 6, *see also* RMB
    Internationalization Index (RII)
investment 35, 99, 164; demand 23, 77, *see
    also* foreign direct investment (FDI);

overseas direct investment (ODI);
   securities investment
iPhone 92
IPO 38–9, 45, 99, 140
Iran 210, 226
Ireland 16
Israel 57

Japan 4, 12, 14, 28, 170–1; current
   situation 37, 54, 56; economists' views
   81–2; historical implications 124–5,
   130, 132, 134; public opinion 92–3
Japanese Offshore Financial Market
   (JOM) 188–90
Jersey 209, 213
Jiangsu 19, 21, 49
Johannesburg 83, 156
Jordan 210
JP Morgan Chase 100, 147
JPY *see* yen
Juncker, J-C. 56

Kazakhstan 17–18, 74
Kenya 57, 157
Kindleberger, C. 124
Konka 47
krona (Swedish) 14, 39
Krugman, P. 124
Kunshan 19, 21, 74
Kuwait 210

Land Bureau 98
language 106, 133–4, 203
Latin America 115
Lebanon 171
legal system 99, 105, 132–3, 168–9, 199,
   203, 209
Lehman Brothers 180
lending relationships 113
letters of credit 15, 147
Li Keqiang 17, 142
Lian Ping 72–3
liberalization 34, 82, 102, 107, 160;
   historical implications 110–11, 118–20;
   vs. convertibility 71
Liberia 209
LIBOR 160
Liechtenstein 211
lion city debt 24
liquidity 51, 113–14, 117, 122, 126, 140;
   challenges 176–7, 179–80; historical
   implications 113–14, 117, 122, 126
liquidity risk 30, 97, 101, 202
localization of currency 72

London 2–4, 180–1, 195, 197–8; current
   situation 43, 45, 51, 58; future of
   offshore market 147–54, 163–4, 172;
   historical implications 110–11, 114,
   125, 132; internationalization index 15,
   24, 29–30; public opinion 86, 89, 106
London Metal Exchange (LME) 78, 147
London Stock Exchange 147, 149
Longyuan Power Group 141
Luxembourg 15, 24, 58–9, 81, 148, 165,
   170, 219; tax preference 212–13

Macao 4, 16, 24, 139, 147, 161, 179, 209
Mainland China 15, 146
Malaysia 4, 62, 106, 209
Malta 170
managed float 59
manufacturing 81
Maritime Silk Road 16–17
market economy 13
marketization 82, 190; of exchange rate
   60–1, 64, 72, 163
Matthew effect 115
Mauritius 4, 156, 171, 213
media 84–93, 99
Memorandum 137
mergers and acquisition 19
Micronesia 208
Middle East 170–1, 191
Ministry of Commerce 22, 35, 98
Monetary Authority of Singapore 165
monetary market funds 68
monetary policy 56–7, 61, 104, 116;
   domestic 4–5, 184–7, 199; economists'
   views 76, 80–1; unconventional 122–3
money laundering 199, 203
money multiplier 187
monopoly 181
Montserrat 210
moral hazard 76
Morgan Stanley 147
Morocco 171
Moscow 83
multinational corporations 110, 158

Nanning 17
Nanyang Commercial Bank 143
National Development Bank 157
National Development and Reform
   Commission 98, 173
Negotiable Certificates of Deposit
   (NCD) 20, 229
Netherlands 170, 212
Netherlands Antilles 110, 210–11

network externality 135, 197
New Caledonia 208
New Hebrides 208
New York 3, 83, 105–6, 114, 125, 132, 198
New York Stock Exchange 43, 78
New Zealand 133
news 84–5, 90
Nicaragua 209
Nigeria 157
Nikkei 38
no fish bait 153–4
nominal exchange rate 61–4
non-deliverable forward (NDF) 62, 64–5, 173
non-trade RMB 176–7
North Africa 170–1, 191
North America 88, 92, *see also* USA, Canada
Norway 159
NRA 48, 50, 74
Nuggets National Development Bank 18
NYMEX 78

Oceania 93
OECD 122
offshore 2–5, 45, 58–9, 194, 196–203; Africa 150–1, 155–7; Chinese-funded banks 72–3; development opportunities 157–9; features/functions 112–15; financial center taxation comparison 208–14; historical implications 127–8, 132–6; Hong Kong 99–103, 137–46; inevitability 109–12; influence 115–16; inner logic 116–23; interaction with onshore 181–2; Japan 188–90; loans 47; location choice model 165–73; London 29–30, 147–54; opportunities/challenges 105–6; public opinion 82–3, 97–9; reform/innovation 159–65; regulation 190–2; RMB internationalization index 13–15, 19–21, 24; role/risk 104–5
offshore RMB *see* CNH
offshore units 178
oil 43, 45, 93, 116, 225–7
Oman 210
one country, two systems 171
onshore markets 181; interaction with offshore 102–3, 188–90
operability 8
operational research 166
options 56, 173
Osbourne, G. 30, 225
OTC derivatives 39, 41

Oversea-Chinese Banking Company 164
overseas direct investment (ODI) 22, 34–5, 153, 158–9, 164

Panama 171, 209
Paraguay 209
Paris 4, 58, 106, 165
payment 198
payment transaction platform 114
PE 22
peer regulation 180
peg 59
People's Bank of China (PBOC) 11, 16, 20–2, 26, 30; bait problem 151–3; challenges 178, 183, 187; current situation 31, 34–5, 47, 50–1, 59–60, 64; future of offshore market 137, 139, 144, 163–4; public opinion 76, 96–8
peso 62
petrodollars 116
Philippines 62, 170–1, 225
pilot projects 19, 21, 31, 83, 139, 194, *see also* free trade zones
Ping An Bank 96, 161–2
Poland 57
policy 76, 97–9, 105, *see also* monetary policy
political factors 126–7
political stability 132, 157–8
pools 151–4
population 129
Port of Dalian 141
pound crisis 109
pound sterling (GBP) 27–8, 79, 194–5; current situation 36–7, 39, 46, 51, 61–2; historical implications 123, 125–6, 129, 133
price discovery 100, 104
pricing 1–2, 9, 78
prisoner's dilemma 71
profitability 180–1
protectionism 57, 109
prudential supervision 180, 191
public debt 76
public opinion 84–93, 195–7, 200–1
public relations 99
Pudong Development Bank 17, 161–2, 178

QDII3 143
QFII 24, 45, 118, 120
Qianhai 19, 21, 47, 93, 96–9, 142–3, 160
Qianhai Bonded Port 96

quantitative easing (QE) 12, 18, 22–3, 27, 51, 56, 61, 80, 119
questionnaire 103

R&D 76
ratings 102, 177
real economy 7, 12–13, 19, 80–1, 102, 124; internationalization 5, 200; relation to offshore 4
real effective exchange rate 62, 64–5
real estate 70
Real Estate Investment Trust (REIT) 140
real-time gross settlement (RTGS) 138, 143, 172, 202
recovery 12, 15, 27–8, 123
refinancing game 190
reflux *see* backflow mechanism
reforms 16, 31, 80, 82, 107, 159–60, 194; exchange rate 59–61
Regional Comprehensive Economic Partnership (RCEP) 17, 159
regional cooperation 16–18
regulation 97–9, 118, 180, 190–2, 199, 203; lax 111–12
remittances 179
Renmin University of China 100, 193, 205–7
Reserve Bank of Australia 26, 61, 143
reserve currencies 2–3, 104–7, 122, 157; comparison 27–8; current situation 47, 50–4; economists' views 73, 75–7, 79; internationalization index 6–7, 10–11, 18, 24, 26–7
reserve requirements 111–12, 114, 184, 186–7, 189
review process 16
Ricardo, D. 154
ringgit 61
risk 104–5, 123
risk management 114
risk premium 160
RMB Internationalization Index (RII) 1–2, 118, 193–5; calculation 11; comparison of major currencies 27–30; compilation principles 7–8; definition 6–7; financial settlement/ clearing 19–23; increase 11–12; indicator system 8–11; international bonds/notes 23–4; reasons for increase 12–15; reserve currency 24–7; trade settlement 15–18
RMB Qualified Foreign Institutional Investors (RQFII) 20, 24, 30, 117; chronology 220, 225–6; current

situation 43, 45–6, 48, 58; future 143, 152, 164, 175
Rongmaoda 48
Rongyuantong 48
RQFLP 22–3, 222
ruble 61, 93
RUC 7
rupee 62
rupiah 222
Russia 53, 119, 143, *see also* BRICs; ruble

SAFE 67–70, 217–18
Saint Pierre Island 208
Saudi Arabia 88, 93, 210
securities investment 9, 67–8; bonds and bills 35–7; derivatives market 39, 41–3; RQFII 43, 45–6; stock market 37–40
securitization 25
seigniorage 76, 127
separation mode 182
September 11th 114
service activities 76
service trade 16, 32–3
services, financial 117
settlement 1–2, 5, 78, 99–100, 194, 198–9; challenges 179, 183–5; current situation 31–4; future 138, 144–5, 155–6, 163–4; historical implications 114–15, 132, 134; internationalization index 9, 13, 15–23
SF Express 47
SFC 175
Shanghai 5; chronology 219, 227; current situation 34–5, 37, 43, 45, 47–8; future of offshore market 139, 160; internationalization index 13, 19, 21–2; public opinion 71–2, 75, 83, 104
Shanghai Bank 23
Shanghai Composite Index 38
Shanghai Eastday Electronic Business 21
Shanghai Futures Exchange 43, 227
Shanghai International Energy Trading Center 43, 45
Shenzhen 47, 49, 96, 98–9, 139, 142–3, 160, 178
Shenzhen Composite Index 38
Shenzhen Development Bank (SDB) 178
Shenzhen Petrochemical Exchange 47
Shenzhen Qianhai 19, 21
Shenzhen Stock Exchange 37, 99
Shibor 42, 176
Silk Road 16–17, 203–4
Singapore 4; challenges 184–5; chronology 215, 219; current situation

45, 51, 58; economists' views 74–5,
82–3; future of offshore market 163–
5, 170–1, 173; historical implications
128, 133–4; internationalization index
14–15, 24; public opinion 99, 106; tax
209, 213
Singapore Exchange 24, 43
social policy 76
Society for Worldwide Interbank
Financial Telecommunication
(SWIFT) 13, 15, 165
Somalia 208
South Africa 2, 38
South African Reserve Bank 26, 50, 157,
216, 226
South America 92, 196
South Asia 88, 92–3
South Korea 16, 57, 128, 159, 170–1;
public opinion 92
Southeast Asia 14, 16, 62, 88, 92–3, 123,
195–6
sovereign wealth funds 118
Soviet Union 114
Special Drawing Rights (SDR) 79–80,
164
special international financial accounts
189–90
Sri Lanka 57
stability 8, *see also* political stability
Standard Bank of South Africa 155
Standard Chartered Bank 21, 24, 143,
151, 154–5, 165, 176–7, 217, 220,
228–9
State Administration of Foreign
Exchange 46, 60, 164, 178, 192
statistics 11, *see also* RMB
Internationalization Index (RII)
sterling *see* pound sterling
stock indicator 9–10
stock markets 9, 25, 40, 67, 98–9, 146,
175; current situation 37–40; index
futures 43–4
strategy 8, 82
*Supplementary Provision to Expand the
RMB Business in Hong Kong and the
Mainland* 138
surpluses 77, 109, 117, 124
Suzhou Industrial Park 74–5
swaps 55–6, 60, 173, *see also* currency
swaps
Swedish krona 14, 39
Swiss franc 39, 51, 133
Switzerland 4, 53, 170–1, 213
Sydney 143

synthetic bonds 175
Syria 210
systemic importance 81

Taipei 58, 75
Taiwan 2, 4, 58, 128, 174, 179, 215, 224;
future of offshore market 147–8, 161,
169; internationalization index 14, 16,
21, 24, 26; public opinion 74–5, 93,
99, 106
Taiwan Stock Exchange 24
Tanzania 157
target layer 166–7
tax 76, 99, 203; comparison of offshore
financial centers 208–14
tax avoidance 110–11
tax environment 169, 171
tax havens 121–2, 200, 208–9, 211–12
Tencent 47, 96
term structure 140
TF1312 25
Thailand 185–6
Third Plenary Session 13, 31, 80–1, 107
third-party use 3, 115–16
three powers 19
time zones 106, 114
Tokyo 125
TPP 81
trade 1, 8–9, 13, 15–16, 106, 123–4, 130;
with Africa 150–1, 155–6; deficits
75–6, 109; financing 109, 147, 149–50;
public sentiment 89–90, 93; route to
internationalization 80–1; settlement
15–18, 31–4, 155–6, 194; surplus
countries 109, 117
Trade and Industry Bureau 98
trading entry 164
trading exit 163
trading time 100–1, 106, 114
traditional trade finance 15, 147
transaction costs 126–8, 134–5
transit transactions 113
transmission mechanism 187
Treasure Island bonds 24
Treasury bonds 25–6; futures 25–6, 44;
yield curve 82
Triennial Survey 128–9
Triffin dilemma 117
Turkey 86
Turks and Caicos 208

UBS 58
UK 14, 16, 27–9, 180–1, 194–5; bait
problem 152–4; chronology 225, 228;

current situation 51, 54, 61; historical
  implications 109, 111, 124, 129, 134;
  public opinion 81, 86, 89; tax 212–13,
  see also London
underwriters 26
unemployment 169
UnionPay 229
United Nations Trade and Development
  Organization 11
United Overseas Bank 164
Uruguay 171
USA 3, 54, 61, 196; economists' views
  77–8, 81; historical implications
  110, 114–15, 123–4, 127, 130, 134;
  internationalization index 12, 14, 25,
  27; public opinion 88, 92, 105
USD *see* dollar (US)

Vanuatu 208
Venezuela 209
Vietnam 57
Virgin Islands 208
virtual economy 7, 80–1, 125
volatility 177

Wang Qishan 147
Web sites 84
weighting 8–9
West Asia 92–3, 196
Westpac 60
Wilmar (Shanghai) International Trade
  Co. 21

wine 93
Wing Lung Bank 143
World Bank 11, 24, 168–9
World Economic Outlook 15
World War I 105
WTO 59, 81, 84
Wyoming 212

Xi Jinping 13, 17
Xiang Songzuo 80–2
Xinjiang 17–18

yen 79, 124, 133, 188–90, 195; current
  situation 36–7, 51; derivatives
  39; exchange rate 59–62;
  internationalization index 14, 27–8;
  overseas loans in domestic financial
  institutions 46
Yifan Hu 73, 75–7
Yiwu 31, 223
yuan 116–17, 196–7
Yuandai 48

Zambia 156
Zeng Songhua 79–80
Zhan Xiangyang 82–3
Zhejiang 18, 31
Zhou Xiaochuan 51
Zhuhai 139
Zi Lu 208
ZTE 47, 96
Zurich 4, 81

Taylor & Francis eBooks

Helping you to choose the right eBooks for your Library

Add Routledge titles to your library's digital collection today. Taylor and Francis ebooks contains over 50,000 titles in the Humanities, Social Sciences, Behavioural Sciences, Built Environment and Law.

Choose from a range of subject packages or create your own!

Benefits for you

» Free MARC records
» COUNTER-compliant usage statistics
» Flexible purchase and pricing options
» All titles DRM-free.

Benefits for your user

» Off-site, anytime access via Athens or referring URL
» Print or copy pages or chapters
» Full content search
» Bookmark, highlight and annotate text
» Access to thousands of pages of quality research at the click of a button.

eCollections – Choose from over 30 subject eCollections, including:

Archaeology	Language Learning
Architecture	Law
Asian Studies	Literature
Business & Management	Media & Communication
Classical Studies	Middle East Studies
Construction	Music
Creative & Media Arts	Philosophy
Criminology & Criminal Justice	Planning
Economics	Politics
Education	Psychology & Mental Health
Energy	Religion
Engineering	Security
English Language & Linguistics	Social Work
Environment & Sustainability	Sociology
Geography	Sport
Health Studies	Theatre & Performance
History	Tourism, Hospitality & Events

For more information, pricing enquiries or to order a free trial, please contact your local sales team:
www.tandfebooks.com/page/sales

For Product Safety Concerns and Information please contact our EU
representative GPSR@taylorandfrancis.com
Taylor & Francis Verlag GmbH, Kaufingerstraße 24, 80331 München, Germany

www.ingramcontent.com/pod-product-compliance
Ingram Content Group UK Ltd.
Pitfield, Milton Keynes, MK11 3LW, UK
UKHW021003180425
457613UK00019B/795